HIPPOCRENE HANDY DICTIONARIES

Turkish

HIPPOCRENE HANDY DICTIONARIES

For the traveler of independent spirit and curious mind, this practical series will help you to communicate, not just get by. Easier to use than a dictionary, the comprehensive listing of words and phrases is arranged alphabetically by key word. More versatile than a phrasebook, words frequently met in stores, on signs, or needed for standard replies, are conveniently presented by subject.

ARABIC
ISBN 0-87052-960-9

CHINESE
ISBN 0-87052-050-4

DUTCH
ISBN 0-87052-049-0

GREEK
ISBN 0-87052-961-7

JAPANESE
ISBN 0-87052-962-5

PORTUGUESE
ISBN 0-87052-053-9

THAI
ISBN 0-87052-963-3

TURKISH
ISBN 0-87052-982-X

SERBO-CROATIAN
ISBN 0-87052-051-2

SWEDISH
ISBN 0-87052-054-7

Books may be ordered directly from the publisher. Each book costs $6.95. Send the total amount plus $3.50 for shipping and handling to: Hippocrene Books, Inc.
171 Madison Avenue
New York, NY 10016.

HIPPOCRENE HANDY DICTIONARIES

Turkish

compiled by

LEXUS

with

Ahmet T Türkistanlı and Felicity J Ünlü

HIPPOCRENE BOOKS
New York

Published in the United States of America in 1991 by
HIPPOCRENE BOOKS, INC., New York,
by arrangement with Routledge, London

For information, address:
HIPPOCRENE BOOKS, INC.
171 Madison Ave.
New York, NY 10016

ISBN 0-87052-982-X

Contents

Pronunciation Guide

Because you are likely to want to speak most of the Turkish given in this book, rather than just understand its meaning, an indication of the pronunciation has been given in square brackets. If you pronounce this as though it were English, the result will be clearly comprehensible to a Turk.

In some cases, however, we have decided it was not necessary to give the entire pronunciation for a word or phrase. This may be because it would more or less duplicate the ordinary Turkish spelling, or because the pronunciation of a particular word or words has already been given within the same entry. In these cases we have simply shown how to pronounce the problematic parts of the word or phrase.

Some comments on the pronunciation system used:

VOWELS

a	as in 'and'
ay	as in 'say'
e	as in 'fed'
ee	as in 'feed'
ew	as in 'few' (or the German ü)
o	as in 'hot'
o-	as in 'so'
oo	as in 'too'
oy	as in 'boy'
uh	like the 'i' in 'sir' or the 'er' in 'father'
ur	like the 'ur' sound in 'further' (or the German ö)

CONSONANTS

ch	as in 'church'
gh	as in 'get'
j	as in 'jam'
J	like the 's' in 'pleasure'

Note that the letter ğ in Turkish has nothing to do with the English 'g' sound — its function is to lengthen the preceding vowel (as in soğuk *[so-**ook**]*).

English-Turkish

A

a bir *[beer]*; **3000 liras a bottle** bir şişesi 3000 lira *[beer sheeshessee ewch been leera]*; *see page 116*

about: about 25 aşağı yukarı 25 *[asha-uh yookaruh yeermee besh]*; **about 6 o'clock** aşağı yukarı saat 6'da *[sa-at altuhda]*; **is the manager about?** müdür buralarda mı? *[mew-dewr booralarda muh]*; **I was just about to leave** ben de şimdi çıkıyordum *[ben de sheemdee chuh-kuh-yordoom]*; **how about a drink?** bir şey içer misiniz? *[beer shay eecher mee-seeneez]*

above üstünde *[ewst-ewndeh]*; **above the village** köyün üstünde

abroad yurt dışında *[yoort duhsh-uhnda]*

abscess çıban *[chuhban]*

absolutely: it's absolutely perfect tam mükemmel *[mewkemmel]*; **you're absolutely right** tamamen haklısınız *[hakluh-suhnuhz]*; **absolutely!** kesinlikle! *[kesseen-leekleh]*

absorbent cotton hidrofil pamuk *[heedrofeel pamook]*

accelerator gaz pedalı *[pedaluh]*

accept kabul etmek *[kabool etmek]*

accident kaza; **there's been an accident** kaza oldu *[oldoo]*; **sorry, it was an accident** affedersiniz, yanlışlıkla oldu *[affeder-seeneez yanluhsh-luhkla]*

accommodation(s) kalacak yer *[kalajak]*; **we need accommodation(s) for four** dört kişi için kalacak yer istiyoruz *[durrt keeshee eecheen … eesteeyorooz]*

accurate doğru *[do-roo]*

ache: I have an ache here buramda bir ağrı var *[booramda beer a-ruh]*; **it aches** ağrıyor *[a-ruh-yor]*

across: across the street/river sokağın/nehrin karşı tarafında *[soka-uhn/nehreen karshuh tarafuhnda]*

actor erkek oyuncu *[erkek oyoonjoo]*

actress kadın oyuncu *[kaduhn oyoonjoo]*

adapter (*elec*) adaptör *[adapturr]*

address adres *[adress]*; **what's your address?** adresiniz nedir? *[—eeneez nedeer]*

address book adres defteri *[adress defteree]*

admission: how much is admission? giriş ücreti ne kadar? *[gheereesh ewjretee neh kadar]*

adore: I adore ... ...-i çok seviyorum *[...-ee chok seveeyoroom]*

adult yetişkin *[yeteesh-keen]*

advance: I'll pay in advance peşin ödeyeceğim *[pesheen urday-yejeh-eem]*

advertisement reklam

advise: what would you advise? ne tavsiye edersiniz? *[neh tavseeyeh eder-seeneez]*

Aegean Ege *[egheh]*

aeroplane uçak *[oochak]*

affluent müreffeh *[mewref-feh]*

afraid: I'm afraid of heights yüksekten korkarım *[yewk-sekten korkaruhm]*; **don't be afraid** korkma; **I'm not afraid** korkmuyorum *[korkmoo-yoroom]*; **I'm afraid I can't help you** maalesef size yardım edemeyeceğim *[malesef seezeh yar-duhm edemay-yejeh-eem]*; **I'm afraid so** maalesef öyle *[urleh]*; **I'm afraid not** maalesef hayır *[h-'eye'-yuhr]*

after: after you sizden sonra *[seezden sonra]*; **after 9 o'clock** saat 9'dan sonra *[sa-at dokoozdan]*

afternoon öğleden sonra *[urleden sonra]*; **in the afternoon** öğleden sonra; **good afternoon** iyi günler *[eeyee ghewnler]*; **this afternoon** bugün öğleden sonra *[booghewn]*

aftershave tıraş losyonu *[tuhrash lossyonoo]*

afterwards sonra

again tekrar

against karşı *[karshuh]*
age yaş *[yash]*; **under age** yaşı küçük *[yashuh kewchewk]*; **not at my age!** benim yaşımda olmaz! *[beneem yashuhmda olmaz]*; **it takes ages** saatlerce sürüyor *[sa-atlerjeh sewrew-yor]*; **I haven't been here for ages** ne zamandır buraya gelmedim *[neh zamanduhr boo-'eye'-ya ghelmedeem]*
agency acente *[ajenteh]*
aggressive saldırgan *[salduhrgan]*
ago: a year/week ago bir yıl/hafta önce *[beer yuhl/hafta urnjeh]*; **it wasn't long ago** çok olmadı *[chok olmaduh]*
agony: it's agony büyük azap *[bew-yewk azap]*
agree: do you agree? razı mısınız? *[razuh muh-suhnuhz]*; **I agree** razıyım *[razuh-yuhm]*; **I don't agree** razı değilim *[deh-eeleem]*; **it doesn't agree with me** bana dokunuyor *[bana dokoonooyor]*
AIDS AIDS *[aydz]*
air hava; **by air** uçakla *[oochakla]*
airbed (*camping*) şişme şilte *[sheesh-meh sheelteh]*
air-conditioning klima *[kleema]*
air hostess hostes *[hostess]*
airmail: by airmail uçak postasıyla *[oochak postassuhla]*
airmail envelope uçak zarfı *[oochak zarfuh]*
airplane uçak *[oochak]*
airport havalimanı *[havaleemanuh]*
airport bus havalimanı otobüsü *[hava-leemanuh otobewssew]*
airport tax havalimanı vergisi *[hava-leemanuh vergheessee]*
airsick uçak tutması *[oochak toot-massuh]*; **I get airsick** beni uçak tutar *[benee oochak tootar]*
alarm alarm
alarm clock çalar saat *[chalar sa-at]*
Albania Arnavutluk *[arnavootlook]*
alcohol alkol
alcoholic: is it alcoholic? alkollü mü? *[alkol-lew mew]*
alive canlı *[janluh]*; **is he still alive?** hâlâ hayatta mı? *[hala h-'eye'-yat-ta muh]*
all: all the hotels bütün oteller *[bewtewn otel-ler]*; **all my friends** bütün arkadaşlarım *[arkadash-laruhm]*; **all my money** tüm param *[tewm param]*; **all of it** hepsi *[hepsee]*; **all of them** onların hepsi *[onlaruhn]*; **all right** peki *[pekee]*; **I'm all right** (*nothing wrong*) ben iyiyim *[eeyeeyeem]*; **that's all** hepsi bu kadar *[boo kadar]*; **it's all changed** hep değişti *[deh-eeshtee]*; **thank you — not at all** teşekkür ederim — bir şey değil *[beer shay deh-eel]*
allergic: I'm allergic to ... ...-e alerjim var *[...-eh alerJeem]*
allergy alerji *[alerJee]*
all-inclusive her şey dahil *[shay daheel]*
allowed serbest; **is it allowed?** serbest mi? *[mee]*; **I'm not allowed to eat salt** bana tuz yasak *[tooz yassak]*
all-risks (*insurance*) bütün rizikolar *[bewtewn reezeekolar]*
almost hemen hemen
alone yalnız *[yalnuhz]*; **are you alone?** yalnız mısınız? *[muh-suhnuhz]*; **leave me alone** beni rahat bırak *[benee rahat buhrak]*
already: we have already bought tickets biz bilet aldık *[beez beelet alduhk]*; **it's already five o'clock!** saat beş olmuş bile! *[sa-at besh olmoosh beeleh]*
also de/da *[deh/da]*; **he came also** o da geldi *[gheldee]*; *see page 118*
alteration değişiklik *[deh-eesheekleek]*
alternative: is there an alternative? başka yolu var mı? *[bashka yoloo var muh]*; **we had no alternative** başka çaremiz yoktu *[charemeez yoktoo]*
alternator alternatör *[alternaturr]*
although gerçi *[gherchee]*
altogether tümüyle *[tewmewleh]*; **what does that come to altogether?** hepsi ne kadar tutuyor? *[hepsee neh kadar tootooyor]*
always daima *[da-eema]*
amazing şaşılacak *[shashuhlajak]*; (*very good*) şahane *[shahaneh]*
ambassador elçi *[elchee]*
ambulance cankurtaran *[jank-oortaran]*; **get an ambulance!** bir cankurtaran çağırın! *[cha-uhruhn]*
American (*man, woman*) Amerikalı *[amereekaluh]*; (*adjective*) Amerikan *[amereekan]*; **the Americans** Ameri-

kalılar *[amereekal-luhlar]*
American plan tam pansiyon *[pansseeyon]*
among arasında *[arassuhnda]*
amp: a 13-amp fuse 13 amperlik sigorta *[on ewch amperleek seegorta]*
an(a)esthetic anestetik *[anesteteek]*
ancestor ata
anchor çapa *[chapa]*
anchovies ançüez *[anchew-ez]*
ancient eski *[esskee]*
and ve *[veh]*
angina anjin *[anJeen]*
angry kızgın *[kuhz-guhn]*; **I'm very angry about it** bu konuda çok kızgınım *[boo konooda chook —uhm]*
animal hayvan *[h-'eye'-van]*
Ankara Ankara
ankle ayak bileği *['eye'-yak beeleh-ee]*
anniversary: it's our (wedding) anniversary today bugün evlenme yıldönümümüz *[booghewn evlenmeh yuhl-durnewm-ewmewz]*
annoy: he's annoying me beni taciz ediyor *[benee tajeez edeeyor]*; **it's so annoying** ne kadar can sıkıcı bir şey *[neh kadar jan suhkuhjuh beer shay]*
anorak anorak
another (*different*) başka *[bashka]*; (*extra*) daha; **can we have another room?** bize başka bir oda verebilir misiniz? *[beezeh bashka beer oda verebeeleer mee-seeneez]*; **another bottle, please** bir şişe daha, lüften *[beer sheesheh daha lewtfen]*
answer: there was no answer kimse cevap vermedi *[keemseh jevap vermedee]*; **what was his answer?** ne cevap verdi? *[neh ... verdee]*
ant: ants karıncalar *[karuhnjalar]*
antibiotics antibiyotikler *[anteebeeyoteekler]*
antifreeze antifriz *[anteefreez]*
antihistamine antihistamin *[anteeheestameen]*
antique: is it an antique? bu antika mı? *[boo anteeka muh]*
antique shop antikacı *[antekajuh]*
antisocial: don't be antisocial oyun bozanlık yapmayın *[oyoon bozanluhk yapm-'eye'-yuhn]*
any: have you got any ...? ... var mı? *[muh]*; **have you got any rolls/milk?** sandviç ekmeği/süt var mı? *[sandveech ekmeh-ee/sewt var muhl]*; **I haven't got any** hiç yok *[heech yok]*
anybody kimse *[keemseh]*; **can anybody help?** kimse yardım edebilir mi? *[yarduhm edebeeleer mee]*; **there wasn't anybody there** orada kimse yoktu *[orada ... yoktoo]*
anything bir şey *[beer shay]*; **I don't want anything** hiç bir şey istemiyorum *[heech ... eestemeeyoroom]*; **don't you have anything else?** başka bir şeyiniz yok mu? *[bashka ...-eeneez yok moo]*
apart from ... ... dışında *[duhshuhnda]*
apartment apartman dairesi *[apartman da-eeressee]*
aperitif aperitif *[apereeteef]*
apology tarziye *[tarzeeyeh]*; **please accept my apologies** özür dilerim *[urzewr deelereem]*
appalling korkunç *[korkoonch]*
appear: it would appear that ... anlaşılan ... *[anlash-uhlan]*
appendicitis apandisit *[apandeesseet]*
appetite iştah *[eeshtah]*; **I've lost my appetite** iştahım kaçtı *[—uhm kachtuh]*
apple elma
apple pie elmalı tart *[elmaluh]*
application form başvuru formu *[bashvooroo formoo]*
appointment randevu *[randevoo]*; **I'd like to make an appointment** randevu almak istiyorum *[eesteeyoroom]*
appreciate: thank you, I appreciate it çok çok teşekkür ederim *[chok chok teshek-kewr edeereem]*
approve: she doesn't approve hoş karşılamıyor *[hosh karshuhlamuhyor]*
apricot kayısı *[k-'eye'-uhssuh]*
April Nisan *[neessan]*
aqualung balıkadam hava tüpü *[baluhk-adam hava tewpew]*
arch(a)eology arkeoloji *[arkeh-oloJee]*
are *see page 114*
area: I don't know the area bu bölgeyi bilmiyorum *[boo burlgayee beelmeeyoroom]*
area code şehir kodu *[sheheer kodoo]*
arm kol
Armenian (*adjective, person*) Ermeni *[ermenee]*
around *see* **about**

arrangement: will you make the arrangements? düzenlemeleri siz yapar mısınız? *[dewzenleme-leree seez yapar muh-suhnuhz]*
arrest tutuklamak *[tootooklamak]*; **he's been arrested** o tutuklandı *[—duh]*
arrival varış *[varuhsh]*
arrive: when do we arrive? ne zaman varacağız? *[neh zaman varaja-uhz]*; **has my parcel arrived yet?** paketim geldi mi? *[paketeem gheldee mee]*; **let me know as soon as they arrive** onlar gelir gelmez bana haber verin *[gheleer ghelmez bana haber vereen]*; **we only arrived yesterday** henüz dün geldik *[henewz dewn gheldeek]*
art sanat
art gallery sanat galerisi *[sanat galereessee]*
arthritis mafsal iltihabı *[mafsal eelteehabuh]*
artificial yapma
artist sanatçı *[sanatchuh]*
as: as fast as you can mümkün olduğu kadar çabuk *[mewmkewn oldoo-oo kadar chabook]*; **as much as you can** mümkün olduğu kadar çok *[chok]*; **as you like** istediğiniz gibi *[eestedee-eeneez gheebee]*; **as it's getting late** geç olduğu için *[ghech oldoo-oo eecheen]*
ashore: to go ashore karaya çıkmak *[kar-'eye'-ya chuhkmak]*
ashtray kül tablası *[kewl tablassuh]*
Asia Asya
aside from ... ... dışında *[duhshuhnda]*
ask sormak; **that's not what I asked for** bunu istemedim *[boonoo eestemedeem]*; **could you ask him to phone me back?** lüften beni aramasını söyleyin *[lewtfen benee aramassuhnuh surlayeen]*
asleep: he's still asleep hâlâ uyuyor *[hala ooyoo-yor]*
asparagus kuşkonmaz *[koosh-konmaz]*
aspirin aspirin *[aspeereen]*
assault: she's been assaulted saldırıya uğradı *[salduhruhya oo-raduh]*; **indecent assault** elle sarkıntılık *[el-leh sarkuhntuhluhk]*
assistant (*helper*) yardımcı *[yarduhmjuh]*; (*in shop*) satıcı *[satuhjuh]*
assume: I assume that ... sanırım ... *[sanuhruhm]*
asthma astım *[astuhm]*
astonishing şaşırtıcı *[shashuhr-tuhjuh]*
at: at the café kahvede *[kahvedeh]*; **at the hotel** otelde *[oteldeh]*; **at 8 o'clock** saat 8'de *[sa-at sekeezdeh]*
Athens Atina *[ateena]*
Atlantic Atlantik *[atlanteek]*
atmosphere atmosfer
attractive cazip *[jazeep]*; **you're very attractive** çok cazipsiniz *[chok jazeepseeneez]*
aubergine patlıcan *[patluhjan]*
auction açık artırma *[achuhk artuhrma]*
audience seyirci *[sayeerjee]*
August Ağustos *[a-oostoss]*
aunt teyze *[tayzeh]*; **my aunt** teyzem *[tayzem]*
Australia Avustralya *[avoostralya]*
Australian (*person*) Avustralyalı *[avoostralyaluh]*; (*adjective*) Avustralya *[avoostralya]*; **the Australians** Avustralyalılar *[avoostralyaluhlar]*
Austria Avusturya *[avoostoorya]*
authorities resmi makamlar *[ressmee]*
automatic otomatik *[otomateek]*
automobile otomobil *[otomobeel]*
autumn sonbahar; **in the autumn** sonbaharda
available: when will it be available? ne zaman hazır olacak? *[neh zaman hazuhr olajak]*; **when will he be available?** onunla ne zaman görüşebilirim? *[onoonla neh zaman ghurrewsheh-beeleereem]*
avenue cadde *[jad-deh]*
average: the average Turk sıradan Türk vatandaşı *[suhradan tewrk vatandashuh]*; **an above average hotel** ortalamanın üstünde bir otel *[ortalamanuhn ewstewndeh beer]*; **a below average hotel** ortalamanın altında bir otel *[altuhnda]*; **the food was only average** yemekler sadece ortalama düzeydeydi *[sadejeh ortalama dewzay-daydee]*; **on average** ortalama olarak
awake: is she awake? uyanık mı? *[ooyanuhk muh]*
away: is it far away? uzakta mı? *[oozakta muh]*; **go away!** çekil! *[chekeel]*

awful berbat

axle aks

B

baby bebek
baby-carrier portbebe *[portbebeh]*
baby-sitter çocuk bakıcısı *[chojook bakuhjuhssuh]*; **can you get us a baby-sitter?** bize bir çocuk bakıcısı bulabilir misiniz? *[beezeh beer ... boolabeeleer mee-seeneez]*
bachelor bekar
back: I've got a bad back sırtım tutuldu *[suhrtuhm tootooldool]*; **at the back** arkada; **in the back of the car** otomobilin arka tarafında *[otomobeeleen arka tarafuhnda]*; **I'll be right back** hemen döneceğim *[hemen durnejeh-eem]*; **when do you want it back?** bunu ne zaman geri istiyorsunuz? *[boonoo neh zaman gheree eesteeyorsoonooz]*; **can I have my money back?** paramı geri alabilir miyim? *[paramuh gheree alabeeleer meeyeem]*; **come back!** geri gel! *[gheree ghel]*; **I go back home tomorrow** yarın eve dönüyorum *[yaruhn eveh durnew-yoroom]*; **we'll be back next year** gelecek yıl tekrar geleceğiz *[ghelejek yuhl tekrar ghelejeh-eez]*; **when is the last bus back?** dönüş için son otobüs kaçta? *[durnewsh eecheen son otobewss kachta]*
backache: I have a backache sırtım ağrıyor *[suhrtuhm a-ruhyor]*
back door arka kapı *[arka kapuh]*
backgammon tavla
backpack sırt çantası *[suhrt chantassuh]*
back seat arka koltuk *[arka koltook]*
back street arka sokak
bacon beykın *[baykuhn]*
bad kötü *[kurtoo]*; **this meat's bad** bu et kokmuş *[boo et kokmoosh]*; **a bad headache** şiddetli bir baş ağrısı *[sheedetlee beer bash a-ruhssuh]*; **it's not bad** bu fena değil *[boo fena deh-eel]*; **too bad!** vah vah!
badly: he's been badly injured ağır yaralandı *[a-uhr yaralanduh]*

bag (*suitcase*) bavul *[bavool]*; (*carrier bag*) naylon torba *[n-'eye'-lon torba]*; (*handbag*) el çantası *[chantassuh]*
baggage bagaj *[bagaȷ]*
baggage allowance bagaj hakkı *[bagaȷ hak-kuh]*
baggage checkroom emanet
bakery fırın *[fuhruhn]*
balcony balkon; **a room with a balcony** balkonlu bir oda *[—loo beer]*; **on the balcony** balkonda *[—da]*
bald kel
ball top
ballet bale *[baleh]*
ball-point pen tükenmez kalem *[tewkenmez kalem]*
banana muz *[mooz]*
band (*music*) orkestra
bandage sargı *[sarguh]*; **could you change the bandage?** sargıyı değiştirir misiniz? *[—yuh deh-eeshteereer mee-seeneez]*
bandaid plaster
bank banka; **when are the banks open?** bankalar saat kaçtan kaça kadar açık? *[—lar sa-at kacha kadar achuhk]*
bank account banka hesabı *[banka hessabuh]*
bar bar; **let's meet in the bar** barda buluşalım *[barda boolooshaluhm]*; **a bar of chocolate** bir tablet çikolata *[beer tablet cheekolata]*
barbecue ızgara *[uhzgara]*
barber berber
bargain: it's a real bargain gerçekten çok ucuz *[gherchekten chok oojooz]*
barman barmen
barrette saç tokası *[sach tokassuh]*
bartender barmen
basic: the hotel is rather basic bu otel oldukça basit *[boo otel oldookcha basseet]*; **will you teach me some basic phrases?** bana birkaç temel deyim öğretir misiniz? *[bana beerkach temel dayeem ur-reteer*

mee-seeneez]
basket sepet
bath banyo; **can I take a bath?** banyo yapabilir miyim? *[yapabeeleer meeyeem]*; **could you give me a bath towel?** bana bir banyo havlusu verir misiniz? *[bana beer ... havloossoo vereer mee-seeneez]*
bathing deniz banyosu *[deneez banyossoo]*
bathing costume mayo *[m-'eye'-yo]*
bathrobe bornoz
bathroom banyo; **a room with a private bathroom** banyolu oda *[—loo oda]*; **can I use your bathroom?** banyonuzu kullanabilir miyim? *[—noozoo kool-lanabeeleer meeyeem]*
battery (*radio etc*) pil *[peel]*; (*in car*) akü *[akew]*; **the battery's flat** akü boşalmış *[akew boshalmuhsh]*
bay koy; (*large*) körfez *[kurrfez]*
be olmak; **be reasonable** makul ol *[makool]*; **don't be lazy** tembellik yapma *[tembel-leek yapma]*; **where have you been?** neredeydin? *[neredaydeen]*; **I've never been to Antalya** Antalya'ya hiç gitmedim *[antal-y-'eye'-ya heech gheetmedeem]*; *see page 114*
beach plaj *[plaJ]*; **on the beach** plajda *[plaJda]*; **I'm going to the beach** plaja gidiyorum *[plaJa gheedeeyoroom]*
beach mat plaj yaygısı *[plaJ y-'eye'-guhssuh]*
beach towel plaj havlusu *[plaJ havloossoo]*
beach umbrella plaj şemsiyesi *[plaJ shem-seeyessee]*
beads boncuk *[bonjook]*
beans fasulye *[fassoolyeh]*
bear (*animal*) ayı *['eye'-yuh]*
beard sakal
beautiful güzel *[ghewzel]*; (*meal*) nefis *[nefeess]*; **thank you, that's beautiful** çok çok teşekkür ederim *[chok chok teshek-kewr edereem]*
beauty salon kuaför *[koo-afurr]*
because çünkü *[chewnkew]*; **I can't go today because I'm ill** bugün gidemem, çünkü hastayım *[booghewn gheedeemem ... hast-'eye'-yuhm]*; **because of the weather** hava nedeniyle *[hava nedeneeleh]*
bed yatak; **single bed** tek kişilik yatak *[tek keesheeleek]*; **double bed** iki kişilik yatak *[eekee]*; **you haven't made my bed** yatağım yapılmamış *[yata-uhm yapuhlmamuhsh]*; **he's still in bed** hâlâ yatıyor *[hala yatuhyor]*; **I'm going to bed** ben yatıyorum *[yatuhyoroom]*
bed and breakfast kahvaltılı pansiyon *[kahvaltuhluh pansseeyon]*
bed linen yatak takımları *[yatak takuhmlar]*
bedroom yatak odası *[yatak odassuh]*
bee arı *[aruh]*
beef sığır eti *[suh-uhr etee]*
beer bira *[beera]*; **two beers, please** iki bira, lütfen *[eekee ... lewtfen]*
before önce *[urnjeh]*; **before breakfast** kahvaltıdan önce *[kahvaltuhdan]*; **before I leave** ayrılmadan önce *['eye'-ruhlmadan]*; **I haven't been here before** buraya daha önce hiç gelmemiştim *[boor-'eye'-ya daha ... heech ghelmemeeshteem]*
begin: when does it begin? ne zaman başlıyor? *[neh zaman bashluhyor]*
beginner acemi *[ajemee]*; **I'm just a beginner** ben bu işin acemisiyim *[boo eesheen —seeyeem]*
beginning: at the beginning başlangıçta *[bashlanguhchta]*
behavio(u)r davranış *[davranuhsh]*
behind arkada; **the driver behind me** arkamdaki şoför *[arkamdakee shoffurr]*
beige bej *[beJ]*
Belgium Belçika *[belcheeka]*
believe: I don't believe you size inanmıyorum *[seezeh eenanmuh-yoroom]*; **I believe you** size inanıyorum *[eenanuh-yoroom]*; **I don't believe it!** inanmıyorum! *[eenanmuh-yoroom]*
bell (*door*) zil *[zeel]*; (*church*) çan *[chan]*
belong: that belongs to me o benim *[beneem]*; **who does this belong to?** bunun sahibi kim? *[boonoon saheebee keem]*
belongings: all my belongings bütün eşyalarım *[bewtewn esh-yalaruhm]*
below altında *[altuhnda]*; **below the knee** dizin altında *[deezeen]*
belt (*clothing*) kemer
bend (*in road*) viraj *[veeraJ]*

berth kuşet *[kooshet]*
beside: beside the church kilisenin yanında *[keeleesseneen yanuhnda]*; **sit beside me** yanımda otur *[yanuhmda otoor]*
besides: besides that onun dışında *[onoon duhshuhnda]*
best en iyi *[eeyee]*; **the best hotel in town** şehirdeki en iyi otel *[sheheerdekee ... otel]*; **that's the best meal I've ever had** bu yediğim en iyi yemekti *[boo yedee-eem ... yemektee]*
bet: I bet you 5000 liras sizinle 5000 lirasına bahse girerim *[seezeenleh besh been leerassuhna bahseh gheerereem]*
better daha iyi *[daha eeyee]*; **that's better!** hah, şöyle! *[shurleh]*; **are you feeling better?** nasıl, biraz iyileştiniz mi? *[nassuhl beeraz eeyeelesh-teeneez mee]*; **I'm feeling a lot better** kendimi çok daha iyi hissediyorum *[kendeemee chok ... heessedee-yoroom]*; **I'd better be going now** artık gitmem lazım *[artuhk gheetmem lazuhm]*
between arasında *[arassuhnda]*
beyond ardında *[arduhnda]*; **beyond the mountains** dağların ardında
bicycle bisiklet *[beesseeklet]*; **can we rent bicycles here?** burada bisiklet kiralayabilir miyiz? *[boorada ... keeral-'eye'-yabeeleer meeyeez]*
big büyük *[bew-yewk]*; **a big ...** büyük bir ... *[beer]*; **that's too big** o fazla büyük; **it's not big enough** yeterince büyük değil *[yetereenjeh ... deh-eel]*
bigger daha büyük *[daha bew-yewk]*
bike bisiklet *[beeseeklet]*; (*motorbike*) motosiklet *[motosseeklet]*
bikini bikini
bill hesap *[hessap]*; **could I have the bill, please?** lütfen hesabı getirir misiniz? *[lewtfen hessabuh gheteereer mee-seeneez]*
billfold para cüzdanı *[para jewzdanuh]*
billiards bilardo *[beelardo]*
bird kuş *[koosh]*
biro (*tm*) tükenmez *[tewkenmez]*
birthday doğum günü *[do-oom ghewnew]*; **it's my birthday today** bugün benim doğum günüm *[booghewn beneem ... ghewnewm]*; **when is your birthday?** doğum gününüz ne zaman? *[ghewnewnewz neh zaman]*; **happy birthday!** doğum gününüz kutlu olsun! *[kootloo olsoon]*
biscuit bisküvi *[beeskewvee]*
bit: just a little bit for me bana yalnız bir lokma *[bana yalnuhz beer lokma]*; **a big bit** büyükçe bir parça *[bew-yewkcheh beer parcha]*; **a bit of that cake** o pastadan birazcık *[pastadan beeraz-juhk]*; **it's a bit too big for me** bana biraz büyük *[beeraz bew-yewk]*; **it's a bit cold today** bugün hava biraz soğuk *[booghewn hava ... so-ook]*
bite (*by insect*) sokma; **I've been bitten** beni böcek soktu *[benee burjek soktoo]*; **do you have something for bites?** böcek sokması için bir şey var mı? *[sokmassuh eecheen beer shay var muh]*
bitter (*taste*) acı *[ajuh]*
bitter lemon 'bitter lemon'
black siyah *[seeyah]*
black and white film siyah beyaz filim *[seeyah bayaz feeleem]*
blackout: he's had a blackout kendinden geçti *[kendeenden ghechtee]*
Black Sea Karadeniz *[karadeneez]*
bladder mesane *[messaneh]*
blanket battaniye *[bat-taneeyeh]*; **I'd like another blanket** bir battaniye daha rica ediyorum *[beer ... daha reeja edeeyoroom]*
blazer bleyzır *[blayzuhr]*
bleach (*for toilet etc*) çamaşır suyu *[chamashuhr sooyoo]*
bleed kanamak; **his nose is bleeding** burnu kanıyor *[boornoo kanuhyor]*
bless you! (*after sneeze*) çok yaşa! *[chok yasha]*
blind kör *[kurr]*
blinds jaluzi *[ʒaloozee]*
blind spot (*driving*) ölü mıntıka *[urlew muhntuhka]*
blister kabarcık *[kabarjuhk]*
blocked (*road, drain*) tıkalı *[tuhkaluh]*
block of flats apartman
blond (*adjective*) sarışın *[saruhshuhn]*
blonde (*woman*) sarışın *[saruhshuhn]*
blood kan; **his blood group is ...** onun kan grubu ...-dır *[onoon ...*

grooboo ...-duhr]; **I have high blood pressure** yüksek tansiyonum var *[yewksek tanseeyonoom]*
blouse bluz *[blooz]*
blue mavi *[mavee]*
blusher (*cosmetic*) allık *[al-luhk]*
board: full board tam pansiyon *[pansseeyon]*; **half-board** yarım pansiyon *[yaruhm]*
boarding house pansiyon *[pansseeyon]*
boarding pass biniş kartı *[beeneesh kartuh]*
boat gemi *[ghemee]*; (*small*) kayık *[k-'eye'-yuhk]*
body vücut *[vewjoot]*
boil (*on body*) çıban *[chuhban]*; **to boil the water** su kaynatmak *[soo k-'eye'-natmak]*
boiled egg haşlanmış yumurta *[hashlanmuhsh yoomoorta]*
boiling hot (*weather*) hamam gibi *[hamam gheebee]*; (*food*) çok sıcak *[chok suhjak]*
bomb (*noun*) bomba
bone (*in meat, body*) kemik *[kemeek]*; (*in fish*) kılçık *[kuhlchuhk]*
bonnet (*of car*) kaporta
book kitap *[keetap]*; **I'd like to book a table for two** iki kişilik bir masa ayırtmak istiyorum *[eekee keesheeleek beer massa 'eye'-yuhrtmak eesteeyoroom]*
bookshop, bookstore kitapçı *[keetapchuh]*
boot (*on foot*) bot; (*riding etc*) çizme *[cheezmeh]*; (*of car*) bagaj *[bagaJ]*
booze içki *[eechkee]*; **I had too much booze** çok fazla içtim *[chok fazla eechteem]*
border (*of country*) sınır *[suhnuhr]*
bored: I'm bored canım sıkılıyor *[januhm suhkuhluhyor]*
boring sıkıcı *[suhkuhjuh]*
born: I was born in ... (*date/place*) ...-de doğdum *[...-deh do-doom]*
borrow: may I borrow ...? ...-i ödünç alabilir miyim? *[...-ee urdewnch alabeeleer meeyeem]*
Bosporus İstanbul Boğazı *[eestanbool bo-azuh]*
boss patron
both ikisi de *[eekeessee deh]*; **I'll take both of them** ikisini de alacağım *[eekeesseenee deh alaja-uhm]*; **we'll both come** ikimiz de geleceğiz *[eekeemeez deh ghelejeh-eez]*; **both ... and ...** hem ... hem de ...
bother: sorry to bother you rahatsız ettiğim için özür dilerim *[rahatsuhz et-tee-eem eecheen urzewr deelereem]*; **it's no bother** zararı yok *[zararuh yok]*; **it's such a bother** ne kadar can sıkıcı bir şey *[neh kadar jan suhkuhjuh beer shay]*
bottle şişe *[sheesheh]*; **a bottle of wine** bir şişe şarap *[beer ... sharap]*; **another bottle, please** bir şişe daha, lütfen, *[daha lewtfen]*
bottle-opener şişe açacağı *[sheesheh achaja-uh]*
bottom (*of person*) popo; **at the bottom of the hill** tepenin eteğinde *[tepeneen eteheendeh]*
bottom gear birinci vites *[beereenjee veetess]*
bouncer (*at club*) fedai *[feda-ee]*
bowels bağırsaklar *[ba-uhrssaklar]*
box kutu *[kootoo]*; (*big*) sandık *[sanduhk]*
box lunch kumanya *[koomanya]*
box office bilet gişesi *[beelet gheeshessee]*
boy oğlan *[o-lan]*
boyfriend: my boyfriend erkek arkadaşım *[erkek arkadashuhm]*
bra sütyen *[sootyen]*
bracelet bilezik *[beelezeek]*
brake fluid hidrolik fren yağı *[heedroleek fren ya-uh]*
brake lining fren balatası *[fren balatassuh]*
brakes frenler; **there's something wrong with the brakes** frenler iyi çalışmıyor *[eeyee chaluhshmuh-yor]*; **can you check the brakes?** frenleri muayene eder misiniz? *[—ee moo-'eye'-yeneh eder mee-seeneez]*; **I had to brake suddenly** aniden fren yapmak zorunda kaldım *[aneeden fren yapmak zoroonda kalduhm]*
brandy konyak
brass pirinç *[peereench]*
brave cesur *[jesoor]*
bread ekmek; **could we have some bread and butter?** biraz ekmek ve tereyağı getirir misiniz? *[beeraz ... veh tereya-uh gheteereer mee-*

seeneez]; **some more bread, please** biraz daha ekmek lütfen *[lewtfen]*; **white bread** has ekmek *[hass]*; **brown bread** kara ekmek; **wholemeal bread** tam ekmek; **rye bread** çavdar ekmeği *[chavdar ekmeh-ee]*

break kırmak *[khuhrmak]*; (*string, rope etc*) kopmak; **I think I've broken my ankle** galiba ayak bileğim kırıldı *[galeeba 'eye'-yak beeleh-eem kuhruhlduh]*; **it keeps breaking** durmadan kopuyor *[doormadan kopooyor]*

breakdown: I've had a breakdown arabam arıza yaptı *[arabam aruhza yaptuh]*; **nervous breakdown** sinir krizi *[seeneer kreezee]*

breakfast kahvaltı *[kahvaltuh]*; **English/full breakfast** İngiliz kahvaltısı *[eengheeleez —ssuh]*; **continental breakfast** normal kahvaltı

break in: somebody's broken in hırsız girmiş *[huhrsuhz gheermeesh]*

breast göğüs *[gur-ewss]*

breast-feed meme vermek *[memeh]*

breath nefes *[nefess]*; **out of breath** nefes nefese *[—eh]*

breathe nefes almak *[nefess almak]*; **I can't breathe** nefes alamıyorum *[alamuhyoroom]*

breathtaking nefis *[nefeess]*

breeze hafif rüzgar *[hafeef rewzgar]*

breezy rüzgarlı *[rewzgarluh]*

bridal suite gelin dairesi *[gheleen daeeressee]*

bride gelin *[gheleen]*

bridegroom damat

bridge (*over river etc*) köprü *[kurprew]*

brief (*stay, visit*) kısa *[kuhssa]*

briefcase evrak çantası *[chantassuh]*

bright (*colour*) canlı *[janluh]*; **bright red** ateş kırmızısı *[atesh kuhrmuhzuhssuh]*

brilliant (*idea, colour*) parlak

bring getirmek *[gheteermek]*; **could you bring it to my hotel?** otelime getirebilir misiniz? *[oteleemeh gheteereh-beeleer mee-seeneez]*; **I'll bring it back** ben geri getiririm *[gheree gheteereereem]*; **can I bring a friend too?** bir arkadaşımı da beraber getirebilir miyim? *[beer arkadashuhmuh da beraber … meeyeem]*

Britain İngiltere Adaları *[engheeltereh adalaruh]*

British İngiliz *[engheeleez]*; **the British** İngilizler *[eengheeleezler]*

brochure broşür *[broshewr]*; **do you have any brochures on ...?** ... hakkında broşür var mı? *[... hakkuhnda … muh]*

broke: I'm broke meteliksizim *[meteleekseezeem]*

broken bozuk *[bozook]*; **you've broken it** onu bozmuşsunuz *[onoo bozmoosh-soonooz]*; **it's broken** bozulmuş *[bozoolmoosh]*; **broken nose** kırık burun *[kuhruhk booroon]*

brooch broş *[brosh]*

brother: my brother erkek kardeşim *[erkek kardesheem]*

brother-in-law (*husband's brother*) kayınbirader *[k-'eye'-yuhn-beerader]*; (*sister's husband*) enişte *[eneeshteh]*; (*wife's sister's husband*) bacanak *[bajanak]*

brown kahverengi *[kahveh-renghee]*; **I don't go brown** bronzlaşmıyorum *[bronzlashmuhyoroom]*

browse: may I just browse around? biraz bakınmak istiyorum *[beeraz bakuhnmak eesteeyoroom]*

bruise (*noun*) çürük *[chewrewk]*

brunette esmer

brush (*noun*) fırça *[fuhrcha]*

bubble bath köpüklü banyo *[kurpewklew banyo]*

bucket kova

buffet büfe *[bewfeh]*

bug (*insect*) böcek *[burjek]*; **she's caught a bug** mikrop almış *[meekrop almuhsh]*

building bina *[beena]*

bulb (*elec*) ampul *[ampool]*; **a new bulb** yeni bir ampul *[yenee beer]*

Bulgaria Bulgaristan *[boolgareestan]*

Bulgarian (*person, adjective*) Bulgar *[boolgar]*

bull boğa *[bo-a]*

bump: I bumped my head başımı vurdum *[bashuhmuh voordoom]*

bumper tampon

bumpy sarsıntılı *[sarssuhntuhluh]*

bunch of flowers çiçek buketi *[cheechek booketee]*

bungalow tek katlı ev *[katluh]*

bunion nasır *[nassuhr]*

bunk yatak
bunk beds ranzalar
buoy şamandıra *[shamanduhra]*
burglar hırsız *[huhrsuhz]*
burn: do you have an ointment for burns? yanığa karşı bir merhem var mı? *[yanuh-a karshuh beer merhem var muh]*
burnt: this meat is burnt bu et yanmış *[boo et yanmuhsh]*; **my arms are so burnt** kollarım o kadar yanmış ki *[kol-laruhm o kadar yanmuhsh kee]*
burst: a burst pipe patlak boru *[patlak boroo]*
bus otobüs *[otobewss]*; **is this the bus for...?** bu ... otobüsü mü? *[boo ... otobewssew mew]*; **when's the next bus?** bir sonraki otobüs kaçta? *[beer sonrakee ... kachta]*
bus driver otobüs şoförü *[otobewss shofurrew]*
business isş *[eesh]*; **I'm here on business** iş için geldim *[eecheen gheldeem]*; **it's a pleasure to do business with you** sizinle iş yapmaktan kıvanç duyuyorum *[seezeenleh ... yapmaktan kuhvanch dooyooyoroom]*
bus station otobüs terminali *[otobewss termeenalee]*
bus stop otobüs durağı *[otobewss doora-uh]*; **will you tell me which bus stop I get off at?** hangi otobüs durağında inmem gerektiğini bana söyler misiniz? *[hanghee ... ...-nda eenmem gherektee-eenee bana* surler mee-seen*eez]*
bust (*of body*) göğüs *[gur-ewss]*
bus tour otobüs turu *[otobewss tooroo]*
busy (*street*) işlek *[eeshlek]*; (*restaurant*) kalabalık *[kalabaluhk]*; **I'm busy this evening** bu akşam meşgulüm *[boo aksham meshgooloom]*; **the line was busy** meşgul çıktı *[meshgool chuhktuh]*
but fakat; **not ... but ...** ... değil ... *[deh-eel]*
butcher kasap *[kassap]*
butter tereyağı *[tereya-uh]*
butterfly kelebek
button düğme *[dew-meh]*
buy: I'll buy it bunu alıyorum *[boonoo aluhyoroom]*; **where can I buy ...?** nerede ... bulabilirim? *[neredeh ... boola-beeleereem]*
by: by train/car/boat tren/otomobil/vapur ile *[otomobeel/vapoor eeleh]*; **who's it written by?** yazarı kim? *[yazaruh keem]*; **it's by Picasso** Picasso'ya ait *[—'ya 'eye'-yeet]*; **I came by myself** yalnız geldim *[yalnuhz gheldeem]*; **a seat by the window** pencere yanı *[penjereh yanuh]*; **by the sea** deniz kenarında *[deneez kenaruhnda]*; **can you do it by Wednesday?** Çarşambaya yetiştirebilir misiniz? *[charshamb-'eye'-ya yeteeshteereh-beeleer mee-seeneez]*
bye-bye (*when going oneself*) hoşça kal *[hoshha kal]*; (*when seeing someone off*) güle güle *[ghewleh]*
bypass (*road*) baypas *[b-'eye'-pass]*
Byzantine Bizans *[beezanss]*

C

cab (*taxi*) taksi *[taksee]*
cabaret kabare *[kabareh]*
cabbage lahana
cabin kamara
cable (*elec*) kablo
cablecar teleferik *[telefereek]*
café kahvehane *[kahvehaneh]*
caffeine kafein
cake pasta; **a piece of cake** bir dilim pasta *[beer deeleem]*
calculator hesap makinesi *[hessap makeenessee]*
calendar takvim *[takveem]*
call: what is this called? buna ne denir? *[boona neh deneer]*; **call the manager!** şefinizle görüşmek istiyorum *[shefeeneezleh ghurewshmek eesteeyoroom]*; **I'd like to make a call to England** İngiltere ile görüşmek istiyorum *[eengheeltereh*

eeleh]; **I'll call back later** (*come back*) sonra tekrar uğrarım *[sonra tekrar oo-raruhm]*; (*phone back*) sonra tekrar ararım *[araruhm]*; **I'm expecting a call from London** Londra'dan bir telefon bekliyorum *[londradan beer telefon bekleeyoroom]*; **would you give me a call at 7.30?** bana saat 7.30'da bir telefon eder misiniz? *[bana sa-at yedee boochookta ... eder mee-seeneez]*; **it's been called off** iptal edildi *[eeptal edeeldee]*

call box telefon kulübesi *[telefon koolewbessee]*

calm (*person, sea*) sakin *[sakeen]*; **calm down!** sakin olun! *[oloon]*

Calor gas tüpgaz *[tewpgaz]*

calories kalori *[kaloree]*

camel deve *[deveh]*

camera (*photo*) fotoğraf makinesi *[foto-raf makeenessee]*; (*film*) sinema kamerası *[seenema kamerassuh]*

camp: is there somewhere we can camp? buralarda kamp yapabileceğimiz bir yer var mı? *[booralarda kamp yapabeelejeh-eemeez beer yer var muh]*; **can we camp here?** burada kamp yapabilir miyiz? *[boorada ... yapabeeleer meeyeez]*

campbed portatif yatak *[portateef]*

camping kamping

campsite kamping

can (*tin*) teneke kutu *[tenekeh kootoo]*; **a can of beer** bir kutu bira

can: can I go/come? gide-/gele-bilir miyim? *[gheedeh-/gheleh-beeleer meeyeem]*; **can he swim?** yüzebilir mi? *[yewzebeeleer mee]*; **can we see?** görebilir miyiz? *[gurrebeeleer meeyeez]*; **can they play?** oynayabilirler mi? *[oyn-'eye'-yabeeleerler mee]*; **I can't see/hear** göremiyorum/duyamıyorum *[gurremeeyoroom/doo-yamuh-yoroom]*; **he can't stay** kalamaz; **can I keep it?** bu bende kalabilir mi? *[boo bende kalabeeleer mee]*; **if I can** elimden gelirse *[eleemden gheleer-seh]*; **that can't be right** bu doğru olamaz *[boo do-roo olamaz]*; *see page 119*

Canada Kanada

Canadian Kanadalı *[kanadaluh]*; (*adjective*) Kanada; **the Canadians** kanadalılar

cancel iptal etmek *[eeptal etmek]*; **can I cancel my reservation?** rezervasyonumu iptal edebilir miyim? *[rezervass-yonoomoo ... edebeeleer meeyeem]*; **can we cancel dinner for tonight?** bu akşamki yemek rezervasyonumuzu iptal edebilir miyiz? *[boo akshamkee yemek ... meeyeez]*; **I cancelled it** onu iptal ettim *[onoo ... et-teem]*

cancellation iptal *[eeptal]*

candies şeker *[sheker]*; **a piece of candy** bir şeker *[beer]*

candle mum *[moom]*

canoe kano

can-opener konserve açacağı *[konser-veh achaja-uh]*

cap (*headwear*) kasket *[kasket]*; (*of bottle, radiator*) kapak; **bathing cap** bone *[boneh]*

capital city başkent *[bashkent]*

capital letters büyük harfler *[bew-yewk harfler]*

capsize: it capsized alabora oldu *[alabora oldoo]*

captain kaptan

car otomobil *[otomobeel]*

carafe sürahi *[sewrahee]*

carat: is it 9/14 carat gold? bu 9/14 ayar altın mı? *[boo dokooz/on durt ayar altuhn muh]*

caravan karavan

carbonated gazlı *[gazluh]*

carburet(t)or karbüratör *[karbew-raturr]*

card: do you have a (business) card? kartvizitiniz var mı? *[kartveezee-teeneez var muh]*

cardboard box karton kutu *[karton kootoo]*

cardigan hırka *[huhrka]*

cards oyun kağıdı *[oyoon ka-uhduh]*; **do you play cards?** kağıt oynar mısınız *[ka-uht oynar muhsuhnuhz]*

care: goodbye, take care hoşça kalın *[hosh-cha kaluhn]*; **will you take care of this bag for me?** lütfen bu paketi benim için saklar mısınız? *[lewtfen boo paketee beneem eecheen saklar muhsuhnuhz]*; **care of ...** eliyle *[eleeleh]*

careful: be careful dikkatli olun *[deek-katlee oloon]*

careless: that was careless of you dikkatsizce davrandınız *[deekkatseezjeh davranduhnuhz]*; **careless driving** dikkatsizce araba sürmek *[araba sewrmek]*
car ferry araba vapuru *[vapooroo]*
care hire kiralık otomobil *[keeraluhk otomobeel]*
car keys otomobil anahtarları *[otomobeel anahtarlaruh]*
carnation karanfil *[karanfeel]*
carnival şenlik *[shenleek]*
car park otopark
carpet halı *[haluh]*
car rental (*place*) kiralık otomobil *[keeraluhk otomobeel]*
carrot havuç *[havooch]*
carry taşımak *[tashuhmak]*; **could you carry this for me?** lütfen şunu taşıyabilir misiniz? *[lewtfen shoonoo tashuh-yabeeleer mee-seeneez]*
carry-all çanta *[chanta]*
carry-cot portbebe *[portbebeh]*
car-sick: I get car-sick beni otomobil tutar *[benee otomobeel tootar]*
carton (*of cigarettes*) karton; **a carton of milk** bir kutu süt *[kootoo sewt]*
carving oyma
carwash otomobil yıkama yeri *[otomobeel yuhkama yeree]*
case (*suitcase*) bavul *[bavool]*; **in any case** her halde *[haldeh]*; **in that case** o halde; **it's a special case** bu özel bir durum *[boo urzel beer dooroom]*; **in case he comes back** eğer dönerse *[eh-er durnersheh]*; **I'll take two just in case** her ihtimale karşı iki tane alıyorum *[eehteemaleh karshuh eekee taneh aluh-yoroom]*
cash nakit *[nakeet]*; **I've no cash** yanımda nakit para yok *[yanuhmda]*; **I'll pay cash** nakit olarak ödeyeceğim *[olarak urdayejeh-eem]*; **will you cash a cheque/check for me?** benim için bir çek bozar mısınız? *[beneem eecheen beer chek bozar muhsuhnuhz]*
cashdesk kasa *[kassa]*
cash dispenser otomatik para çekme makinesi *[otomateek para chekmeh makeenessee]*
cash register yazar kasa *[yazar kassa]*
casino kumarhane *[koomarhaneh]*
cassette kaset *[kasset]*
cassette player, cassette recorder kasetli teyp *[kassetlee tayp]*
castle kale *[kaleh]*
casual: casual clothes günlük giysiler *[ghewnlewk gheeseeler]*
cat kedi *[kedee]*
catamaran katamaran
catastrophe felaket *[felaket]*
catch: where do we catch the bus? otobüse nerede binebiliriz? *[otobewsseh neredeh beeneh-beeleereez]*; **he's caught some strange illness** garip bir hastalığa tutuldu *[gareep beer hastaluh-a tootooldoo]*
catching: is it catching? bulaşıcı mı? *[bulashuhjuh muh]*
cathedral katedral
Catholic (*adjective*) Katolik *[katoleek]*
cauliflower karnabahar
cause sebep
cave mağara *[ma-ara]*
caviar havyar
ceiling tavan
celebrations kutlama şenliği *[kootlama shenlee-ee]*
celery sap kerevizi *[kereveezee]*
cellophane selofan
cemetery mezarlık *[mezarluhk]*
center merkez; *see also* **centre**
centigrade santigrat *[santeegrat]*; *see page 121*
centimetre, centimeter santimetre *[santeemetreh]*; *see page 120*
central merkezi *[merkezee]*; **we'd prefer something more central** daha merkezi bir yerde istiyoruz *[daha ... beer yerdeh eesteeyorooz]*
central heating kalorifer *[kaloreefer]*
central station ana istasyon *[ana eestassyon]*
centre merkez; **how do we get to the centre?** şehir merkezine nasıl gidilir? *[sheheer merkezeeneh nassuhl gheedeeleer]*; **in the centre** (*of town*) şehir merkezinde *[merkezeendeh]*
century yüzyıl *[yewz-yuhl]*; **in the 19th/20th century** 19uncu/20nci yüzyılda *[on dokoozoonjoo/yeermeeyeenjee yewz-yuhlda]*
ceramics seramik *[serameek]*
certain: are you certain? emin misiniz? *[emeen meesseeneez]*; **he is certain to come** geleceği kesindir

[ghelejeh-ee kesseendeer]

certainly kesinlikle *[kesseenleekleh]*; **certainly not** kesinlikle öyle değil *[urleh deh-eel]*

certificate belge *[belgheh]*; **birth certificate** nüfus kâğıdı *[newfoos ka-uhduh]*

chain zincir *[zeenjeer]*

chair iskemle *[eeskemleh]*

chambermaid oda hizmetçisi *[oda heezmet-cheessee]*

champagne şampanya *[shampanya]*

chance: quite by chance tesadüfen *[tessadewfen]*; **no chance!** imkânsız! *[eemkansuhz]*

change: could you change this into liras? bunu Türk lirasıyla değiştire-bilir misiniz? *[boonoo tewrk leerassuhla deh-eeshteereh-beeleer mee-seeneez]*; **I haven't got any change** hiç bozuk param yok *[heech bozook param yok]*; **can you give me change for a 1,000 lira note?** bana 1000 lira bozabilir misiniz? *[bana been leera bozabeeleer mee-seeneez]*; **do we have to change (trains)?** aktarma yapmamız lazım mı? *[yapmamuhz lazuhm muh]*; **for a change** değişiklik olsun diye *[deh-eesheekleek olsoon deeyeh]*; **you haven't changed the sheets** çarşafları değiştirmediniz *[charshaflaruh deh-eeshteer-medeeneez]*; **the place has changed so much** burası o kadar değişmiş ki *[boorassuh o kadar deh-eeshmeesh kee]*; **do you want to change places with me?** benimle yer değiştirmek ister misiniz? *[beneemleh yer deh-eeshteermek eester mee-seeneez]*; **can I change this for ...?** bunu ... ile değiştirebilir miyim? *[eeleh deh-eeshteereh-beeleer meeyeem]*

changeable değişken *[deh-eeshken]*

channel: the English Channel Manş Denizi *[mansh deneezee]*

chaos keşmekeş *[keshmekesh]*

chap adam

chapel kilise *[keeleesseh]*

charge: is there an extra charge? bunun için ayrıca ücret alıyor musunuz? *[boonoon eecheen 'eye'-ruhja ewjret aluhyor moo-soonooz]*; **what do you charge?** ne kadar ücret istiyorsunuz? *[neh kadar ewjret eesteeyor-soonooz]*; **who's in charge here?** buranın sorumlusu kim? *[booranuhn soroomloossoo keem]*

charming cana yakın *[jana yakuhn]*

chart şema *[shema]*; (*navigation*) deniz haritası *[deneez hareetassuh]*

charter flight çarter seferi *[charter seferee]*

chassis şasi *[shassee]*

cheap ucuz *[oojooz]*; **do you have something cheaper?** daha ucuz bir şey var mı? *[beer shay var muh]*

cheat: I've been cheated aldatıldım *[aldatuhlduhm]*

check: will you check? gözden geçirir misiniz? *[gurzden ghecheereer mee-seeneez]*; **will you check the steering?** direksiyonu muayene eder misiniz? *[deerekseeyonoo moo-'eye'-yeneh eder mee-seeneez]*; **will you check the bill?** hesabı kontrol eder misiniz? *[hessabuh]*; **I've checked it** kontrol ettim *[et-teem]*

check (*money*) çek *[chek]*; **will you take a check?** çek kabul ediyor musunuz? *[kabool edeeyor moossoonooz]*

check (*bill*) hesap *[hessap]*; **may I have the check please?** lütfen hesabı getirir misiniz? *[lewtfen hessabuh gheteereer mee-seeneez]*

checkbook çek defteri *[chek defteree]*

checked (*shirt*) kareli *[karelee]*

checkers dama

check-in bagaj kayıt *[bagaȷ k-'eye'-yuht]*

checkroom (*for coats*) vestiyer *[vesteeyer]*

cheek (*on face*) yanak; **what a cheek!** yüzsüzlüğün daniskası! *[yewz-sewzlew-ewn daneeskassuh]*

cheeky (*person*) küstah *[kewstah]*

cheerio (*bye-bye*) eyvallah *[ayval-lah]*

cheers (*thank you*) teşekkürler *[teshek-kewrler]*; (*toast*) şerefe *[sherefeh]*

cheer up! hadi, üzülme! *[hadee ewzewlmeh]*

cheese peynir *[payneer]*

chef ahçıbaşı *[ahchuh-bashuh]*

chemist (*shop*) eczane *[ejzaneh]*

cheque çek *[chek]*; **will you take a cheque?** çek kabul eder misiniz? *[kabool eder mee-seeneez]*

cheque book çek defteri *[chek*

defteree]
cheque card çek kartı *[chek kartuh]*
cherry kiraz *[keeraz]*
chess satranç *[satranch]*
chest (*body*) göğüs *[gur-ewss]*
chewing gum çiklet *[cheeklet]*
chicken tavuk *[tavook]*
chickenpox suçiçeği *[soocheecheh-ee]*
child çocuk *[chojook]*; **children** çocuklar *[choojooklar]*
child minder çocuk bakıcısı *[chojook bakuhjuhssuh]*
child minding service çocuk bakım servisi *[chojook bakuhm serveessee]*
children's playground çocuk bahçesi *[chojook bahchessee]*
children's pool çocuk havuzu *[chojook havoozoo]*
children's portion çocuk porsiyonu *[chojook porseeyonoo]*
children's room çocuk odası *[chojook odassuh]*
chilled (*wine*) soğutulmuş *[so-ootoolmoosh]*; **it's not properly chilled** yeterince soğutulmamış *[yetereenjeh so-ootoolmamuhsh]*
chilly serin *[sereen]*
chimney baca *[baja]*
chin çene *[cheneh]*
china porselen *[porselen]*
chips patates kızartması *[patatess kuhzartmassuh]*; **potato chips** cips *[jeeps]*
chiropodist ayak bakımı uzmanı *['eye'-yak bakuhmuh oozmanuh]*
chocolate çikolata *[cheekolata]*; **a chocolate bar** tablet çikolata; **a box of chocolates** bir kutu çikolata *[beer kootoo]*; **a hot chocolate** kakao *[kaka-o]*
choke (*on car*) jikle *[ʒeekleh]*
choose: it's hard to choose seçmek zor *[sechmek]*; **you choose for us** bizim için siz seçin *[beezeem eecheen seez secheen]*
chop: a lamb chop kuzu pirzolası *[domooz/koozoo peerzolassuh]*
Christian Hıristiyan *[huhreesteeyan]*
Christian name öz ad *[urz]*
Christmas Noel; **merry Christmas** Noeliniz kutlu olsun *[no-eleeneez kootloo olsoon]*
church kilise *[keeleesseh]*; **where is the Protestant/Catholic church?** Protestan/Katolik kilisesi nerede? *[katoleek keelees-sessee neredeh]*
cider elma şarabı *[elma sharabuh]*
cigar puro *[pooro]*
cigarette sigara *[seegara]*; **tipped/plain cigarettes** filtreli/filtresiz sigara *[feeltrelee/feeltresseez]*
cigarette lighter çakmak *[chakmak]*
cine-camera sinema kamerası *[seenema kamerassuh]*
cinema sinema *[seenema]*
circle daire *[da-eereh]*; (*in theatre*) balkon
citizen: I'm a British/American citizen ben İngiliz/Amerikan vatandaşıyım *[eengheeleez/amereekan vatandashuh-yuhm]*
city şehir *[sheheer]*
city centre, city center şehir merkezi *[sheheer merkezee]*
claim (*noun: insurance*) talep
claim form talep formüleri *[formewleree]*
clarify açıklamak *[achuhklamak]*
classical klasik *[klasseek]*
clean (*adjective*) temiz *[temeez]*; **may I have some clean sheets?** lütfen temiz çarşaf verir misiniz? *[lewtfen ... charshaf vereer mee-seeneez]*; **our apartment hasn't been cleaned today** dairemiz bugün temizlenmedi *[da-eereemeez booghewn temeezlenmedee]*; **it's not clean** bu temiz değil *[boo ... deh-eel]*; **can you clean this for me?** lütfen bunu temizler misiniz? *[boonoo temeezler]*
cleaning solution (*for contact lenses*) temizleme sıvısı *[temeezlemeh suhvuhssuh]*
cleansing cream (*cosmetic*) temizleyici krem *[temeezlayeejee]*
clear: it's not very clear o kadar iyi anlaşılmıyor *[o kadar eeyee anlashuhl-muhyor]*; **ok, that's clear** tamam, anlaşıldı *[anlashuhlduh]*
clever akıllı *[akuhl-luh]*
cliff yar
climate iklim *[eekleem]*
climb: it's a long climb to the top tepeye çıkmak uzun zaman alıyor *[tepayeh chuhkmak oozoon zaman aluhyor]*; **we're going to climb ...** biz ...-e tırmanacağız *[beez ...-eh tuhrmanaja-uhz]*

climber dağcı *[da-juh]*
climbing boots dağcı botları *[da-juh botlaruh]*
clinic klinik *[kleeneek]*
clip (*ski*) klip *[kleep]*
cloakroom (*for coats*) vestiyer *[vesteeyer]*; (*WC*) tuvalet *[toovalet]*
clock saat *[sa-at]*
close: is it close? yakında mı? *[yakuhnda muh]*; **close to the hotel** otelin yakınında *[oteleen yakuhnuhnda]*; **close by** yakında
close: when do you close? saat kaçta kapatıyorsunuz? *[sa-at kachta kapatuhyor-soonooz]*
closed kapalı *[kapaluh]*; **they were closed** kapalıydılar *[kapaluhduhlar]*
closet dolap
cloth (*material*) kumaş *[koomash]*; (*rag*) bez
clothes elbiseler *[elbeesseler]*
clothes line çamaşır ipi *[chamashuhr eepee]*
clothes peg, clothespin çamaşır mandalı *[chamashuhr mandaluh]*
clouds bulutlar *[boolootlar]*; **it's clouding over** hava kapanıyor *[hava kapanuhyor]*
cloudy bulutlu *[boolootloo]*
club klüp *[klewp]*
clubhouse klüp binası *[klewp beenassuh]*
clumsy beceriksiz *[bejereekseez]*
clutch (*car*) debriyaj *[debreeyaJ]*; **the clutch is slipping** debriyaj kaçırıyor *[kachuhruhyor]*
coach (*bus*) otobüs *[otobewss]*
coach party otobüs grubu *[otobewss grooboo]*
coach trip otobüsle gezi *[otobewssleh ghezee]*
coast sahil *[saheel]*; **at the coast** sahilde *[saheeldeh]*
coastguard sahil muhafaza *[saheel moohafaza]*
coat (*overcoat etc*) palto; (*jacket*) ceket *[jeket]*
coathanger elbise askısı *[elbeesseh askuhssuh]*
cobbled street arnavut kaldırımı *[arnavoot kalduhruhmuh]*
cobbler ayakkabı tamircisi *['eye'-yakkabuh tameerjeessee]*
cockroach tahta kurusu *[tahta kooroossoo]*
cocktail kokteyl *[koktayl]*
cocktail bar kokteyl barı *[koktayl baruh]*
cocoa kakao *[kaka-o]*
coconut hindistancevizi *[heendeestan-jeveezee]*
code: what's the (dialling) code for ...? ...-in kodu nedir? *[...-een kodoo nedeer]*
coffee kahve *[kahveh]*; **a white coffee, a coffee with milk** bir sütlü kahve *[beer sewtlew]*; **a black coffee** sütsüz kahve *[sewtsewz]*; **two coffees, please** iki kahve, lütfen *[eekee ... lewtfen]*; **Turkish coffee** Türk kahvesi *[tewrk kahvessee]*; **a sweet/medium/unsweetened Turkish coffee** bir şekerli/orta şekerli/sade Türk kahvesi *[beer shekerlee/orta/sadeh]*
coin madeni para *[madenee para]*
Coke (*tm*) Koka Kola
cold (*adjective*) soğuk *[so-ook]*; **I'm cold** üşüyorum *[ewshew-yoroom]*; **I have a cold** soğuk aldım *[alduhm]*
coldbox (*for carrying food*) buz kutusu *[booz kootoossoo]*
cold cream yüz kremi *[yewz kremee]*
collapse: he's collapsed yıkılıverdi *[yuhkuhluh-verdee]*
collar yaka
collarbone köprücük kemiği *[kurprewjewk kemee-ee]*
colleague: my colleague meslektaşım *[meslektashuhm]*; **your colleague** meslektaşınız *[...-uhnuhz]*
collect: I've come to collect ... ...-i almaya geldim *[...-uh alm-'eye'-ya gheldeem]*; **I collect ...** (*stamps etc*) ... koleksiyonu yapıyorum *[kolekssee-yonoo yapuh-yoroom]*; **I want to call New York collect** New York'u ödemeli aramak istiyorum *[New York'oo urdemelee aramak eesteeyoroom]*
collect call ödemeli konuşma *[urdemelee konooshma]*
college kolej *[koleJ]*
collision çarpışma *[charpuhshma]*
cologne kolonya
colo(u)r renk; **do you have any other colo(u)rs?** başka renkleriniz var mı? *[bashka renklereeneez var muh]*
colo(u)r film renkli filim *[renklee*

feeleem]
comb (*noun*) tarak
come gelmek *[ghelmek]*; **I come from London** ben Londra'lıyım *[ben londraluhyuhm]*; **where do you come from?** siz nerelisiniz? *[seez nereleeseeneez]*; **when are they coming?** ne zaman geliyorlar? *[neh zaman gheleeyorlar]*; **come here** buraya gelin *[boor-'eye'-ya gheleen]*; **come with me** benimle gelin *[beneemleh]*; **come back!** geri dönün! *[gheree durnewn]*; **I'll come back later** sonra tekrar gelirim *[sonra tekrar gheleereem]*; **come in!** giriniz! *[gheereeneez]*; **he's coming on very well** (*improving*) iyi gelişme gösteriyor *[eeyee gheleeshmeh gurstereeyor]*; **come on!** hadi! *[hadee]*; **do you want to come out this evening?** bu akşam dışarı çıkmak ister misiniz? *[boo aksham duhsharuh chuhkmak eester meeseeneez]*; **these two pictures didn't come out** bu iki fotoğraf çıkmamış *[boo eekee foto-raf chuhkmamuhsh]*; **the money hasn't come through yet** para henüz gelmemiş *[para henewz ghelmemeesh]*
comfortable (*hotel etc*) rahat; **it's not very comfortable** o kadar rahat değil *[deh-eel]*
Common Market Ortak Pazar
company (*firm*) şirket *[sheerket]*
comparison: there's no comparison mukayese götürmez *[mook-'eye'-yesseh gurtewrmez]*
compartment (*train*) kompartıman *[kompartuhman]*
compass pusula *[poossoola]*
compensation tazminat *[tazmeenat]*
complain şikayet etmek *[sheek-'eye'-yet etmek]*; **I want to complain about my room** odamla ilgili şikayetim var *[odamla eelgheelee ...-eem]*
complaint şikayet *[sheek-'eye'-yet]*; **I have a complaint** bir şikayette bulunmak istiyorum *[beer ...-teh booloonmak eesteeyoroom]*
complete: the complete set komple takım *[kompleh takuhm]*; **it's a complete disaster** tam bir felaket *[beer felaket]*
completely tamamen
complicated: it's very complicated çok karmaşık *[chok karmashuhk]*
compliment övgü *[urvghew]*; **my compliments to the chef** ahçıbaşının eline sağlık *[ahchuh-bashuhnuhn eeleneh sa-luhk]*
comprehensive (*insurance*) kapsamlı *[kapsamluh]*
compulsory mecburi *[mejborree]*
computer bilgisayar *[beelghee-s-'eye'-yar]*
concern: we are very concerned çok endişeliyiz *[chok endeesheleeyeez]*
concert konser
concussion sarsıntı *[sarsuhntuh]*
condenser (*in car*) kondensatör *[kondensaturr]*
condition durum *[dooroom]*; **it's not in very good condition** pek iyi durumda değil *[eeyee dooroomda deheel]*
conditioner balsam *[balssam]*
condom prezervatif *[prezervateef]*
conductor kondüktör *[kondewkturr]*
conference konferans
confirm: can you confirm the reservation? rezervasyonu teyid edebilir misiniz? *[rezervassyonoo tayeed edebeeleer mee-seeneez]*
confuse: it's very confusing çok kafa karıştırıcı *[chok kafa karuhshtuhruhjuh]*
congratulations tebrikler *[tebreekler]*
conjunctivitis konjonktivit *[konJonkteeveet]*
connection (*in travelling*) bağlantı *[ba-lantuh]*
connoisseur erbap
conscious (*medically*) bilinçli *[beeleenchlee]*
consciousness: he's lost consciousness kendinden geçti *[kendeenden ghechtee]*
constipation kabızlık *[kabuhzluhk]*
consul konsolos *[konsoloss]*
consulate konsolosluk *[konsolosslook]*
contact: how can I contact ...? ... ile nasıl temas kurabilirim? *[eeleh nassuhl temass koorabeeleereem]*; **I'm trying to contact ...** ... ile temas kurmaya çalışıyorum *[koorm-'eye'-ya chaluhshuh-yoroom]*
contact lenses kontak lensleri *[kontak lensleree]*
contraceptive gebeliği önleyici

[ghebelee-ee urnlayeejee]
convenient (*time, location*) uygun *[ooy-goon]*; **that's not convenient** bu uygun değil *[boo ... deh-eel]*
cook: it's not properly cooked (*is underdone*) yeterince pişmemiş *[yetereenjeh peeshmemeesh]*; **it's beautifully cooked** çok güzel pişmiş *[chok ghewzel peeshmeesh]*; **he's a good cook** o iyi ahçıdır *[eeyee ahchuhduhr]*
cooker ocak *[ojak]*
cookie bisküvi *[beeskewvee]*
cool (*day, weather*) serin *[sereen]*
copper bakır *[bakuhr]*
corduroy fitilli kadife *[feeteel-lee kadeefeh]*
cork (*in bottle*) mantar
corkscrew tirbuşon *[teerbooshon]*
corn (*on foot*) nasır *[nassuhr]*
corner: on the corner köşede *[kurshedeh]*; **in the corner** köşede; **a corner table** köşede bir masa *[beer massa]*
cornflakes mısırlı kahvaltılık *[muhsuhrluh kahvaltuhluhk]*
coronary enfarktüs *[enfarktews]*
correct (*adjective*) doğru *[do-roo]*; **please correct me if I make a mistake** hata yaparsam lütfen düzeltin *[hata yaparsam lewtfen dewzelteen]*
corridor koridor *[koreedor]*
corset korse *[korseh]*
cosmetics kozmetik *[kozmeteek]*
cost: what does it cost? fiyatı nedir? *[feeyatuh nedeer]*
cot (*for baby*) çocuk yatağı *[chojook yata-uh]*; (*for camping*) portatif yatak *[portateef yatak]*
cottage sayfiye evi *[s-'eye'-feeyeh evee]*
cotton pamuk *[pamook]*
cotton buds pamuklu çubuk *[pamookloo choobook]*
cotton wool hidrofil pamuk *[heedrofeel pamook]*
couch divan *[deevan]*
couchette kuşet *[kooshet]*
cough (*noun*) öksürük *[urksewrewk]*
cough tablets öksürük hapları *[urksewrewk haplaruh]*
cough medicine öksürük ilacı *[urksewrewk eelajuh]*
could: could you help me? bana yardım edebilir misiniz? *[bana yarduhm edebeeleer mee-seeneez]*; **could you read it out?** yüksek sesle okuyabilir misiniz? *[yewk-sek sessleh okoo-yabeeleer]*; **I couldn't understand** anlayamadım *[anl-'eye'-yamaduhm]*; **he couldn't come** gelemedi *[ghelemedee]*; *see page 119*
country (*nation*) ülke *[ewlkeh]*; **in the country** (*countryside*) kırda *[kuhrda]*
countryside kırsal alanlar *[kuhrsal alanlar]*
couple (*man and woman*) çift *[cheeft]*; **a couple of ...** bir çift ... *[beer]*
courier kurye *[koor-yeh]*
course (*of meal*) servis *[serveess]*; **of course** elbette *[elbet-teh]*; **of course not** tabii değil *[tabee-ee deh-eel]*
court (*law*) mahkeme *[mahkemeh]*; (*tennis*) kort
courtesy bus (*airport to hotel etc*) ücretsiz otobüs *[ewjretseez otobewss]*
cousin: my cousin (*male*) kuzenim *[koozeneem]*; (*female*) kuzinim *[koozeeneem]*
cover charge masa ücreti *[massa ewjretee]*
cow inek *[eenek]*
crab yengeç *[yenghech]*
cracked: it's cracked (*plate etc*) bu çatlamış *[boo chatlamuhsh]*
cracker (*biscuit*) krik krak *[kreek]*
craftshop el sanatları dükkanı *[sanatlaruh dewk-kanuh]*
cramp (*in leg etc*) kramp
crankshaft krank mili *[meelee]*
crash: there's been a crash kaza olmuş *[kaza olmoosh]*
crash course yoğun kurs *[yo-oon koors]*
crash helmet koruyucu başlık *[koroo-yoojoo bashluhk]*
crawl (*swimming*) kulaç *[koolach]*
crazy deli *[delee]*
cream (*on milk*) kaymak *[k-'eye'-mak]*; (*in cake*) krema; (*for face*) krem
creche (*for babies*) kreş *[kresh]*
credit card kredi kartı *[kredee kartuh]*
Crete Girit *[gheereet]*
crib (*baby's cot*) çocuk yatağı *[chojook yata-uh]*
crisis kriz *[kreez]*
crisps cips *[jeeps]*

crockery yemek takımları *[yemek takuhmlaruh]*
crook; he's a crook o düzenbazdır *[dewzenbazduhr]*
crossing (*by sea*) geçiş *[ghecheesh]*
crossroads kavşak *[kavshak]*
crosswalk yaya geçidi *[y-'eye'-ya ghecheedee]*
crowd kalabalık *[kalabaluhk]*
crowded kalabalık *[kalabaluhk]*
crown (*on tooth*) kuron *[kooron]*
crucial: it's absolutely crucial son derece önemlidir *[derejeh urnemleedeer]*
cruise (*by ship*) sefer
crutch (*of body*) kasık *[kassuhk]*
crutches koltuk değnekleri *[koltook deh-nekleree]*
cry ağlamak *[a-lamak]*; **don't cry** ağlamayın *[a-lam-'eye'-yuhn]*
cucumber salatalık *[salataluhk]*
cuisine mutfak *[mootfak]*
cultural kültürel *[kewltewrel]*
cup fincan *[feenjan]*; **a cup of coffee** bir fincan kahve *[beer ... kahveh]*
cupboard dolap
cure: have you got something to cure it? buna iyi gelecek bir şey var mı? *[boona eeyee ghelejek beer shay var muh]*
curlers bigudi *[beegoodee]*
current (*elec*) akım *[akuhm]*; (*in water*) akıntı *[akuhntuh]*
curtains perdeler
curve (*noun: in road*) viraj *[veeraJ]*
cushion yastık *[yastuhk]*
custom gelenek *[ghelenek]*
Customs Gümrük *[ghewmrewk]*
cut: I've cut my hand elimi kestim *[eleemee kesteem]*; **could you cut a little off here?** buradan biraz alabilir misiniz? *[booradan beeraz alabeeleer mee-seeneez]*; **we were cut off** (*telec*) görüşmemiz kesildi *[gurewshmemeez kesseeldee]*; **the engine keeps cutting out** motor durmadan stop ediyor *[motor doormadan stop edeeyor]*
cutlery çatal bıçak *[chatal buhchak]*
cutlets kotlet
cycle: can we cycle there? (*is it far?*) oraya bisikletle gidebilir miyiz? *[or-'eye'-ya bee-seekletleh gheedebeeleer meeyeez]*
cyclist bisikletli *[bee-seekletlee]*
cylinder (*of car*) silindir *[seeleendeer]*
cylinder-head gasket motor kapak contası *[motor kapak jontassuh]*
cynical sinik *[seeneek]*
Cypriot (*person*) Kıbrıslı *[kuhbruhsluh]*; (*adjective*) Kıbrıs *[kuhbruhss]*
Cyprus Kıbrıs *[kuhbruhss]*
cystitis sistit *[seesteet]*

D

damage: you've damaged it onu bozdunuz *[onoo bozdoonooz]*; **it's damaged** hasara uğramış *[hassara oo-ramuhsh]*; **there's no damage** bir şey olmamış *[beer shay olmamuhsh]*
damn! Allah kahretsin! *[Allah kahretseen]*
damp (*adjective*) nemli *[nemlee]*
dance: a Turkish dance bir Türk dansı *[beer tewrk dansuh]*; **folk dance** halk oyunu *[oyoonoo]*; **do you want to dance?** dans etmek ister misiniz? *[eester mee-seeneez]*
dancer: he's a good dancer o iyi dans eder *[eeyee dans eder]*
dancing: we'd like to go dancing dansa gitmek istiyoruz *[dansa gheetmek eesteeyorooz]*; **traditional (Turkish) dancing** geleneksel oyun *[gheleneksel oy-yoon]*
dandruff kepek
dangerous tehlikeli *[tehleekelee]*
Dardanelles Çanakkale Boğazı *[chanak-kaleh bo-azuh]*
dare: I don't dare kendime güvenemiyorum *[kendeemeh ghewvenemeeyoroom]*
dark (*adjective*) karanlık *[karanluhk]*; (*colour*) koyu *[koyoo]*; **dark blue** lacivert *[lajeevert]*; **when does it get dark?** hava saat kaçta kararıyor? *[saat kachta kararuh-yor]*; **after dark** hava kararınca *[kararuhnja]*
darling sevgili *[sevgheelee]*

dashboard kumanda tablosu *[koomanda tablosoo]*
date: what's the date? bugün ayın kaçı? *[booghewn ayuhn kachuh]*; **on what date?** hangi tarihte? *[hanghee tareehteh]*; **can we make a date?** (*romantic*) buluşalım mı? *[booloo-shaluhm muh]*; (*to business partner*) bir tarih saptayabilir miyiz? *[beer tareeh sapt-'eye'-yabeeleer meeyeez]*
dates (*to eat*) hurma *[hoorma]*
daughter kız *[kuhz]*; **my daughter** kızım *[kuhzuhm]*
daughter-in-law gelin *[gheleen]*
dawn (*noun*) şafak *[shafak]*; **at dawn** gün ağarırken *[ghewn a-aruhrken]*
day gün *[ghewn]*; **the day after** ertesi gün *[ertessee]*; **the day before** evvelki gün *[evvelkee]*; **every day** her gün; **one day** bir gün; **can we pay by the day?** günlük ödeme yapabilir miyiz? *[ghewnlewk urdemeh yapabeeleer meeyeez]*; **have a good day!** iyi günler! *[eeyee ghewnler]*
daylight robbery kazıkçılık *[kazuhk-chuhluhk]*
day trip günlük gezi *[ghewnlewk ghezee]*
dead ölü *[urlew]*
deaf sağır *[sa-uhr]*
deaf-aid işitme cihazı *[eesheetmeh jeehazuh]*
deal (*business*) iş *[eesh]*; **it's a deal** tamam, anlaştık *[tamam anlashtuhk]*; **will you deal with it?** siz meşgul olur musunuz? *[seez meshgool oloor moo-soonooz]*
dealer (*agent*) satıcı *[satuhjuh]*
dear (*expensive*) pahalı *[pahaluh]*; **Dear Sir** Sayın Bay (+ *surname*) *[s-'eye'-yuhn b-'eye']*; **Dear Madam** Sayın Bayan (+ *surname*) *[b-'eye'-yan]*; **Dear Hasan** Sevgili Hasan *[sevgheelee hassan]*; **Dear Ayşe** Sevgili Ayşe *['eye'-sheh]*
death ölüm *[urlewm]*
decadent yozlaşmış *[yozlashmuhsh]*
December Aralık *[araluhk]*
decent: that's very decent of you çok naziksiniz *[chok nazeekseeneez]*
decide: we haven't decided yet henüz karar vermedik *[henewz karar vermedeek]*; **you decide for us** siz bizim yerimize karar verin *[seez beezeem yereemeezeh ... vereen]*; **it's all decided** artık herşey karara bağlandı *[artuhk her shay karara ba-landuh]*
decision karar
deck (*on ship*) güverte *[ghew-verteh]*
deckchair şezlong *[shezlong]*
declare: I have nothing to declare beyan edecek bir şeyim yok *[bayan edejek beer shayeem yok]*
decoration (*in room*) dekorasyon
deduct düşmek *[dewshmek]*
deep derin *[dereen]*; **is it deep?** derin mi? *[mee]*
definitely kesinlikle *[kesseenleekleh]*; **definitely not** kesinlikle öyle değil *[urleh deh-eel]*
degree (*univ*) diploma *[deeploma]*; (*temperature*) derece *[derejeh]*
dehydrated (*person*) su kaybetmiş *[soo k-'eye'-betmeesh]*
de-icer buz giderici *[booz gheedereejee]*
delay: the flight was delayed uçak rötar yaptı *[oochak rurtar yaptuh]*
deliberately bile bile *[beeleh]*
delicacy: a local delicacy yöresel yiyecek *[yurressel yeeyejek]*
delicious nefis *[nefeess]*
deliver: will you deliver it? adresime teslim eder misiniz? *[adresseemeh tessleem eder meeseeneez]*
delivery: is there another mail delivery? başka posta dağıtımı var mı? *[bashka posta da-uhtuhmuh var muh]*
de luxe lüks *[lewks]*
denims blucin *[bloojeen]*
Denmark Danimarka *[daneemarka]*
dent: there's a dent in it berelenmiş *[berelenmeesh]*
dental floss diş floşu *[dish floshoo]*
dentist dişçi *[deesh-chee]*
dentures protez
deny: he denies it inkâr ediyor *[eenkar edeeyor]*
deodorant deodoran
department store büyük mağaza *[bew-yewk ma-aza]*
departure kalkış *[kalkuhsh]*
departure lounge giden yolcular salonu *[gheeden yoljoolar salonoo]*
depend: it depends duruma göre *[doorooma gurreh]*; **it depends on ...** ...-e bağlıdır *[—eh ba-luhduhr]*

deposit (*downpayment*) depozito
depressed kederli *[kederlee]*
depth derinlik *[dereenleek]*
description tanım *[tanuhm]*
deserted (*beach, area*) ıssız *[uhs-suhz]*
dessert üstlük *[ewstlewk]*
destination gidilecek yer *[gheedeelejek yer]*
detergent deterjan *[deterɹan]*
detour dolambaçlı yol *[dolambachluh]*
devalued değeri düşürülmüş *[deh-eree dewshewr-ewlmew*sh]
develop: could you develop these films? bu filimleri develope eder misiniz? *[boo feeleemleree developeh eder mee-seeneez]*
diabetic (*noun*) şeker hastası *[sheker hastassuh]*
diagram grafik *[grafeek]*
dialect lehçe *[lehcheh]*
dialling code telefon kodu *[kodoo]*
diamond elmas *[elmass]*
diaper çocuk bezi *[chojook bezee]*
diarrhoea, diarrhea ishal *[eess-hal]*; **do you have something to stop diarrhoea?** ishali önelyici bir ilaç var mı? *[eess-halee urnlayeejee beer eelach var muh]*
diary (*business etc*) acenda *[ajenda]*; (*for personal experiences*) günce *[ghewnjeh]*
dictionary sözlük *[surzlewk]*; **a Turkish/ English dictionary** Türkçe/İngilizce sözlük *[tewrkjeh/ eengheeleezjeh]*
didn't *see* **not** *and page 117*
die ölmek *[urlmek]*; **I'm absolutely dying for a drink** susuzluktan ölüyorum *[soossoozlooktan urlew-yoroom]*
diesel (*fuel*) mazot
diet perhiz *[perheez]*; **I'm on a diet** perhiz yapıyorum *[yapuh-yoroom]*
difference fark; **what's the difference between ...?** ... ile arasında ne fark var? *[eeleh arasuhnda neh]*; **I can't tell the difference** bir fark göremiyorum *[beer ... gurremee-yoroom]*; **it doesn't make any difference** hiç fark etmez *[heech]*
different: they are different aynı değiller *['eye'-nuh deh-eel-ler]*; **they are very different** çok farklılar *[chok farkluhlar]*; **it's different from this one** bundan farklı *[boondan farkluh]*; **may we have a different table?** bize başka bir masa verebilir misiniz? *[beezeh bashka beer massa verebeeleer mee-seeneez]*; **ah well, that's different** ha, o zaman başka
difficult zor
difficulty zorluk *[zorlook]*; **without any difficulty** hiç zorluk çekmeden *[heech ... chekmeden]*; **I'm having difficulties with ...** ... ile başım bela-da *[eeleh bashuhm belada]*
digestion sindirim *[seendeereem]*
dining car vagon restoran
dining room yemek salonu *[salonoo]*
dinner akşam yemeği *[aksham yemeh-ee]*
dinner jacket smokin
dinner party yemekli toplantı *[yemeklee toplantuh]*
dipped headlights kısa far *[kuhssa]*
dipstick yağ seviye çubuğu *[ya seveeyeh chooboo-oo]*
direct (*adjective*) direkt *[deerekt]*; **does it go direct?** direkt sefer mi? *[mee]*
direction yön *[yurn]*; **in which direction is it?** hangi yöndedir? *[hanghee ... dedeer]*; **is it in this direction?** bu yönde mi? *[boo yurndeh mee]*
directory: telephone directory telefon rehberi *[telefon rehberee]*
directory enquiries bilinmeyen numaralar *[beeleenmayen noomaralar]*
dirt pislik *[peessleek]*
dirty kirli *[keerlee]*; (*habit*) pis *[peess]*
disabled özürlü *[urzewrlew]*
disagree: it disagrees with me bana dokunuyor *[bana dokoonoo-yor]*
disappear kaybolmak *[k-'eye'-bol-mak]*; **it's just disappeared** (*I've lost it*) ortadan kayboldu *[k-'eye'-boldoo]*
disappointed: I was disappointed beklediğim gibi çıkmadı *[bekledee-eem gheebee chuhkmaduh]*
disappointing hayal kırıcı *[h-'eye'-yal kuhruhjuh]*
disaster felaket
discharge (*pus*) cerahat *[jerahat]*
disco disko
disco dancing disko dansı *[danssuh]*
discount (*noun*) iskonto *[eeskonto]*
disease hastalık *[hastaluhk]*
disgusting iğrenç *[ee-rench]*
dish (*meal*) yemek; (*plate*) tabak

dishcloth bulaşık bezi *[boolashuhk bezee]*
dishwashing liquid bulaşık deterjanı *[boolashuhk deterjanuh]*
disinfectant (*noun*) dezenfektan
disk of film film disketi *[feelm deesketee]*
dislocated shoulder çıkık omuz *[chuhkuhk omooz]*
dispensing chemist eczane *[ejzaneh]*
disposable nappies kâgit çocuk bezi *[ka-uht chojook bezee]*
distance uzaklık *[oozakluhk]*; **what's the distance from ... to ...?** ... ile ... arasındaki uzaklık ne kadardır? *[eeleh ... arassuhndakee ... neh kadarduhr]*; **in the distance** uzakta *[oozakta]*
distilled water arı su *[aruh soo]*
disturb: the disco is disturbing us diskotek bizi rahatsız ediyor *[deeskotek beezee rahatsuhz edeeyor]*; **please don't disturb** lütfen rahatsız etmeyin *[lewtfen ... etmayeen]*
diversion (*traffic*) geçici güzergah *[ghecheejee ghewzergah]*
diving board tramplen
divorced boşanmış *[boshanmuhsh]*
dizzy: I feel dizzy başım dönüyor *[bashuhm durnew-yor]*; **dizzy spells** ara sıra baş dönmesi *[ara suhra bash durnmessee]*
do yapmak; **what shall I do?** ne yapayım? *[neh yap-'eye'-yuhm]*; **what are you doing tonight?** bu akşam ne yapıyorsunuz? *[boo aksham neh yapuhyor-soonooz]*; **how do you do it?** onu nasıl yapıyorsunuz? *[onoo nassuhl yapuhyor-soonooz]*; **will you do it for me?** benim için bunu yapabilir misiniz? *[beneem eecheen boonoo yapabeeleer mee-seeneez]*; **who did it?** kim yaptı? *[keem yaptuh]*; **the meat's not done** et pişmemiş *[et peeshmemeesh]*; **what do you do?** (*job*) ne iş yapıyorsunuz? *[neh eesh yapuhyor-soonooz]*; **do you have ...?** ... var mı? *[muh]*
docks doklar
doctor doktor; **he needs a doctor** ona doktor lazım *[lazuhm]*; **can you call a doctor?** bir doktor çağırabilir misiniz? *[cha-uhrabeeleer mee-seeneez]*
document belge *[belgheh]*
dog köpek *[kurpek]*
doll bebek
dollar dolar
donkey eşek *[eshek]*
don't! yapma!; *see* **not** *and page 117*
door (*of room, car*) kapı *[kapuh]*
doorman kapıcı *[kapuhjuh]*
dosage doz
double: double room iki kişilik oda *[eekee keesheeleek oda]*; **double bed** iki kişilik yatak; **double brandy** duble konyak *[doobleh]*; **double r** iki r *[eekee reh]*; **it's all double Dutch to me** hiç bir şey anlamıyorum *[heech beer shay anlamuhyoroom]*
doubt: I doubt it sanmam
douche (*medical*) şırınga *[shuhruhnga]*
down: get down! çök! *[chuhk]*; **he's not down yet** (*is in room, bed*) henüz kalkmadı *[henewz kalkmaduh]*; **further down the road** yolun biraz ilerisinde *[yoloon beeraz eeleree-seendeh]*; **I paid 20% down** % 20'sini peşin ödedim *[yewzdeh yeermee-seenee pesheen urdedeem]*
downmarket mütevazi *[mewtevazee]*
downstairs aşağıda *[asha-uhda]*
dozen düzine *[dewzeeneh]*; **half a dozen** yarım düzine *[yaruhm]*
drain (*noun: in sink*) pis su borusu *[peess soo boroossoo]*; (*street*) dren
draughts (*game*) dama
draughty: it's rather draughty oldukça cereyanlı *[oldookcha jerayanluh]*
drawing pin raptiye *[rapteeyeh]*
dreadful berbat
dream (*noun*) rüya *[rew-ya]*; **it's like a bad dream** karabasan gibi *[kara-bassan gheebee]*; **sweet dreams** güzel rüyalar *[ghew-zel rewyalar]*
dress (*woman's*) elbise *[elbeesseh]*; **I'll just get dressed** hemen giyinirim *[hemen gheeyeeneereem]*
dressing (*for wound*) pansuman *[pansooman]*; (*for salad*) sos
dressing gown sabahlık *[sabahluhk]*
drink (*verb*) içmek *[eechmek]*; **can I get you a drink?** içecek bir şey ister misiniz? *[eechejek beer shay eester mee-seeneez]*; **I don't drink** (*alcohol*) alkol almıyorum *[almuh-yoroom]*; **I must have something to drink** (*alcoholic and non-alcoholic*) muhakkak bir

şey içmem lazım *[moohak-kak beer shay eechmem lazuhm]*; **a long cool drink** buzlu içki *[boozloo eechkee]*; **may I have a drink of water?** bir su rica ediyorum *[beer soo reeja edeeyoroom]*; **drink up!** içelim! *[eecheleem]*; **I had too much to drink** fazla içtim *[eechteem]*

drinkable: is the water drinkable? bu su içilebilir mi? *[boo soo eecheeleh-beeleer mee]*

drive: we drove here buraya arabayla geldik *[boor-'eye'-ya arab-'eye'-la gheldeek]*; **I'll drive you home** ben sizi arabayla evinize götürürüm *[seezee ... eveeneezeh gurtewr-ewrewm]*; **do you want to come for a drive?** arabayla gezmek ister misiniz? *[ghezmek eester mee-seeneez]*; **is it a very long drive?** yol çok uzun mu? *[chok oozoon moo]*

driver (*of car, bus*) şoför *[shofurr]*

driver's license şoför ehliyeti *[shofurr ehleeyetee]*

drive shaft kardan mili *[meelee]*

driving licence şoför ehliyeti *[shofurr ehleeyetee]*

drizzle: it's drizzling çiseliyor *[cheesseleeyor]*

drop: just a drop (*of drink*) yalnız bir damla *[yalnuhz beer damla]*; **I dropped it** onu düşürdüm *[onoo dewshewr-dewm]*; **drop in some time** bir ara uğrayın *[oo-r-'eye'-yuhn]*

drown: he's drowning boğuluyor *[bo-ooloo-yor]*

drug (*medical*) ilaç *[eelach]*; (*narcotic*) beyaz zehir *[bayaz zeheer]*

drugstore (*for pharmaceuticals*) eczane *[ejzaneh]*

drunk (*adjective*) sarhoş *[sarhosh]*

drunken driving içkili olarak araba sürmek *[eechkeelee ... sewrmek]*

dry (*adjective*) kuru *[kooroo]*; **where can I dry my washing?** çamaşırlarımı nerede kurutabilirim? *[chamashuhr-laruhmuh neredeh kooroota-beeleereem]*

dry-clean: can I get these dry-cleaned? bunları kuru temizlemeye verebilir miyim? *[boonlaruh kooroo temeezlemayeh verebeeleer meeyeem]*

dry-cleaner kuru temizleyici *[kooroo temeezlayeejee]*

duck ördek *[urrdek]*

due: when is the bus due? otobüs kaçta gelecek? *[otobewss kachta ghelejek]*

dumb (*can't speak*) dilsiz *[deelseez]*; (*stupid*) aptal

dummy (*for baby*) emzik *[emzeek]*

durex (*tm*) prezervatif *[prezervateef]*

during sırasında *[suhrassuhnda]*

dust toz

dustbin çöp tenekesi *[churp tenekessee]*

duty-free (*goods*) gümrüksüz *[ghewmrewk-sewz]*

dynamo dinamo *[deenamo]*

dysentery dizanteri *[deezanteree]*

E

each her; **each of them** her biri *[beeree]*; **one for each of us** hepimize birer tane *[hepeemeezeh beerer taneh]*; **how much are they each?** tanesi kaça? *[tanessee kacha]*; **each time** her seferinde *[sefereendeh]*; **we know each other** tanışıyoruz *[tanuhshuh-yorooz]*

ear kulak *[koolak]*

earache: I have earache kulağım ağrıyor *[koola-uhm a-ruhyor]*

early erken; **early in the morning** sabah erkenden; **it's too early** henüz çok erken *[henewz chok]*; **a day earlier** bir gün önce *[beer ghewn urnjeh]*; **half an hour earlier** bir saat önce *[sa-at]*; **I need an early night** erken yatmam lazım *[lazuhm]*

early riser: I'm an early riser sabahları erken kalkarım *[sabahlaruh erken kalkaruhm]*

earring küpe *[kewpeh]*

earth (*soil*) toprak

earthenware çömlek *[churmlek]*

earwig kulağakaçan *[koola-akachan]*

east doğu *[do-oo]*; **to the east of ...**

...-in doğusunda *[...-een do-oossoonda]*; **in the east** doğuda *[do-ooda]*
Easter Paskalya
easy kolay *[kol-'eye']*; **easy with the cream!** fazla krem kullanmayın! *[fazla ... kool-lanm-'eye'-yuhn]*
eat yemek; **something to eat** yiyecek bir şey *[yeeyejek beer shay]*; **we've already eaten** biz yedik *[beez yedeek]*
eau-de-Cologne kolonya
eccentric tuhaf *[toohaf]*
edible yenebilir *[yenebeeleer]*
efficient (*hotel, organization*) randımanlı *[randuhmanluh]*
egg yumurta *[yoomoorta]*
eggplant patlıcan *[patluhjan]*
Eire İrlanda *[eerlanda]*
either: either ... or ... ya ... ya ...; **I don't like either of them** ikisinden de hoşlanmıyorum *[eekee-seenden deh hoshlanmuh-yoroom]*
elastic (*noun*) lastik *[lasteek]*
elastic band lastik bant *[lasteek]*
Elastoplast (*tm*) plaster
elbow dirsek *[deersek]*
electric elektrikli *[elektreeklee]*
electric blanket elektrikli battaniye *[elektreeklee bat-taneeyeh]*
electric cooker elektrik ocağı *[elektreek oja-uh]*
electric fire elektrik sobası *[elektreek sobassuh]*
electrician elektrikçi *[elektreekchee]*
electricity elektrik *[elektreek]*
electric outlet elektrik prizi *[elektreek preezee]*
elegant zarif *[zareef]*
elevator asansör *[assansurr]*
else: something else başka bir şey *[bashka beer shay]*; **somewhere else** başka bir yer; **let's go somewhere else** başka bir yere gidelim *[yereh gheedeleem]*; **what else?** başka?; **nothing else** hepsi bu kadar *[hepsee boo kadar]*
embarrassed: he's embarrassed utanıyor *[ootanuhyor]*
embarrassing utandırıcı *[ootan-duhruhjuh]*
embassy elçilik *[elcheeleek]*
emergency acil durum *[ajeel dooroom]*; **this is an emergency** bu acildir *[boo ajeeldeer]*
emery board zımparalı törpü *[zuhmparaluh turrpew]*
emotional duygusal *[dooy-goossal]*
empty boş *[bosh]*
end (*noun*) son; **at the end of the road** yolun sonunda *[yoloon sonoonda]*; **when does it end?** ne zaman bitiyor? *[neh zaman beeteeyor]*
energetic (*person*) enerjik *[enerɪeek]*
energy (*of person*) enerji *[enerɪee]*
engaged (*to be married*) nişanlı *[nee-shanluh]*; (*toilet*) meşgul *[meshgool]*
engagement ring nişan yüzüğü *[neeshan yewzew-ew]*
engine motor
engine trouble motor arızası *[motor aruhzassuh]*
England İngiltere *[eengheeltereh]*
English İngiliz *[eengheeleez]*; (*language*) İngilizce *[eengheeleezjeh]*; **the English** İngilizler *[eengheeleezler]*; **I'm English** ben İngilizim *[eengheeleezeem]*; **do you speak English?** İngilizce biliyor musunuz? *[beeleeyor moo-soonooz]*
Englishman İngiliz *[eengheeleez]*
Englishwoman İngiliz kadın *[eengheeleez kaduhn]*
enjoy: I enjoyed it very much çok beğendim *[chok beh-endeem]*; **enjoy yourself!** hoşça vakit geçirin! *[hoshcha vakeet ghecheereen]*
enjoyable zevkli *[zevklee]*
enlargement (*of photo*) agrandisman
enormous muazzam *[moo-az-zam]*
enough yeter; **there's not enough** yetmez; **it's not big enough** yeterince büyük değil *[yetereenjeh bew-yewk deh-eel]*; **thanks, that's enough** teşekkür ederim, bu kadar yeter *[teshek-kewr edereem, boo kadar]*
entertainment eğlence *[eh-lenjeh]*
enthusiastic istekli *[eesteklee]*
entrance (*noun*) giriş *[gheereesh]*
envelope zarf
epileptic saralı *[saraluh]*
equipment (*in apartment*) araç gereç *[arach gherech]*; (*for climbing etc*) donatım *[donatuhm]*
eraser silgi *[seelghee]*
erotic erotik *[eroteek]*
error hata
escalator yürüyen merdiven *[yewrew-yen merdeeven]*

especially özellikle *[urzel-leekleh]*
espresso coffee espreso kahve *[espresso kahveh]*
essential: it is essential that ... ... şarttır *[shart-tuhr]*
estate agent emlakçı *[emlakchuh]*
ethnic (*restaurant etc*) etnik *[etneek]*
Europe Avrupa *[avroopa]*
European Avrupa *[avroopa]*; (*person*) Avrupalı *[avroopaluh]*; **European plan** yarım pansiyon *[yaruhm pansseeyon]*
even: even the English İngilizler bile *[engheeleezler beeleh]*; **even if ...** ...-se bile; **even if you're late** geç kalsan bile *[ghech kalsan]*
evening akşam *[aksham]*; **good evening** iyi akşamlar *[eeyee akshamlar]*; **this evening** bu akşam *[boo]*; **in the evening** akşam; **evening meal** akşam yemeği *[yemeh-ee]*
evening dress (*for man*) smokin *[smokeen]*; (*for woman*) gece elbisesi *[ghejeh elbee-sessee]*
eventually en sonunda *[sonoonda]*
ever: have you ever been to ...? ... hiç ...-e gittiniz mi? *[heech ...-eh gheet-teeneez mee]*; **if you ever come to Britain** eğer İngiltere'ye gelecek olursanız *[eh-er eengheelterayeh ghelejek oloorsanuhz]*
every her; **every day** her gün
everyone herkes *[herkess]*
everything herşey *[—shay]*
everywhere her yerde *[yerdeh]*
exactly! çok doğru! *[chok do-roo]*
exam sınav *[suhnav]*
example örnek *[urrnek]*; **for example** mesela *[messela]*
excellent mükemmel *[mewkem-mel]*; **excellent!** nefis! *[nefeess]*
except dışında *[duhshuhnda]*; **except Sunday** Pazar günleri dışında *[pazar ghewnleree]*
exception istisna *[eesteessna]*; **as an exception** istisna olarak
excess baggage fazla bagaj *[bagaȷ]*
excessive çok fazla *[chok]*; **that's a bit excessive** (*price*) bu biraz fazla *[boo beeraz]*
exchange (*verb: money*) değiştirmek *[de-eeshteermek]*; **in exchange** karşılığında *[karshuhluh-uhnda]*
exchange rate: what's the exchange rate? döviz kuru nedir? *[durveez kooroo nedeer]*
exciting (*day, holiday*) heyecan verici *[hayejan vereejee]*; (*film*) heyecanlı *[hayejanluh]*
exclusive (*club*) seçkin *[sechkeen]*
excursion gezi *[ghezee]*; **is there an excursion to ...?** ...-ye gezi var mı? *[...-yeh ... muh]*
excuse me (*to get past*) pardon; (*to get attention*) affedersiniz *[af-feder-seeneez]*; (*pardon?*) efendim? *[efendeem]*; (*annoyed*) rica ederim! *[reeja edereem]*
exhaust (*on car*) egzos *[egzoss]*
exhausted (*tired*) bitkin *[beetkeen]*
exhibition sergi *[serghee]*
exist: does it still exist? hâlâ var mı? *[hala var muh]*
exit çıkış *[chuhkuhsh]*
expect: I expect so sanırım öyle *[sanuhruhm urleh]*; **she's expecting** bebek bekliyor *[bebek bekleeyor]*
expensive pahalı *[pahaluh]*
experience: an absolutely unforgettable experience asla unutulmayacak bir anı *[assla oonootoolm-'eye'-yajak beer anuh]*
experienced tecrübeli *[tejrewbelee]*
expert uzman *[oozman]*
expire: it's expired (*passport etc*) süresi doldu *[sewressee doldoo]*
explain açıklamak *[achuhklamak]*; **would you explain that to me?** bunu bana açıklar mısınız? *[boonoo bana achuhklar muhsuhnuhz]*
explore araştırmak *[arashtuhrmak]*; **I just want to go and explore** gidip bir görmek istiyorum *[gheedeep beer gurrmek eesteeyoroom]*
export (*verb*) ihraç etmek *[eehrach]*
exposure meter pozometre *[pozometreh]*
express (*mail*) özel ulak *[urzel oolak]*; (*train*) ekspres *[ekspress]*
extra: can we have an extra chair? lütfen bir sandalye daha *[lewtfen beer sandalyeh daha]*; **is that extra?** bu ekstra mı? *[boo ekstra muh]*
extraordinarily: extraordinarily beautiful olağanüstü güzel *[ola-an-ewstew ghewzel]*
extraordinary (*very strange*) çok garip *[chok gareep]*

extremely son derece *[derejeh]*
extrovert dışadönük *[duhsha-durnewk]*
eye göz *[gurz]*; **will you keep an eye on my bags for me?** çantalarıma göz kulak olur musunuz? *[chantalaruhma gurz koolak oloor moo-soonooz]*
eyebrow kaş *[kash]*
eyebrow pencil kaş kalemi *[kash kalemee]*
eye drops göz damlası *[gurz damlassuh]*
eyeliner rimel *[reemel]*
eye shadow far
eye witness görgü tanığı *[gurrghew tanuh-uh]*

F

fabulous fevkalade *[fevkaladeh]*
face yüz *[yewz]*
face cloth (*flannel*) elbezi *[el-bezee]*
face mask (*diving*) başlık *[bashluhk]*
facing: facing the sea deniz manzaralı *[deneez manzaraluh]*
fact olgu *[olgoo]*
factory fabrika *[fabreeka]*
Fahrenheit *see page 121*
faint: she's fainted bayıldı *[b-'eye'-yuhlduh]*; **I'm going to faint** fena oluyorum *[fena oloo-yoroom]*
fair (*fun-fair*) panayır *[pan-'eye'-yuhr]*; (*commercial*) sergi *[serghee]*; **it's not fair** bu haksızlıktır *[boo haksuhzluhktuhr]*; **OK, fair enough** peki, tamam *[pekee tamam]*
fake taklit *[takleet]*
fall: he's had a fall düştü *[dewshtew]*; **he fell off his bike** bisikletten düştü *[beesseeklet-ten]*; **in the fall** (*autumn*) sonbaharda
false sahte *[sahteh]*
false teeth takma dişler *[deeshler]*
family aile *[a-eeleh]*
family hotel aile pansiyonu *[a-eeleh pansseeyonoo]*
family name soyadı *[soyaduh]*
famished: I'm famished açlıktan ölüyorum *[achluhktan urlew-yoroom]*
famous ünlü *[ewnlew]*
fan vantilatör *[vanteelaturr]*; (*hand held*) fön *[furn]*; (*football*) taraftar; (*singer etc*) hayran *[h-'eye'-ran]*
fan belt vantilatör kayışı *[vanteelaturr k-'eye'-yuhshuh]*
fancy: he fancies you senden hoşlanıyor *[senden hoshlanuh-yor]*
fancy dress party kıyafet balosu *[kuh-yafet balossoo]*
fantastic fantastik *[fantasteek]*
far uzak *[oozak]*; **is it far?** uzak mı? *[muh]*; **how far is it to ...?** ...buraya ne kadar çeker? *[boor-'eye'-ya neh kadar cheker]*; **as far as I'm concerned** benim açımdan *[beneem achuhmdan]*
fare taşıma ücreti *[tashuhma ewjretee]*; **what's the fare to ...?** ...-e gidiş ücreti ne kadardır? *[-eh gheedeesh ... neh kadarduhr]*
farewell party veda partisi *[veda parteessee]*
farm çiftlik *[cheeftleek]*
farther daha ötede *[daha urtedeh]*; **farther than ...** ...-den ötede
fashion (*in clothes etc*) moda
fashionable moda
fast hızlı *[huhzluh]*; **not so fast** o kadar hızlı değil *[kadar ... deh-eel]*
fastener (*on clothes*) bağ *[ba]*
fat (*person*) şişman *[sheeshman]*; (*on meat*) yağ *[ya]*
father baba; **my father** babam
father-in-law kayınpeder *[k-'eye'-yuhnpeder]*
fathom kulaç *[koolach]*
fattening şişmanlatıcı *[sheesh-manlatuhjuh]*
faucet musluk *[moosslook]*
fault hata; **it was my fault** hata bendeydi *[bendaydee]*; **it's not my fault** hata bende değil *[bendeh de-eel]*
faulty (*equipment*) arızalı *[aruhzaluh]*
favo(u)rite gözde *[gurzdeh]*; **that's my favo(u)rite** ben en çok onu tutuyorum *[chok onoo tootoo-yoroom]*
fawn (*colour*) açık kahverengi *[achuhk kahveh-renghee]*
February Şubat *[shoobat]*

fed up: I'm fed up bıktım *[buhktuhm]*; **I'm fed up with ...** ...-den bıktım

feeding bottle biberon *[beeberon]*

feel: I feel hot/cold sıcak bastı/üşüyorum *[suhjak bastuh/ewshewyoroom]*; **I feel like a drink/some food** bir şey içmek/yemek istiyorum *[beer shay eechmek/yemek eesteeyoroom]*; **I don't feel like it** canım çekmiyor *[januhm chekmeeyor]*; **how are you feeling today?** bugün kendinizi nasıl hissediyorsunuz? *[booghewn kendeeneezee nassuhl heessedeeyor-soonooz]*; **I'm feeling a lot better** kendimi çok daha iyi hissediyorum *[kendeemee chok daha eeyee heessedeeyoroom]*

felt-tip (*pen*) keçe uçlu kalem *[kecheh oochloo kalem]*

fence parmaklık *[parmakluhk]*

fender (*car*) çamurluk *[chamoorlook]*

ferry feribot *[fereebot]*; **what time's the last ferry?** son feribot saat kaçta? *[sa-at kachta]*

festival festival *[festeeval]*

fetch: I'll go and fetch it ben gidip getiririm *[gheedeep gheteereereem]*; **will you come and fetch me?** gelip beni alır mısınız? *[gheleep benee aluhr muhsuhnuhz]*

fever ateş *[atesh]*

feverish: I'm feeling feverish ateş basıyor *[atesh basuhyor]*

few: only a few yalnız birkaç tane *[yalnuhz beerkach taneh]*; **a few minutes** birkaç dakika *[dakeeka]*; **he's had a good few** (*to drink*) iyice kafayı çekti *[eeyeejeh kaf-'eye'-yuh chektee]*

fez fes

fiancé(e): my fiancé nişanlım *[neeshanluhm]*

fiasco: what a fiasco! tam bir fiyasko! *[beer feeyasko]*

field (*agricultural*) tarla; (*sport*) saha

fifty-fifty yarı yarıya *[yaruh yaruhya]*

fight (*noun*) kavga

figs incir *[eenjeer]*

figure (*of person*) vücut yapısı *[vewjewt yapuhssuh]*; (*number*) sayı *[s-'eye'-yuh]*; **I have to watch my figure** şişmanlamamaya dikkat etmem lazım *[sheeshman-lamam-'eye'-ya deek-kat etmem lazuhm]*

fill doldurmak *[doldoormak]*; **fill her up please** lütfen depoyu doldurun *[lewtfen depo-yoo doldooroon]*; **will you help me fill out this form?** bu formüleri doldurmama yardım eder misiniz? *[boo formewleree doldoormama yarduhm eder meeseeneez]*

fillet fileto *[feeleto]*

filling (*in tooth*) dolgu *[dolgoo]*; **it's very filling** (*food*) çok doyurucu *[chok doyooroorjoo]*

filling station benzin istasyonu *[benzeen eestassyonoo]*

film filim *[feeleem]*; **do you have this type of film?** bu tip filim var mı? *[boo teep ... muh]*; **16mm film** 16 milimetrelik filim *[onaltuh meeleemetreleek]*; **35mm film** 35 milimetrelik filim *[otooz besh]*

filter (*for camera, coffee*) filtre *[feeltreh]*

filter-tipped filtreli *[feeltrelee]*

filthy (*room etc*) pis *[peess]*

find bulmak *[boolmak]*; **I can't find it** bulamıyorum *[boolamuh-yoroom]*; **if you find it** bulursanız *[booloorsanuhz]*; **I've found a ...** bir ... buldum *[beer ... booldoom]*

fine: it's fine weather hava güzel *[hava ghewzel]*; **a 30,000 lira fine** 30,000 lira ceza *[otooz been leera jeza]*; **how are you? - fine** nasılsınız? - iyiyim *[eeyeeyeem]*; **that's fine** tamam

finger parmak

fingernail tırnak *[tuhrnak]*

finish: I haven't finished bitirmedim *[beeteer-medeem]*; **when I've finished** bitirdiğim zaman *[beeteerdee-eem]*; **when does it finish?** ne zaman bitiyor? *[neh zaman beeteeyor]*; **finish off your drink** içkini bitir *[eech-keenee beeteer]*

Finland Finlandiya *[feenlandeeya]*

fire: fire! (*something's on fire*) yangın var! *[yanguhn]*; **may we light a fire here?** burada ateş yakabilir miyiz? *[boorada atesh yakabeeleer meeyeez]*; **it's on fire** yanıyor *[yanuhyor]*; **it's not firing properly** (*car*) doğru ateşlemiyor *[do-roo ateshlemeeyor]*

fire alarm yangın alarmı *[yanguhn alarmuh]*

fire brigade, fire department itfaiye

[eetfa-eeyeh]
fire escape yangın merdiveni *[yanguhn merdeevenee]*
fire extinguisher yangın söndürme cihazı *[yanguhn surndewrmeh jeehazuh]*
firm (*company*) firma *[feerma]*
first ilk *[eelk]*; **I was first** ilk ben geldim *[gheldeem]*; **at first** ilk önce *[urnjeh]*; **this is the first time** bu ilk sefer *[boo ... sefer]*
first aid ilk yardım *[eelk yarduhm]*
first aid kit ilk yardım çantası *[eelk yarduhm chantassuh]*
first class (*travel etc*) birinci sınıf *[beereenjee suhnuhf]*
first name ad
fish (*noun*) balık *[baluhk]*
fisherman balıkçı *[baluhkchuh]*
fishing balıkçılık *[baluhk-chuhluhk]*
fishing boat balıkçı botu *[baluhkchuh botoo]*
fishing net balık ağı *[baluhk a-uh]*
fishing rod olta kamışı *[kamuhshuh]*
fishing tackle balık takımı *[baluhk takuhmuh]*
fishing village balıkçı köyü *[baluhkchuh kur-yew]*
fit (*healthy*) sağlam *[sa-lam]*; **I'm not very fit** sağlığım o kadar iyi değil *[sa-luh-uhm o kadar eeyee deh-eel]*; **he's a keep fit fanatic** aşırı sağlık meraklısıdır *[ashuhruh sa-luhk merakluh-suhduhr]*; **it doesn't fit** uymuyor *[ooy-mooyor]*
fix: can you fix it? (*arrange*) siz ayarlayabilir misiniz? *[seez 'eye'-yarl-'eye'-ya-beeleer mee-seeneez]*; (*repair*) onarabilir misiniz? *[onarabeeleer]*; **let's fix a time** bir gün saptayalım *[beer ghewn sapt-'eye'-yaluhm]*; **it's all fixed up** her şey ayarlandı *[shay 'eye'-yarlanduh]*; **I'm in a bit of a fix** biraz zor durumdayım *[beeraz zor dooroomd-'eye'-yuhm]*
fizzy gazlı *[gazluh]*
fizzy drink gazoz *[gazoz]*
flab (*on body*) yağ *[ya]*
flag bayrak *[b-'eye'-rak]*
flannel elbezi *[el-bezee]*
flash (*for camera*) flaş *[flash]*
flashlight el feneri *[feneree]*
flashy (*clothes etc*) frapan
flat (*adjective*) düz *[dewz]*; **this beer is flat** bu biranın gazı kaçmış *[boo beeranuhn gazuh kachmuhsh]*; **I've got a flat tyre/tire** lastiğim patladı *[lastee-eem patladuh]*; (*apartment*) daire *[da-eereh]*
flatterer dalkavuk *[dalkavook]*
flatware (*cutlery*) çatal bıçak *[chatal buhchak]*; (*crockery*) çanak çömlek *[chanak churmlek]*
flavo(u)r tat
flea pire *[peereh]*
flea bite pire ısırığı *[peereh uhsuhruh-uh]*
flea powder pire tozu *[peereh tozoo]*
flexible (*material, arrangements*) esnek
flies (*on trousers*) pantalon düğmeleri *[pantalon dew-meleree]*; (*zip*) fermuar *[fermoo-ar]*
flight uçak seferi *[oochak seferee]*
flippers paletler
flirt flört etmek *[flurrt etmek]*
float yüzmek *[yewzmek]*
flood sel
floor (*of room*) taban; **on the floor** yerde *[yerdeh]*; **on the second floor** (*UK*) ikinci katta *[eekeenjee kat-ta]*; (*US*) birinci katta *[beereenjee]*
floorshow şov *[shov]*
flop (*failure*) başarısızlık *[basharuh-suhzluhk]*
florist çiçekçi *[cheechek-chee]*
flour un *[oon]*
flower çiçek *[cheechek]*
flu grip *[greep]*
fluent: he speaks fluent Turkish akıcı bir Türkçesi var *[akuhjuh beer tewrkchessee]*
fly (*verb*) uçmak *[oochmak]*; **can we fly there?** oraya uçakla gidebilir miyiz? *[or-'eye'-ya oochakla gheedeh-beeleer meeyeez]*
fly (*insect*) sinek *[seenek]*
fly spray sinek spreyi *[seenek sprayee]*
foggy: it's foggy hava sisli *[seesslee]*
fog lights sis lambaları *[seess lambalaruh]*
folk dancing halk dansları *[danslaruh]*
folk music halk müziği *[mewzee-ee]*
follow takip etmek *[takeep]*; **follow me** beni takip edin *[benee ... edeen]*
fond: I'm quite fond of ... ... çok hoşuma gidiyor *[chok hoshooma gheedeeyor]*

food yiyecek *[yeeyejek]*; **the food's excellent** yemekler mükemmel *[yemekler mewkem-mel]*
food poisoning gıda zehirlenmesi *[ghuhda zeheerlen-messee]*
food store bakkal *[bak-kal]*
fool budala *[boodala]*
foolish aptal
foot ayak *['eye'-yak]*; **on foot** yayan *[y-'eye'-yan]*; *see page 120*
football futbol *[footboll]*; (*ball*) top
for: is that for me? bu benim için mi? *[boo beneem eecheen mee]*; **that's for me** bu benim için **that's for him/her** bu onun için *[onoon]*; **what's this for?** bu ne için? *[neh]*; **for two days** iki gün için *[eekee ghewn]*; **I've been here for a week** bir hafta için geldim *[gheldeem]*; **a bus for ...** ...-e bir otobüs *[-eh beer otobewss]*
forbidden yasak *[yassak]*
forehead alın *[aluhn]*
foreign yabancı *[yabanjuh]*
foreigner yabancı *[yabanjuh]*
foreign exchange (*money*) döviz *[durveez]*
forest orman
forget unutmak *[oonootmak]*; **I forget, I've forgotten** unuttum *[oonoot-toom]*; **don't forget** unutma *[oonootma]*
fork (*for eating*) çatal *[chatal]*; (*in road*) iki yol ağzı *[eekee ... a-zuh]*
form (*to fill out*) formüler *[formewler]*
formal resmi *[ressmee]*
fortnight iki hafta *[eekee hafta]*
fortunately bereket versin *[bereket verseen]*
fortune-teller falcı *[faljuh]*
forward: could you forward my mail? mektuplarımı bana iletir misiniz? *[mektoop-laruhmuh bana eeleteer mee-seeneez]*
forwarding address gönderilecek adres *[gurn-dereelejek adress]*
foundation cream fondöten *[fondurten]*
fountain çeşme *[cheshmeh]*
foyer (*of hotel, theatre*) foyer
fracture (*noun*) kırık *[kuhruhk]*
fractured skull kırık kafatası kemiği *[kuhruhk kafatassuh kemee-ee]*
fragile kırılır *[kuhruhluhr]*
frame (*for picture*) çerçeve *[chercheveh]*
France Fransa *[fransa]*
fraud sahtekârlık *[sahtekarluhk]*
free (*at liberty*) serbest; (*costing nothing*) bedava; **admission free** giriş bedava *[gheereesh]*
freezer buzluk *[boozlook]*
freezing cold buz gibi soğuk *[booz gheebee so-ook]*
French Fransız *[fransuhz]*; (*language*) Fransızca *[fransuhzja]*
French fries patates kızartması *[patatess kuhzartmassuh]*
frequent sık *[suhk]*
fresh (*weather, breeze*) serin *[sereen]*; (*fruit etc*) taze *[tazeh]*; (*cheeky*) küstah *[kewstah]*; **don't get fresh with me** haddini bil *[haddeenee beel]*
fresh orange juice taze portakal suyu *[tazeh portakal soo-yoo]*
friction tape izole bant *[eezoleh]*
Friday Cuma *[jooma]*
fridge buzdolabı *[booz-dolabuh]*
fried egg sahanda yumurta *[sahanda yoomoorta]*
friend arkadaş *[arkadash]*
friendly dost
frog kurbağa *[koorba-a]*
from: from here to the sea buradan denize kadar *[booradan deneezeh kadar]*; **the next boat from ...** ...-den gelecek bir sonraki vapur *[ghelejek beer sonrakee vapoor]*; **as from Tuesday** Salı gününden itibaren *[saluh ghewnewnden eeteebaren]*; **I'm from London/New York** ben Londra'lıyım/New York'luyum *[londraluh-yuhm/...-loo-yoom]*; **this is from me/us** bu da benden/bizden *[boo da benden/beezden]*
front ön *[urn]*; **in front** önde *[urndeh]*; **in front of us** önümüzde *[urnew-mewzdeh]*; **at the front** ön tarafta
frozen donmuş *[donmoosh]*
frozen food dondurulmuş yiyecekler *[dondoorool-moosh yeeyejekler]*
fruit meyva *[mayva]*
fruit juice meyva suyu *[mayva soo-yoo]*
fruit salad meyva salatası *[mayva salatassuh]*
frustrating: it's very frustrating çok can sıkıcı *[chok jan suhkuhjuh]*
fry kızartmak *[kuhzartmak]*; **nothing**

fried kızarmış bir şey olmasın *[kuhzarmuhsh beer shay olmassuhn]*
frying pan tava
full dolu *[doloo]*; **it's full of ...** ... ile dolu *[eeleh]*; **I'm full** (*eating*) doydum *[doydoom]*
full-board tam pansiyon *[pansseeyon]*
full-bodied (*wine*) dolgun *[dolgoon]*
fun: it's fun eğlenceli *[aylenjelee]*; **it was great fun** çok eğlendik *[chok aylendeek]*; **just for fun** sırf hoşça vakit geçirmek için *[suhrf hoshcha vakeet ghecheermek eecheen]*; **have fun** eğlenmek *[aylenmek]*
funeral cenaze *[jenazeh]*
funny (*strange*) garip *[gareep]*; (*amusing*) komik *[komeek]*
furniture mobilya *[mobeelya]*
further ileride *[eelereedeh]*; **2 kilometres further** iki kilometre ileride *[eekee keelometreh]*; **further down the road** yolun ilerisinde *[yoloon eeleree-seendeh]*
fuse sigorta *[seegorta]*; **the lights have fused** sigorta attı *[at-tuh]*
fuse wire sigorta teli *[seegorta telee]*
future gelecek *[ghelejek]*; **in future** gelecekte *[—teh]*

G

gale fırtına *[fuhrtuhna]*
gallon *see page 121*
gallstones safra taşı *[safra tashuh]*
gamble kumar oynamak *[koomar]*; **I don't gamble** kumar oynamam
game oyun *[oyoon]*
games room oyun odası *[oyoon odassuh]*
garage (*petrol*) benzin istasyonu *[benzeen eestassyonoo]*; (*repair*) servis istasyonu *[serveess]*; (*for parking*) garaj *[garaJ]*
garbage çöp *[churp]*
garden bahçe *[bahcheh]*
garlic sarmısak *[sarmuhsak]*
gas gaz; (*gasoline*) benzin *[benzeen]*
gas cylinder (*eg for Calor gas*) gaz şişesi *[sheeshessee]*
gasket conta *[jonta]*
gas pedal gaz pedalı *[pedaluh]*
gas permeable lenses gaz geçirgen lensler *[ghecheerghen lensler]*
gas station benzin istasyonu *[benzeen eestassyonoo]*
gas tank benzin deposu *[benzeen depossoo]*
gastroenteritis gastroenterit *[gastro-entereet]*
gate kapı *[kapuh]*; (*at airport*) çıkış kapısı *[chuhkuhsh kapuhssuh]*
gauge ölçek *[urlchek]*
gay homoseksüel *[homo-seksewel]*
gear (*car*) vites *[veetess]*; (*equipment*) donatım *[donatuhm]*; **the gears keep sticking** vitesler zor geçiyor *[veetessler ... ghecheeyor]*
gearbox vites kutusu *[veetess kootoossoo]*; **I have gearbox trouble** vites kutusu arızalı *[aruhzaluh]*
gear lever, gear shift vites kolu *[veetess koloo]*
general delivery postrestant
generous: that's very generous of you çok naziksiniz *[chok nazeek-seeneez]*
gentleman (*man*) beyefendi *[bay-efendee]*; **that gentleman over there** oradaki beyefendi *[oradakee]*; **he's such a gentleman** çok nazik bir adam *[chok nazeek beer adam]*
gents (*toilet*) erkekler tuvaleti *[erkekler toovaletee]*
genuine gerçek *[gherchek]*
German (*adjective, person*) Alman; (*language*) Almanca *[almanja]*
German measles kızamıkçık *[kuhzamuhk-chuhk]*
Germany Almanya *[almanya]*
get: have you got ...? ... var mı? *[muh]*; **how do I get to ...?** ...-e nasıl gidilir? *[...-eh nassuhl gheedeeleer]*; **where do I get it from?** nereden alabilirim? *[nereden alabeeleereem]*; **can I get you a drink?** içecek bir şey ister misiniz? *[eechejek beer shay eester mee-seeneez]*; **will you get it for me?** onu bana bulabilir misiniz? *[onoo bana boolabeeleer]*; **when do**

we get there? ne zaman varacağız? *[neh zaman varaja-uhz]*; **I've got to ...** ... lazım *[lazuhm]*; **I've got to go** gitmem lazım *[gheetmem]*; **where do I get off?** nerede inmem lazım? *[neredeh eenmem]*; **it's difficult to get to** ulaşılması zor *[oolashuhlmassuh]*; **when I get up** (*in morning*) kalktığım zaman *[kalktuh-uhm]*
ghastly korkunç *[korkoonch]*
ghost hayalet *[h-'eye'-yalet]*
giddy: it makes me giddy başımı döndürüyor *[bashuhmuh durndewrewyor]*
gift hediye *[hedeeyeh]*
gigantic dev
gin cin *[jeen]*; **a gin and tonic** cintonik *[jeentoneek]*
girl kız *[kuhz]*
girlfriend kız arkadaş *[kuhz arkadash]*
give vermek; **will you give me ...?** ... verir misiniz? *[vereer mee-seeneez]*; **I'll give you 10,000 liras** sana 10,000 lira vereceğim *[sana on been leera verejeh-eem]*; **I gave it to him** ona verdim *[ona verdeem]*; **will you give it back?** geri verecek misiniz? *[gheree verejek]*; **would you give this to ...?** bunu ...-e verebilir misiniz? *[boonoo ...-eh verebeeleer]*
glad memnun *[memnoon]*
glamorous (*woman*) dilber *[deelber]*
gland gudde *[good-deh]*
glandular fever gudde iltihabı *[good-deh eelteehabuh]*
glass cam *[jam]*; (*drinking*) bardak; **a glass of water** bir bardak su *[soo]*
glasses (*spectacles*) gözlük *[gurzlewk]*
gloves eldiven *[eldeeven]*
glue (*noun*) zamk
gnat tatarcık *[tatarjuhk]*
go gitmek *[gheetmek]*; **we want to go to ...** ...-e gitmek istiyoruz *[...-eh ... eesteeyorooz]*; **I'm going there tomorrow** ben yarın oraya gidiyorum *[yaruhn or-'eye'-ya gheedeeyoroom]*; **when does it go?** (*bus etc*) ne zaman kalkıyor? *[neh zaman kalkuhyor]*; **where are you going?** nereye gidiyorsunuz? *[nerayeh gheedeeyorsoonooz]*; **let's go** haydi gidelim *[h-'eye'-dee gheedeleem]*; **he's gone** gitti *[gheet-tee]*; **it's all gone** hepsi bitti *[hepsee beet-tee]*; **I went there yesterday** oraya dün gittim *[dewn gheet-teem]*; **a hotdog to go** dışarıya bir sosisli sandviç *[duhsharuhya beer sosseesslee sandveech]*; **go away!** çekil! *[chekeel]*; **it's gone off** (*milk etc*) bozulmuş *[bozoolmoosh]*; **we're going out tonight** bu akşam dışarı çıkıyoruz *[boo aksham duhsharuh chuhkuh-yorooz]*; **do you want to go out tonight?** bu akşam dışarı çıkmak ister misiniz? *[chuhkmak eester meeseeneez]*; **has the price gone up?** fiyatı arttı mı? *[feeyat art-tuh muh]*
goal (*sport*) gol
goat keçi *[kechee]*
goat's cheese keçi peyniri *[kechee payneeree]*
god tanrı *[tanruh]*
goddess tanrıça *[tanruhcha]*
gold altın *[altuhn]*
golf golf
golf clubs golf sopaları *[sopalaruh]*
golf course golf sahası *[sahassuh]*
good iyi *[eeyee]*; **good!** iyi!; **that's no good** bu işe yaramaz *[boo eesheh yaramaz]*; **good heavens!** Allah Allah! *[allah]*
goodbye (*when going oneself*) hoşça kal *[hosh-cha kal]*; (*when seeing someone off*) güle güle *[ghewleh]*
good-looking alımlı *[aluhmluh]*
gooey (*food etc*) yapışkan *[yapuhshkan]*
goose kaz
gooseberries bektaşiüzümü *[bektashee-ewzewmew]*
gorgeous (*meal, woman*) nefis *[nefeess]*
gourmet ağzının tadını bilir *[a-zuhnuhn taduhnuh beeleer]*
government hükümet *[hewkewmet]*
gradually tedricen *[tedreejen]*
grammar gramer
gram(me) gram; *see page 120*
granddaughter kız torun *[kuhz toroon]*
grandfather büyükbaba *[bew-yewk-baba]*
grandmother büyükanne *[bew-yewk-anneh]*
grandson torun *[toroon]*
grapefruit greypfrut *[graypfroot]*
grapefruit juice greypfrut suyu *[graypfroot soo-yoo]*
grapes üzüm *[ewzewm]*
grass ot; (*lawn*) çimen *[cheemen]*

grateful minnettar *[meenet-tar]*; **I'm very grateful to you** size minnettarım *[seezeh —uhm]*
gravy sos
gray gri *[gree]*
grease (*for car*) gres; (*on food*) yağ *[ya]*
greasy (*food*) yağlı *[ya-luh]*
great büyük *[bew-yewk]*; **that's great!** mükemmel! *[mewkem-mel]*
Great Britain Büyük Britanya *[bew-yewk breetanya]*
Greece Yunanistan *[yoonaneestan]*
greedy açgözlü *[ach-gurzlew]*
Greek (*adjective*) Yunan *[yoonan]*; (*ethnic, referring to Turkish subjects of Greek extraction*) Rum *[room]*; **a Greek** Yunanlı *[yoonanluh]*; (*ethnic*) Rum; **Greek woman** Yunanlı kadın *[yoonanluh kaduhn]*; (*ethnic*) Rum kadını *[kaduhnuh]*; **the Greeks** Yunanlılar *[yoonanluhlar]*; (*ethnic*) Rumlar *[roomlar]*
Greek (*language*) Rumca *[roomja]*
Greek islands Yunan Adaları *[yoonan adalaruh]*
Greek Orthodox Rum Ortodoks *[room]*
green yeşil *[yesheel]*
green card (*car insurance*) yeşil kart *[yesheel]*
greengrocer manav
grey gri *[gree]*
grilled ızgara *[uhzgara]*
gristle (*on meat*) sinir *[seeneer]*
grocer bakkal *[bak-kal]*
ground yer; **on the ground** yerde *[yerdeh]*; **on the ground floor** zemin katta *[zemeen kat-ta]*
ground beef sığır kıyması *[suh-uhr kuhy-massuh]*
group grup *[groop]*
group insurance grup sigortası *[groop seegortassuh]*
group leader grup başkanı *[groop bashkanuh]*
guarantee garanti *[garantee]*; **is it guaranteed?** garantili mi? *[—lee mee]*
guardian (*of child*) veli *[velee]*
guest misafir *[meessafeer]*
guesthouse pansiyon *[pansseeyon]*
guest room misafir odası *[meessafeer odassuh]*
guide (*noun*) rehber
guidebook rehber
guilty suçlu *[soochloo]*
guitar gitar *[gheetar]*
gum (*in mouth*) dişeti *[deesh-etee]*; (*chewing gum*) çiklet *[cheeklet]*
gun (*rifle*) tüfek *[tewfek]*; (*pistol*) tabanca *[tabanja]*
gymnasium spor salonu *[salonoo]*
gyn(a)ecologist jinekolog *[ȷeenekolog]*
gypsy çingene *[cheen-ghehneh]*

H

hair saç *[sach]*
hairbrush saç fırçası *[sach fuhrchassuh]*
haircut (*men*) saç tıraşı *[sach tuhrashuh]*; (*women*) saç kesme *[kessmeh]*; **just an ordinary haircut please** lütfen sade saçlarımı kesin *[lewtfen sadeh sachlaruhmuh kesseen]*
hairdresser berber
hairdryer saç kurutma makinesi *[sach koorootma makeenessee]*
hair foam saç köpüğü *[sach kurpew-ew]*
hair gel jel *[ȷel]*
hair grip saç tokası *[sach tokassuh]*
hair lacquer lak
half yarım *[yaruhm]*; **half an hour** yarım saat *[sa-at]*; **a half portion** yarım porsiyon *[porseeyon]*; **half a litre/liter** yarım litre *[leetreh]*; **half as much** yarısı kadar *[yaruhssuh kadar]*; **half as much again** bir yarısı kadar daha; *see page 119*
halfway: halfway to Ankara Ankaraya giderken yarı yolda *[akar-'eye'-ya gheederken yaruh yolda]*
ham jambon *[ȷambon]*
hamburger hamburger *[hamboorger]*
hammer (*noun*) çekiç *[chekeech]*
hand el; **will you give me a hand?** yardım eder misiniz? *[yarduhm eder mee-seeneez]*

handbag el çantası *[chantassuh]*
hand baggage elde taşınan bagaj *[eldeh tashuhnan bagaJ]*
handbrake el freni *[frenee]*
handkerchief mendil *[mendeel]*
handle (*noun*) tutamak *[tootamak]*; **will you handle it?** bu işi siz halleder misiniz? *[boo eeshee seez halleder mee-seeneez]*
hand luggage elde taşınan bagaj *[eldeh tashuhnan bagaJ]*
handmade elişi *[el-eeshee]*
handsome yakışıklı *[yakuh-shuhkluh]*
hanger (*for clothes*) askı *[askuh]*
hangover içki sersemliği *[eechkee sersemlee-ee]*; **I've got a terrible hangover** akşamdan müthiş bir başağrısı kaldı *[akshamdan mewt-heesh beer bash-a-ruhssuh kalduh]*
happen olmak; **how did it happen?** nasıl oldu? *[nassuhl oldoo]*; **what's happening?** ne oluyor? *[neh olooyor]*; **it won't happen again** bir daha olmayacak *[olm-'eye'-yajak]*
happy mutlu *[mootloo]*; **we're not happy with the room** odadan memnun değiliz *[memnoon deh-eeleez]*
harbo(u)r liman *[leeman]*
hard sert; (*difficult*) zor
hard-boiled egg lop yumurta *[yoomoorta]*
hard lenses sert lensler *[lensler]*
hardly ancak *[anjak]*; **hardly ever** hemen hemen hiç *[hemen ... heech]*
hardware store nalbur dükkânı *[nalboor dewk-kanuh]*
harm (*noun*) zarar
hassle: it's too much hassle bu kadar zahmete değmez *[boo kadar zahmeteh deh-mez]*; **a hassle-free trip** kazasız belasız bir seyahat *[kazasuhz belasuhz beer sayahat]*
hat şapka *[shapka]*
hate: I hate ... ...-den nefret ediyorum *[...-den nefret edeeyoroom]*
have: do you have ...? ... var mı? *[muh]*; **can I have ...?** ... istiyorum *[eesteeyoroom]*; **can I have some water?** biraz su istiyorum *[beeraz soo]*; **I have ...** ... var; **I don't have ...** ... yok; **can we have breakfast in our room?** odamızda kahvaltı edebilir miyiz? *[odamuhzda kahvaltuh edebeeleer meeyeez]*; **have another** bir tane daha alın *[beer taneh daha aluhn]*; **I have to leave early** erken gitmem lazım *[gheetmem lazuhm]*; **do I have to ...?** ...-m lazım mı? *[muh]*; **do we have to ...?** ...-memiz lazım mı? *[...-memeez]*; **do I have to pay now?** şimdi ödemem lazım mı? *[sheemdee urdemem]*; *see page 115*
hay fever saman nezlesi *[nezlessee]*
he o; **is he here?** o burada mı? *[boorada muh]*; **where does he live?** nerede oturuyor? *[neredeh otoorooyor]*; *see page 110*
head baş *[bash]*; **we're heading for Antalya** Antalya doğru gidiyoruz *[antaly-'eye'-ya do-roo gheedee-yorooz]*
headache başağrısı *[bash-a-ruhssuh]*
headlights farlar
headphones kulaklıklar *[koolak-luhklar]*
head waiter baş garson *[bash garson]*
head wind rüzgâr baştan *[rewzgar bashtan]*
health sağlık *[sa-luhk]*; **your health!** sağlığınıza! *[sa-luh-uhnuhza]*
healthy sağlıklı *[sa-luhkluh]*
hear duymak *[dooy-mak]*; **can you hear me?** sesimi duyabiliyor musunuz? *[sesseemee doo-yabeeleeyor moo-soonooz]*; **I can't hear you** sesinizi duyamıyorum *[sesseeneezee doo-yamuhyoroom]*; **I've heard about it** duydum *[dooy-doom]*
hearing aid işitme cihazı *[eesheetmeh jeehazuh]*
heart kalp
heart attack kalp krizi *[kreezee]*
heat sıcaklık *[suhjakluhk]*; **not in this heat!** bu sıcakta olmaz! *[boo suhjakta]*
heated rollers ısıtılmış bigudiler *[uhsuhtuhl-muhsh beegoodeeler]*
heater (*in car*) kalorifer *[kaloreefer]*
heating ısıtma *[uhssuhtma]*
heat rash sıcaktan kaynaklanan isilik *[suhjaktan k-'eye'-naklanan eessee-leek]*
heat stroke sıcak çarpması *[suhjak charpmassuh]*
heatwave sıcak dalgası *[suhjak dalgassuh]*
heavy ağır *[a-uhr]*

hectic telaş içinde *[telash eecheendeh]*
heel (*of foot*) topuk *[topook]*; (*of shoe*) ökçe *[urkcheh]*; **could you put new heels on these?** bunların ökçelerini yeniler misiniz? *[boonlaruhn urkchelereenee yeneeler mee-seeneez]*
heelbar kundura tamircisi *[koondoora tameerjeessee]*
height (*of person*) boy; (*of mountain*) rakım *[rakuhm]*
helicopter helikopter *[heleekopter]*
hell: oh hell! Allah kahretsin! *[allah kahretseen]*; **go to hell!** cehennemin dibine kadar! *[jehen-nemeen deebeeneh kadar]*
hello merhaba; (*in surprise*) Allah Allah! *[allah]*; (*on phone*) alo
helmet (*for motorcycle*) kask
help (*verb*) yardım etmek *[yarduhm etmek]*; **can you help me?** bana yardım eder misiniz? *[bana ... eder mee-seeneez]*; **thanks for your help** yardımınız için teşekkür ederim *[yarduhmuhnuhz eecheen teshek-kewr edereem]*; **help!** imdat! *[eemdat]*
helpful: he was very helpful çok yardımcı oldu *[chok yarduhmjuh oldoo]*; **that's helpful** bu yararlı olur *[boo yararluh oloor]*
helping (*of food*) porsiyon *[porsseeyon]*
hepatitis hepatit *[hepateet]*
her: I don't know her onu tanımıyorum *[onoo tanuhmuh-yoroom]*; **will you send it to her?** ona gönderecek misiniz? *[ona gurnderejek mee-seeneez]*; **it's her** odur *[odoor]*; **with her** onunla *[onoonla]*; **for her** onun için *[onoon eecheen]*; **that's her suitcase** bu onun bavulu *[boo onoon bavooloo]*; *see pages 108, 110*
herbs çeşni veren otlar *[cheshnee veren otlar]*
here burada *[boorada]*; **here you are** (*giving something*) al bakalım *[al bakaluhm]*; **here he comes** işte geliyor *[eeshteh gheleeyor]*
hers onun *[onoon]*; **that's hers** bu onun *[boo]*; *see page 110*
hey! hey! *[hay]*
hi! (*hello*) merhaba
hiccups hıçkırık *[huhch-kuhruhk]*
hide saklanmak
hideous berbat
high yüksek *[yewksek]*
highbeam uzak ışıkları *[oozak uhshuhklaruh]*
highchair bebek iskemlesi *[eeskemlessee]*
highway karayolu *[kar-'eye'-yoloo]*
hiking kır yürüyüşü *[kuhr yewrew-yewshew]*
hill tepe *[tepeh]*; **it's further up the hill** daha yukarda *[daha yookarda]*
hillside yamaç *[yamach]*
hilly engebeli *[enghebelee]*
him: I don't know him onu tanımıyorum *[onoo tanuhmuh-yoroom]*; **will you send it to him?** ona gönderecek misiniz? *[ona gurnderejek mee-seeneez]*; **it's him** odur *[odoor]*; **with him** onunla *[onoonla]*; **for him** onun için *[onoon eecheen]*; *see page 110*
hip kalça *[kalcha]*
hire kiralamak *[keeralamak]*; **can I hire a car?** otomobil kiralayabilir miyim? *[otomobeel keeral-'eye'-ya-beeleer meeyeem]*; **do you hire them out?** kiraya veriyor musunuz? *[keer-'eye'-ya vereeyor moo-soonooz]*
his: it's his drink bu onun içkisi *[boo onoon eech-keessee]*; **it's his** onundur *[onoodoor]*; *see pages 108, 110*
history: the history of Istanbul İstanbul'un tarihi *[eestanbooloon tareehee]*
hit vurmak *[voormak]*; **he hit me** bana vurdu *[bana voordoo]*; **I hit my head** başımı çarptım *[bashuhmuh charptuhm]*
hitch: is there a hitch? bir sorun mu var? *[beer soroon moo]*
hitch-hike otostop yapmak
hitch-hiker otostopçu *[otostopchoo]*
hit record çok satan plak *[chok satan]*
hole delik *[deleek]*; (*in ground*) çukur *[chookoor]*
holiday tatil *[tateel]*; **I'm on holiday** tatildeyim *[tateeldayeem]*
Holland Hollanda
home ev; **at home** (*in my house etc*) evde *[evdeh]*; (*in my country*) yurdumda *[yoordoomda]*; **I go home tomorrow** yarın yurda dönüyorum *[yaruhn yoorda durnew-yoroom]*
home address ev adresi *[adressee]*
homemade evde yapılmış *[evdeh yapuhlmuhsh]*

homesick: I'm homesick yurdumu özledim *[yoordoomoo urzledeem]*
honest dürüst *[dewrewst]*
honestly? sahi mi? *[sahee mee]*
honey bal
honeycomb bal peteği *[peteh-ee]*
honeymoon balayı *[bal-'eye'-yuh]*; **it's our honeymoon** balayındayız *[bal-'eye'-yuhnd-'eye'-yuhz]*
honeymoon suite gelin dairesi *[gheleen da-eeressee]*
hood (*of car*) motor kapağı *[kapa-uh]*
hookah nargile *[nargheeleh]*
hoover (*tm*) elektrik süpürgesi *[elektreek sewpewr-ghessee]*
hope umut *[oomoot]*; **I hope so** inşallah *[eenshal-lah]*; **I hope not** inşallah öyle değildir *[urleh-deh-eeldeer]*
horn (*of car*) klakson
horrible korkunç *[korkoonch]*
hors d'oeuvre ordövr *[ordurvr]*
horse at
horse riding binicilik *[beeneejeeleek]*
hose (*car radiator*) hortum *[hortoom]*
hospital hastane *[hastaneh]*
hospitality konukseverlik *[konook-severleek]*; **thank you for your hospitality** konukseverliğiniz için teşekkürler *[konook-severlee-eeneez eecheen teshek-kewrler]*
hostel hostel
hot sıcak *[suhjak]*; (*curry etc*) acı *[ajuh]*; **I'm hot** sıcaktan bunaldım *[suhjaktan boonalduhm]*; **something hot to eat** sıcak bir yemek *[beer yemek]*; **it's so hot today** bugün hava çok sıcak *[booghewn hava chok]*
hotdog sosisli sandviç *[sosseesslee sandveech]*
hotel otel; **at my hotel** otelimde *[oteleemdeh]*; **at your hotel** otelinizde *[oteleeneezdeh]*
hotel clerk resepsiyoncu *[ressepseeyonjoo]*
hotplate (*on cooker*) ocak gözü *[ojak gurzew]*
hot-water bottle buyot *[boo-yot]*
hour saat *[sa-at]*; **on the hour** saat başında *[bashuhnda]*
house ev
housewife ev kadını *[kaduhnuh]*
house wine müessese şarabı *[mew-ess-sesseh sharabuh]*
hovercraft hoverkraft
how nasıl *[nassuhl]*; **how many?** kaç tane? *[kach taneh]*; **how much?** ne kadar? *[neh kadar]*; **how often?** kaç kere? *[kereh]*; **how are you?** nasılsınız? *[nassuhl-suhnuhz]*; **how do you do?** memnun oldum! *[memnoon oldoom]*; **how about a beer?** bir biraya ne dersiniz? *[beer beer-'eye'-ya neh derseeneez]*; **how nice!** ne güzel! *[neh ghewzel]*; **would you show me how to?** nasıl yapıldığını gösterir misiniz? *[nassuhl yapuhlduh-uhnuh gurstereer mee-seeneez]*
humid nemli *[nemlee]*
humidity nem
humo(u)r: where's your sense of humo(u)r? siz şakadan anlamaz mısınız? *[seez shakadan anlamaz muhsuhnuhz]*
hundredweight *see page 121*
hungry: I'm hungry acıktım *[ajuhktuhm]*; **I'm not hungry** aç değilim *[ach deh-eeleem]*
hurry: I'm in a hurry acelem var *[ajelem]*; **hurry up!** çabuk! *[chabook]*; **there's no hurry** aceleye gerek yok *[ajelayeh gherek]*
hurt: it hurts acıyor *[ajuhyor]*; **my back hurts** sırtım ağrıyor *[suhrtuhm a-ruhyor]*
husband koca *[koja]*; **my husband** kocam *[kojam]*
hydrofoil kızaklı tekne *[kuhzakluh tekneh]*

I

I ben; **I am English** ben İngilizim *[eengheeleezeem]*; **I live in Manchester** Manchester'de oturuyorum *[—,deh otooroo-yoroom]*; *see page 110*
ice buz *[booz]*; **with ice** buzlu *[boozloo]*; **with ice and lemon** buz ve limonlu *[veh leemonloo]*
ice cream dondurma *[dondoorma]*
ice-cream cone dondurma külahı *[dondoorma kewlahuh]*
iced almonds badem şekeri *[badem shekeree]*
iced coffee buzlu kahve *[boozloo kahveh]*
ice lolly eskimo (*tm*) *[eskeemo]*
idea fikir *[feekeer]*; **good idea!** iyi bir fikir! *[eeyee beer]*
ideal (*solution, time*) ideal *[eedeh-al]*
identity papers kimlik belgeleri *[keemleek belgheleree]*
idiot ebleh
idyllic pastoral
if eğer *[eh-er]*; **if you could** eğer mümkünse *[mewm-kewnseh]*; **if not** aksi halde *[aksee haldeh]*
ignition kontak
ill hasta; **I feel ill** kendimi iyi hissetmiyorum *[kendeemee eeyee heessetmeeyoroom]*
illegal kanunsuz *[kanoon-sooz]*
illegible okunaksız *[okoonak-suhz]*
illness hastalık *[hastaluhk]*
imitation (*leather etc*) taklit *[takleet]*
immediately hemen
immigration yurt dışından göç *[yoort duhshuhndan gurch]*
import (*verb*) ithal etmek *[eet-hal]*
important önemli *[urnemlee]*; **it's very important** çok önemlidir *[chok —deer]*; **it's not important** önemli değil *[deh-eel]*
impossible imkânsız *[eemkan-suhz]*
impressive etkileyici *[etkeelayeejee]*
improve: it's improving düzeliyor *[dewzeleeyor]*; **I want to improve my Turkish** Türkçe düzeyimi yükseltmek istiyorum *[tewrkcheh dewzayeemee yewkseltmek eesteeyoroom]*
improvement düzelme *[dewzelmeh]*
in: in my room odamda; **in your room** odanızda *[odanuhzda]*; **in the town centre** şehir merkezinde *[sheheer merkezeendeh]*; **in London** Londra'da *[londrada]*; **in one hour's time** bir saat içinde *[sa-at eecheendeh]*; **in August** Ağustosta *[a-oostosta]*; **in English** İngilizce *[eengheeleezjeh]*; **in Turkish** Türkçe *[tewrk-cheh]*; **is he in?** evde mi? *[evdeh mee]*
inch inç *[eench]*; *see page 120*
include dahil olmak *[daheel olmak]*; **is that included in the price?** fiyata dahil mi? *[feeyata ... mee]*
incompetent beceriksiz *[bejereekseez]*
inconvenient elverişsiz *[elvereesh-seez]*
increase (*noun*) artış *[artuhsh]*
incredible (*very good, amazing*) inanılmaz *[eenanuhlmaz]*
indecent hayasız *[h-'eye'-yassuhz]*
independent (*adjective*) bağımsız *[ba-uhmssuhz]*
India Hindistan *[heendeestan]*
Indian (*adjective*) Hint; (*person*) Hintli *[heentlee]*
indicator (*on car*) sinyal *[seenyal]*
indigestion hazımsızlık *[hazuhm-suhzluhk]*
indoor pool kapalı havuz *[kapaluh havooz]*
indoors içerde *[eecherdeh]*
industry sanayi *[san-'eye'-yee]*
inefficient verimsiz *[vereemsseez]*
infection enfeksiyon *[enfeksseeyon]*
infectious bulaşıcı *[boolashuhjuh]*
inflammation iltihap *[eelteehap]*
inflation enflasyon *[enflassyon]*
informal gayri resmi *[g-'eye'-ree resmee]*
information bilgi *[beelghee]*
information desk danışma masası *[danuhshma massassuh]*
information office danışma bürosu

[danuhshma bewrossoo]
injection enjeksiyon *[enjeksseyon]*
injured yaralı *[yaraluh]*; **she's been injured** yaralandı *[yaralanduh]*
injury yara
innocent masum *[massoom]*
inquisitive meraklı *[merakluh]*
insect böcek *[burjek]*
insect bite böcek sokması *[burjek sokmassuh]*
insecticide haşere ilacı *[hashereh eelajuh]*
insect repellent böcek kaçıran *[burjek kachuhran]*
inside: inside the tent çadırın içinde *[chaduhruhn eecheendeh]*; **let's sit inside** içerde oturalım *[eecherdeh otooraluhm]*
insincere samimiyetsiz *[sameemeeyetseez]*
insist: I insist ısrar ediyorum *[uhssrar edeeyoroom]*
insomnia uykusuzluk *[ookoosoozlook]*
instant coffee neskafe (*tm*) *[neskafeh]*
instead yerine *[yereeneh]*; **I'll have that one instead** yerine onu istiyorum *[onoo eesteeyoroom]*; **instead of ...** ... yerine
insulating tape izolebant *[eezolebant]*
insulin insülin *[eenssewleen]*
insult (*noun*) hakaret
insurance sigorta *[seegorta]*; **write the name of your insurance company here** sigorta şirketinin adını buraya yazın *[sheerketeeneen aduhnuh boor-'eye'-ya yazuhn]*
insurance policy sigorta poliçesi *[seegorta poleechessee]*
intellectual (*noun*) aydın *['eye'-duhn]*
intelligent zeki *[zekee]*
intentional: it wasn't intentional kasdi değildi *[kassdee deh-eeldee]*
interest: places of interest görülmeye değer yerler *[gurrewlmayeh deh-er]*
interested: I'm very interested in ... ... ile yakından ilgileniyorum *[... eeleh yakuhndan eelgheeleneeyoroom]*
interesting ilginç *[eelgheench]*; **that's very interesting** çok ilginç *[chok]*
international uluslararası *[oolooss-lararassuh]*
international driving licence/driver's license uluslararası şoför ehliyeti *[oolooss-lararassuh shofurr ehleeyetee]*
interpret tercüme etmek *[terjewmeh]*; **would you interpret?** tercüme eder misiniz? *[eder mee-seeneez]*
interpreter tercüman *[terjewman]*
intersection kavşak *[kavshak]*
interval (*during play etc*) ara
into -e *[eh]*; **put it into the box** kutuya koyun *[kootooya koyoon]*; **go into the house** eve girin *[eveh gheereen]*; **I'm not into that** (*don't like*) ilgimi çekmiyor *[eelgheemee chekmeeyor]*
introduce: may I introduce ...? size ...-i takdim edebilir miyim? *[seezeh ...-ee takdeem edebeeleer meeyeem]*
introvert içedönük *[eecheh-durnewk]*
invalid malul *[malool]*
invalid chair tekerlekli sandalye *[tekerleklee sandalyeh]*
invitation davet; (*card etc*) davetiye *[daveteeyeh]*; **thank you for the invitation** davet ettiğiniz için teşekkürler *[et-tee-eeneez eecheen teshek-kewrler]*
invite davet etmek; **can I invite you out?** birlikte çıkabilir miyiz? *[beerleekteh chuhkabeeleer meeyeez]*
involved: I don't want to get involved in it bu işe karışmak istemiyorum *[boo eesheh karuhshmak eestemeeyoroom]*
iodine tentürdiyot *[tentewrdeeyot]*
Iran İran *[eeran]*
Iranian (*man, woman*) İranlı *[eeranluh]*; (*adjective*) İran *[eeran]*
Iraq Irak *[uhrak]*
Iraqi (*man, woman*) Iraklı *[uhrakluh]*; (*adjective*) Iraklı
Ireland İrlanda *[eerlanda]*
Irish İrlanda *[eerlanda]*
Irishman İrlandalı *[eerlandaluh]*
Irishwoman İrlandalı kadın *[eerlandaluh kaduhn]*
iron (*metal*) demir *[demeer]*; (*for clothes*) ütü *[ewtew]*; **can you iron these for me?** bunları benim için ütüler misiniz? *[boonlaruh beneem eecheen ewtewler mee-seeneez]*
ironmonger hırdavatçı *[huhrdavatchuh]*
is *see page 114*
Islam İslam *[eeslam]*

Islamic İslami *[eeslamee]*
island ada
isolated ücra *[ewjra]*
Istanbul İstanbul *[eestanbool]*
it o; **is it ...?** ... mu? *[moo]*; **where is it?** nerede? *[neredeh]*; **it's her** odur *[odoor]*; **it was ...** ... idi *[eedee]*; **that's just it** (*just the problem*) zaten mesele burada *[zaten messeleh boorada]*; **that's it** (*that's right*) doğru *[do-roo]*; *see page 110*
Italy İtalya *[eetalya]*
itch: it itches kaşınıyor *[kashuhnuhyor]*
itinerary gezi programı *[ghezee programuh]*

J

jack (*for car*) kriko *[kreeko]*
jacket ceket *[jeket]*
jam (*to eat*) reçel *[rechel]*; **I jammed on the brakes** frene abandım *[freneh abanduhm]*
January Ocak *[ojak]*
jaundice sarılık *[saruhluhk]*
jaw çene *[cheneh]*
jazz caz *[jaz]*
jazz club caz klübü *[jaz klewbew]*
jealous kıskanç *[kuhskanch]*; **he's jealous** kıskanıyor *[kuhskanuhyor]*
jeans blucin *[bloojeen]*
jellyfish denizanası *[deneez-anassuh]*
jetlag: I'm/he's suffering from jetlag uzun uçak yolculuğu başıma/başına vurdu *[oozoon oochak yoljooloo-oo bashuhma/bashuhna voordoo]*
jet-set jet sosyete *[Jet sossyeteh]*
jetty iskele *[eeskeleh]*
Jew Yahudi *[yahoodee]*
jewel(le)ry mücevherat *[mewjevherat]*
Jewish Yahudi *[yahoodee]*
jiffy: just a jiffy bir dakikacık *[beer dakeekajuhk]*
job iş *[eesh]*; **just the job!** (*just right*) tam uygun! *[ooy-goon]*; **it's a good job you told me!** iyi ki söyledin *[eeyee kee surledeen]*
jog: I'm going for a jog koşuya çıkıyorum *[koshooya chuhkuh-yoroom]*
jogging hafif koşu *[hafeef koshoo]*
join: I'd like to join ben de katılmak isterim *[deh katuhlmak eestereem]*; **can I join you?** (*go with*) sizinle gelebilir miyim? *[seezeenleh ghelebeeleer meeyeem]*; (*sit with*) müsaade eder misiniz? *[mewsa-adeh eder meeseeneez]*; **do you want to join us?** (*go with*) bizimle gelmek ister misiniz? *[beezeemleh ghelmek eester]*; (*sit with*) buyurmaz mısınız? *[booyoormaz muhsuhnuhz]*
joint (*in body*) eklem; (*to smoke*) çifte kâğıt *[cheefteh ka-uht]*
joke şaka *[shaka]*; **you've got to be joking!** şaka mı ediyorsunuz! *[muh edeeyor-soonooz]*; **it's no joke** şakası yok *[shakassuh]*
jolly: it was jolly good gayet iyiydi *[g-'eye'-yet eeyeedee]*; **jolly good!** çok iyi! *[chok eeyee]*
journey yolculuk *[yoljoolook]*; **have a good journey!** iyi yolculuklar! *[eeyee]*; **safe journey!** yolunuz açık olsun! *[yoloonooz achuhk olsoon]*
jug sürahi *[sewrahee]*; **a jug of water** bir sürahi su *[beer ... soo]*
July Temmuz *[tem-mooz]*
jump: you made me jump ödümü kopardın *[urdewmew koparduhn]*; **jump in!** (*to car*) bin! *[been]*
jumper kazak
jump leads, jumper cables buji telleri *[booJee tel-leree]*
junction kavşak *[kavshak]*
June Haziran *[hazeeran]*
junk (*rubbish*) çöp *[churp]*
just: just one yalnız bir tane *[yalnuhz beer taneh]*; **just me** yalnız ben; **just for me** yalnız benim için *[beneem eecheen]*; **just a little** birazcık *[beerazjuhk]*; **just here** (*right here*) hemen burada *[hemen boorada]*; **not just now** simdi değil *[sheemdee deh-eel]*; **that's just right** tam öyle *[urleh]*; **it's just as good** bu da onun kadar iyidir *[boo da onoon kadar eeyeedeer]*; **he was here just now** şimdi buradaydı *[sheemdee boorad-*

'eye'-duh]; **I've only just arrived** ben henüz geldim *[henewz gheldeem]*

K

kagul rüzgârlık *[rewzgarluhk]*
kebab kebap
keen: I'm not keen pek istekli değilim *[eesteklee deh-eeleem]*
keep: can I keep it? bende kalabilir mi? *[bendeh kalbeeleer mee]*; **please keep it** lütfen sizde kalsın *[lewtfen seezdeh kalsuhn]*; **keep the change** üstü kalsın *[ewstew]*; **will it keep?** (*food*) dayanır mı? *[dayanuhr muh]*; **it's keeping me awake** beni uyutmuyor *[benee oo-yootmooyor]*; **it keeps on breaking** durmadan kırılıyor *[doormadan kuhruhluhyor]*; **I can't keep anything down** (*food*) ne yesem çıkarıyorum *[neh yessem chuhkaruh-yoroom]*
kerb yaya kaldırımı *[y-'eye'-ya kalduhruhmuh]*
kerosene gazyağı *[gaz-ya-uh]*
ketchup keçap *[kechap]*
kettle güğüm *[ghew-ewm]*
key anahtar
kid: the kids çocuklar *[chojooklar]*; **I'm not kidding** ciddi söylüyorum *[jeedee surlew-yoroom]*
kidneys (*in body*) böbrekler *[burbrekler]*; (*food*) böbrek *[burbrek]*
kill öldürmek *[urldewrmek]*; **my feet are killing me** ayaklarım çok fena *['eye'- yaklaruhm chok fena]*
kilo kilo *[keelo]*; *see page 120*
kilometre, kilometer kilometre *[keelometreh]*; *see page 120*
kind: that's very kind çok naziksiniz *[chok nazeek-seeneez]*; **this kind of ...** bu tür ... *[boo tewr]*
kiosk kulübe *[koolewbeh]*
kiss (*noun*) öpücük *[urpewjewk]*; (*verb*) öpmek *[urpmek]*
kitchen mutfak *[mootfak]*
kitchenette mutfakçık *[mootfakchuhk]*
Kleenex (*tm*) kâğıt mendil *[ka-uht mendeel]*
knee diz *[deez]*
kneecap dizkapağı *[deez-kapa-uh]*
knickers don
knife bıçak *[buhchak]*
knitting (*act*) örgü *[urghew]*; (*material*) triko *[treeko]*
knitting needles örgü şişleri *[urghew sheeshleree]*
knock: there's a knocking noise from the engine motordan vuruntu duyuluyor *[vooroontoo doo-yoolooyor]*; **he's had a knock on the head** başına vurulmuş *[bashuhna vooroolmoosh]*; **he's been knocked over** araba çarpmış *[charpmuhsh]*
knot (*in rope*) düğüm *[dew-ewm]*
know (*somebody*) tanımak *[tanuhmak]*; (*something*) bilmek *[beelmek]*; **I don't know** bilmiyorum *[beelmeeyoroom]*; **do you know a good restaurant?** iyi bir lokanta biliyor musunuz? *[eeyee beer lokanta beeleeyor moo-soonooz]*; **who knows?** kim bilir? *[keem beeleer]*; **I didn't know that** bunu bilmiyordum *[boonoo beelmeeyor-doom]*; **I don't know him** onu tanımıyorum *[onoo tanuhmuh-yoroom]*

L

label etiket *[eteeket]*
laces (*for shoes*) ayakkabı bağları *['eye'-yak-kabuh ba-laruh]*
lacquer (*for hair*) sprey *[spray]*
ladies (*room*) bayanlar *[b-'eye'-yanlar]*
lady bayan *[b-'eye'-yan]*; **ladies and gentlemen!** sayın bayanlar ve baylar! *[s-'eye'-yuhn b-'eye'-yanlar veh b-'eye'-lar]*
lager pilsen bira *[beera]*
lake göl *[gurl]*
lamb kuzu *[koozoo]*
lamp lamba
lamppost lamba direği *[lamba deereh-ee]*
lampshade abajur *[abaJoor]*
land (*not sea*) kara; **when does the plane land?** uçak kaçta inecek? *[oochak kachta eenejek]*
landscape manzara
lane (*on motorway*) şerit *[shereet]*; (*in city*) sokak; **a country lane** köy yolu *[kur yoloo]*
language dil *[deel]*
language course dil kursu *[deel koorsoo]*
large büyük *[bew-yewk]*
laryngitis larenjit *[larenJeet]*
last son; **when's the last bus?** son otobüs kaçta? *[otobewss kachta]*; **one last drink** son bir kadeh *[beer kadeh]*; **when were you last in London?** en son Londra'ya ne zaman gittiniz? *[Londr-'eye'-ya neh zaman gheet-teeneez]*; **last year** geçen yıl *[ghechen yuhl]*; **last night** dün gece *[dewn ghejeh]*; **at last!** nihayet! *[nee-h-'eye'-yet]*; **how long does it last?** ne kadar sürer? *[neh kadar sewrer]*
last name soyadı *[soyaduh]*
late geç *[ghech]*; **sorry I'm late** geciktiğim için özür dilerim *[ghejeektee-eem eecheen urzewr deelereem]*; **don't be late** geç kalmayın *[kalm-'eye'-yuhn]*; **the bus was late** otobüs gecikti *[otobewss ghejeektee]*; **we'll be back late** geç döneceğiz *[durnejeh-eez]*; **it's getting late** geç oluyor *[olooyor]*; **is it that late!** o kadar geç mi? *[o kadar ... mee]*; **it's too late now** artık çok geç *[artuhk chok]*; **I'm a late riser** sabahları geç kalkarım *[sabahlaruh ... kalkaruhm]*
lately son zamanlarda
later daha sonra; **later on** daha sonra; **I'll come back later** sonra tekrar gelirim *[tekrar gheleereem]*; **see you later** görüşmek üzere *[gurrewshmek ewzereh]*; **no later than Tuesday** en geç Salı günü *[ghech saluh ghewnew]*
latest: the latest news son haberler; **at the latest** en geç *[ghech]*
laugh gülmek *[ghewlmek]*; **don't laugh** gülmeyin *[ghewlmayeen]*; **it's no laughing matter** bu iş şakaya gelmez *[boo eesh shak-'eye'-ya ghelmez]*
launderette, landromat otomatlı çamaşırhane *[otomatluh chamashuhr-haneh]*
laundry (*clothes*) çamaşır *[chama-shuhr]*; (*place*) çamaşırhane *[—haneh]*; **could you get the laundry done?** çamaşırları yıkatabilir misiniz? *[chamashuhrlaruh yuhkatabeeleer mee-seeneez]*
lavatory tuvalet *[toovalet]*
law kanun *[kanoon]*; **against the law** kanuna aykırı *[kanoona 'eye'-kuhruh]*
lawn çimen *[cheemen]*
lawyer avukat *[avookat]*
laxative müshil *[mewss-heel]*
lay-by dinlenme yeri *[deenlenmeh yeree]*
laze around: I just want to laze around biraz yan gelip yatmak istiyorum *[beeraz yan gheleep yatmak eesteeyoroom]*
lazy tembel; **don't be lazy** üşenme *[ewshenmeh]*; **a nice lazy holiday** güzel, dertsiz bir tatil *[ghewzel dertseez beer tateel]*
lead (*electric*) kablo; **where does this**

road lead? bu yol nereye çıkıyor? *[boo yol nerayeh chuhkuhyor]*
leaf yaprak
leaflet broşür *[broshewr]*; **do you have any leaflets on ...?** ... konusunda broşür var mı? *[konoossoonda ... muh]*
leak kaçak *[kachak]*; **the roof leaks** dam akıyor *[akuhyor]*
learn: I want to learn ... ...-i öğrenmek istiyorum *[...-ee urrenmek eesteeyoroom]*
learner: I'm just a learner bu işin acemisiyim *[boo eesheen ajemesseeyeem]*
lease (*verb*) kiralamak *[keeralamak]*
least: not in the least hiç de değil *[heech deh deh-eel]*; **at least 50** en azından 50 *[en azuhndan el-lee]*
leather deri *[deree]*
leave: when does the bus leave? otobüs ne zaman kalkıyor? *[otobewss neh zaman kalkuhyor]*; **I leave tomorrow** yarın hareket ediyorum *[yaruhn hareket edeeyoroom]*; **he left this morning** bu sabah hareket etti *[boo sabah ... et-tee]*; **may I leave this here?** bunu burada bırakabilir miyim? *[boonoo boorada buhraka-beeleer meeyeem]*; **I left my bag in the bar** çantamı barda bıraktım *[chantamuh barda buhraktuhm]*; **she left her bag here** çantasını burada bıraktı *[chantassuhnuh ... buhraktuh]*; **leave the window open please** lütfen pencereyi açık bırakın *[lewtfen penjerayee achuhk buhrakuhn]*; **there's not much left** pek fazla kalmadı *[kalmaduh]*; **I've hardly any money left** hemen hiç param kalmadı *[hemen heech param kalmaduh]*; **I'll leave it up to you** siz karar verin *[seez karar vereen]*
lecherous zampara
left sol; **on the left** solda
left-hand drive soldan direksiyonlu *[soldan deerek-sseeyonloo]*
left-handed solak
left luggage office emanet
leg bacak *[bajak]*
legal yasal *[yassal]*
lemon limon *[leemon]*
lemonade limonata *[leemonata]*
lemon tea limonlu çay *[leemonloo ch-'eye']*
lend: would you lend me your ...? ...-inizi ödünç verir misiniz? *[...-eeneezee urdewnch vereer mee-seeneez]*
lens objektif *[obɹekteef]*; (*contact*) lens
lens cap objektif kapağı *[obɹekteef kapa-uh]*
lesbian sevici *[seveejee]*
less: less than an hour bir saatten az *[sa-at-ten]*; **less than that** ondan daha az; **less hot/expensive** o kadar sıcak/pahalı değil *[shuhjak pahaluh deh-eel]*
lesson ders; **do you give lessons?** ders veriyor musunuz? *[vereeyor moo-soonooz]*
let: would you let me use it? kullanabilir miyim? *[kool-lanabeeleer meeyeem]*; **will you let me know?** bana haber verir misiniz? *[bana haber vereer mee-seeneez]*; **I'll let you know** ben size haber veririm *[seezeh haber vereereem]*; **let me try** bir deneyeyim *[beer denay-ayeem]*; **let me go!** bırak beni! *[buhrak benee]*; **let's leave now** haydi gidelim *[h-'eye'-dee gheedeleem]*; **let's not go yet** biraz daha kalalım *[beeraz daha kalaluhm]*; **will you let me off at ...?** beni ...-de indirir misiniz? *[...-eh eendeereer mee-seeneez]*; **rooms to let** kiralık oda *[keeraluhk oda]*
letter (*in mail*) mektup *[mektoop]*; (*of alphabet*) harf; **are there any letters for me?** bana mektup var mı? *[muh]*
letterbox mektup kutusu *[mektoop kootoossoo]*
lettuce marul *[marool]*
level crossing hemzemin geçit *[hemzemeen ghecheet]*
lever (*noun*) manivela *[maneevela]*
liable (*responsible*) sorumlu *[soroomloo]*
liberated: a liberated woman özgürleşmiş bir kadın *[urzghewr-leshmeesh beer kaduhn]*
library kütüphane *[kewtewp-haneh]*
licence, license (*driving*) ehliyet *[ehleeyet]*
license plate (*on car*) plaka
lid kapak
lie (*untruth*) yalan; **can he lie down for a while?** biraz uzanabilir mi? *[beeraz oozana-beeleer mee]*; **I want**

to go and lie down biraz uzanmak istiyorum *[oozanmak eesteeyoroom]*

lie-in: I'm going to have a lie-in tomorrow yarın sabah iyi bir uyku çekeceğim *[yaruhn sabah eeyee beer ooykoo chekejeh-eem]*

life hayat *[h-'eye'-yat]*; **not on your life!** dünyada olmaz! *[dewn-yada olmaz]*; **that's life!** olacağına varır! *[olaja-uhna varuhr]*

lifebelt emniyet kemeri *[emneeyet kemeree]*

lifeboat cankurtaran filikası *[jankoortaran feeleekassuh]*

lifeguard cankurtaran *[jankoortaran]*

life insurance hayat sigortası *[h-'eye'-yat seegortassuh]*

life jacket cankurtaran yeleği *[jankoortaran yeleh-ee]*

lift (*in hotel etc*) asansör *[assansurr]*; **could you give me a lift?** beni de götürebilir misiniz? *[benee deh gurtewreh-beeleer mee-seeneez]*; **do you want a lift?** sizi de götürebilir miyim? *[seezee deh ... meeyeem]*; **thanks for the lift** beni arabanıza aldığınız için teşekkürler *[arabanuhza alduh-uhnuhz eecheen teshekkewrler]*; **I got a lift** birisi beni arabasına aldı *[beereessee arabassuhna alduh]*

light (*noun*) ışık *[uhshuhk]*; (*not heavy*) hafif *[hafeef]*; **the light was on** ışık yanıyordu *[yanuh-yordoo]*; **do you have a light?** bir ateş verir misiniz? *[beer atesh vereer mee-seeneez]*; **a light meal** hafif bir yemek; **light blue** açık mavi *[achuhk mavee]*

light bulb ampul *[ampool]*

lighter (*cigarette*) çakmak *[chakmak]*

lighthouse deniz feneri *[deneez feneree]*

light meter pozometre *[pozometreh]*

lightning şimşek *[sheemshek]*

like: I'd like a ... bir ... istiyorum *[beer ... eesteeyoroom]*; **I'd like to ...** ... istiyorum; **would you like a ...?** bir ... ister misiniz? *[eester mee-seeneez]*; **would you like to come too?** siz de gelmek ister misiniz? *[seez deh ghelmek]*; **I'd like to** çok isterdim *[chok eesterdeem]*; **I like it** beğendim *[bayendeem]*; **I like you** sizden hoşlanıyorum *[seezden hoshlanuh-yoroom]*; **I don't like it** hoşuma gitmiyor *[hoshooma gheetmeeyor]*; **he doesn't like it** hoşlanmıyor *[hoshlanmuhyor]*; **do you like ...?** ... sever misiniz? *[... sever mee-seeneez]*; **I like swimming** yüzmeyi severim *[yewzmayee severeem]*; **OK, if you like** eğer istiyorsanız, olur *[eh-er eesteeyorsanuhz oloor]*; **what's it like?** nasıl bir şey? *[nassuhl beer shay]*; **do it like this** böyle yapın *[burleh yapuhn]*; **one like that** onun benzeri *[onoon benzeree]*

lilo şişirme şilte *[sheesheermeh sheelteh]*

line (*on paper*) çizgi *[cheezghee]*; (*tel*) hat; (*of people*) sıra *[suhra]*; **would you give me a line?** (*tel*) bana bir hat verir misiniz? *[bana beer hat vereer mee-seeneez]*

linen (*for beds*) yatak çarşafları *[yatak charshaflaruh]*

linguist dilci *[deeljee]*; **I'm no linguist** yabancı dil yeteneğim azdır *[yabanjuh deel yeteneh-eem azduhr]*

lining astar

lip dudak *[doodak]*

lip brush dudak fırçası *[doodak fuhrchassuh]*

lip pencil dudak kalemi *[dookak kalemee]*

lip salve dudak merhemi *[doodak merhemee]*

lipstick ruj *[rooJ]*

liqueur likör *[leekurr]*

liquor içki *[eechkee]*

lira lira *[leera]*

list liste *[leesteh]*

listen: I'd like to listen to ... ...-i dinlemek istiyorum *[...-ee deenlemek eesteeyoroom]*; **listen!** dinle! *[deenleh]*

litre, liter litre *[leetreh]*; *see page 121*

litter (*rubbish*) çöp *[churp]*

little (*size*) küçük *[kewchewk]*; (*quantity*) az; **just a little, thanks** biraz, lütfen *[beeraz lewtfen]*; **just a very little** azıcık *[azuhjuhk]*; **a little cream** biraz krema; **a little more** biraz daha; **a little better** biraz daha iyi *[eeyee]*; **that's too little** (*not enough*) çok az *[chok]*

live yaşamak *[yashamak]*; **I live in ...**

...-de oturuyorum *[...-deh otooroo-yoroom]*; **where do you live?** nerede oturuyorsunuz? *[neredeh otooroo-yorsoonooz]*; **where does he live?** o nerede oturuyor? *[otoorooyor]*; **we live together** birlikte yaşıyoruz *[beerleekteh yashuh-yorooz]*

lively (*person, town*) canlı *[janluh]*

liver (*in body*) karaciğer *[karajee-er;* (*food*) ciğer *[jee-er]*

lizard kertenkele *[kertenkeleh]*

loaf somun *[somoon]*

lobby (*of hotel*) lobi *[lobee]*

lobster istakoz *[eestakoz]*

local: local wine yerel şarap *[sharap]*; **a local newspaper** yerel gazete *[gazeteh]*; **a local restaurant** yerel lokanta

lock (*noun*) kilit *[keeleet]*; **it's locked** kilitli *[keeleetlee]*; **I locked myself out of my room** odamın anahtarını içerde unuttum *[odamuhn anahta-ruhnuh eecherdeh oonoot-toom]*

locker (*for luggage etc*) kilitli dolap *[keeleetlee dolap]*

log: I slept like a log ölü gibi uyu-dum *[urlew gheebee oo-yoodoom]*

lollipop lolipop

London Londra *[londra]*

lonely yalnız *[yalnuhz]*; **are you lonely?** yalnızlık çekiyor musunuz? *[yalnuhzluhk chekeeyor moossoonooz]*

long uzun *[oozoon]*; **how long does it take?** ne kadar sürer *[neh kadar sewrer]*; **is it a long way?** uzak mı? *[oozak muh]*; **a long time** uzun süre *[sewreh]*; **I won't be long** hemen döneceğim *[hemen durnejeh-eem]*; **don't be long** hemen dön *[durn]*; **that was long ago** ondan beri çok zaman geçti *[ondan beree chok zaman ghechtee]*; **long time no see!** ne zamandır görüşmedik! *[neh zamanduhr gurrewsh-medeek]*; **so long!** hoşça kalın! *[hosh-cha kaluhn]*

long distance call şehirlerarası konuşma *[sheheerler-arassuh konoosh-ma]*

loo: where's the loo? tuvalet nerede? *[toovalet neredeh]*; **I want to go to the loo** tuvalete gitmek istiyorum *[toovaleteh gheetmek eesteeyoroom]*

look: that looks good bu iyiye benziyor *[boo eeyeeyeh benzeeyor]*; **you look tired** yorgun görünüyorsun *[yorgoon gurrewnew-yorsoon]*; **you don't look your age** yaşınızı göstermiyorsunuz *[yashuh-nuhzuh gurster-meeyor-soonooz]*; **look at him** şuna bak *[shoona]*; **I'm looking for ...** ...-i arıyorum *[...-ee aruhyoroom]*; **look out!** dikkat! *[deek-kat]*; **can I have a look?** bakabilir miyim? *[bakabeeleer meeyeem]*; **can I have a look around?** etrafa bir bakabilir miyim? **I'm just looking, thanks** şöyle bir bakıyorum *[shurleh beer bakuhyoroom]*

loose (*button, handle etc*) gevşemiş *[ghevshemeesh]*

loose change bozuk para *[bozook]*

lorry kamyon

lorry driver kamyon şoförü *[kamyon shofurrew]*

lose kaybetmek *[k-'eye'-betmek]*; **I've lost my ...** ...-imi kaybettim *[...-eemee k-'eye'-bet-teem]*; **I'm lost** yolumu kaybettim *[yoloomoo]*

lost property office, lost and found kayıp eşya bürosu *[k-'eye'-yuhp eshya bewrossoo]*

lot: a lot, lots çok *[chok]*; **not a lot** o kadar çok değil *[kadar... deh-eel]*; **a lot of money** çok para *[para]*; **a lot of women** çok sayıda kadın *[s-'eye'-yuhda kaduhn]*; **a lot cooler** çok daha serin *[daha sereen]*; **I like it a lot** çok beğendim *[bayendeem]*; **is it a lot further?** çok ötede mi? *[urtedeh mee]*; **I'll take the (whole) lot** hepsini alacağım *[hepseenee alaja-uhm]*

lotion losyon *[lossyon]*

loud yüksek sesle *[yewksek sessleh]*; **the music is rather loud** müziğin sesi biraz fazla yüksek *[mewzee-een sessee beeraz fazla yewksek]*

lounge (*in house, hotel*) salon

lousy (*not good*) berbat

love: I love you seni seviyorum *[senee seveeyoroom]*; **he's fallen in love** aşık oldu *[ashuhk oldoo]*; **I love Turkey** Türkiye'ye aşığım *[tewrkee-yay-yeh ashuh-uhm]*; **let's make love** aşk yapalım *[ashk yapaluhm]*

lovely nefis *[nefeess]*

low (*prices*) düşük *[dewshewk]*; (*bridge*) alçak *[alchak]*

low beam yakın far *[yakuhn]*

LP uzunçalar *[oozoon-chalar]*
luck şans *[shans]*; **hard luck!** vah vah!; **good luck!** talihin açık olsun! *[taleeheen achuhk olsoon]*; **just my luck!** benim kötü şansım! *[beneem kurtew shansuhm]*; **it was pure luck** sırf talih eseri *[suhrf taleeh esseree]*
lucky: that's lucky! ne şans! *[neh shans]*
lucky charm uğur *[oo-oor]*
luggage bagaj *[bajaJ]*
lumbago lumbago *[loombago]*
lump (*medical*) yumru *[yoomroo]*
lunch öğle yemeği *[urleh yemeh-ee]*
lungs ak ciğerler *[jee-erler]*
luxurious lüks *[lewks]*
luxury lüks *[lewks]*

M

macaroon acıbadem kurabiyesi *[ajuhbadem koorabee-yessee]*
mad deli *[delee]*
madam madam
magazine dergi *[derghee]*
magnificent şahane *[shahaneh]*
maid (*in hotel*) oda hizmetçisi *[oda heezmet-cheessee]*
maiden name kızlık adı *[kuhzluhk aduh]*
mail (*noun*) posta; **is there any mail for me?** bana mektup var mı? *[bana mektoop ... muh]*; **where can I mail this?** bunu nereden postalayabilirim? *[boonoo nereden postal-'eye'-yabeeleereem]*
mailbox mektup kutusu *[mektoop kootoossoo]*
main esas *[essass]*; **where's the main post office?** merkez postanesi nerede? *[merkez postanessee neredeh]*
main road ana yol
make yapmak; **do you make them yourself?** bunları kendiniz mi yapıyorsunuz? *[boonlaruh kendeeneez mee yapuh-yorsoonooz]*; **it's very well made** çok iyi yapılmış *[chok eeyee yapuhlmuhsh]*; **what does that make altogether?** hepsi ne kadar tutuyor? *[hepsee neh kadar tootoo-yor]*; **I make it only ... liras** benim hesabıma göre ... lira tutuyor *[beneem hessabuhma gurreh ... leera]*
make-up makyaj *[makyaJ]*
make-up remover makyaj silme losyonu *[makyaJ seelmeh lossyonoo]*
male chauvinist pig erkek şovenisti *[erkek shoveneestee]*
man adam
manager yönetici *[yurneteejee]*; **may I see the manager?** yöneticiyle görüşmek istiyorum *[yurneteejeeleh gurreshmek eesteeyoroom]*
manicure manikür *[manikewr]*
many çok *[chok]*
map: a map of ... ... haritası *[hareetassuh]*; **it's not on this map** bu haritada görülmüyor *[boo hareetada gurrewlmew-yor]*
marble (*noun*) mermer
March Mart
marijuana esrar *[essrar]*
mark: there's a mark on it üzerinde bir leke var *[ewzereendeh beer lekeh]*; **could you mark it on the map for me?** benim için haritada işaretler misiniz? *[beneem eecheen hareetada eesharetler mee-seeneez]*
market (*noun*) çarşı *[charshuh]*
marmalade portakal reçeli *[rechelee]*
married: are you married? evli misiniz? *[evlee mee-seeneez]*; **I'm married** ben evliyim *[evleeyeem]*
mascara rimel *[reemel]*
mass: I'd like to go to mass ayine gitmek istiyorum *['eye'-yeeneh gheetmek eesteeyorum]*
mast direk *[deerek]*
masterpiece başyapıt *[bash-yapuht]*
matches kibrit *[keebreet]*
material (*cloth*) kumaş *[koomash]*
matter: it doesn't matter farketmez *[farketmez]*; **what's the matter** ne oldu? *[neh oldoo]*
mattress şilte *[sheelteh]*
maximum (*noun*) azami *[azamee]*
May Mayıs *[m-'eye'-yuhss]*
may: may I have another bottle/beer?

bir şişe/bira daha verir misiniz? *[beer sheesheh/beera daha vereer mee-seeneez]*; **may I?** müsaade eder misiniz? *[mewsa-adeh eder]*

maybe belki *[belkee]*; **maybe not** belki değil *[deh-eel]*

mayonnaise mayonez *[m-'eye'-yonez]*

me: come with me benimle gelin *[beneemlee gheleen]*; **it's for me** benim için *[beneem eecheen]*; **it's me** benim; **me too** ben de *[deh]*; *see page 110*

meal: that was an excellent meal yemek mükemmeldi *[yemek mewkem-meldee]*; **does that include meals?** buna yemekler de dahil mi? *[boona yemekler deh daheel mee]*

mean: what does this word mean? bu kelimenin anlamı nedir? *[boo keleemeneen anlamuh nedeer]*; **what does he mean?** ne demek istiyor? *[neh demek esteeyor]*; **what does that mean?** bu ne demek?

measles kızamık *[kuhzamuhk]*

measurements ölçüler *[urlchewler]*

meat et

mechanic: do you have a mechanic here? burada tamirci var mı? *[boorada tameerjee var muh]*

medicine ilaç *[eelach]*

medieval ortaçağa ait *[orta-cha-a 'eye'-yeet]*

Mediterranean Akdeniz *[akdeneez]*

medium (*adjective*) orta

medium-sized orta büyüklükte *[orta bew-yewk-lewkteh]*

meet: pleased to meet you memnun oldum *[memnoon oldoom]*; **where shall we meet?** nerede buluşalım? *[neredeh boolooshaluhm]*; **let's meet up again** tekrar görüşelim *[tekrar gurrewsheleem]*

meeting toplantı *[toplantuh]*

meeting place buluşma yeri *[boolooshma yeree]*

melon kavun *[kavoon]*

member üye *[ew-yeh]*; **I'd like to become a member** üye olmak istiyorum *[olmak eesteeyoroom]*

men adamlar

mend: can you mend this? bunu onarabilir misiniz? *[boonoo onara-beeleer mee-seeneez]*

men's room erkekler tuvaleti *[erkekler toovaletee]*

mention: don't mention it bir şey değil *[beer shay deh-eel]*

menu yemek listesi *[yemek leestessee]*; **may I have the menu please?** yemek listesini verir misiniz? *[leesteh-seenee vereer mee-seeneez]*

mess: it's a mess berbat durumda *[berbat dooroomda]*

message: are there any messages for me? bana mesaj bırakan oldu mu? *[bana mesaj buhrakan oldoo moo]*; **I'd like to leave a message for ...** ...için bir mesaj bırakmak istiyorum *[eecheen beer ... buhrakmak eesteeyoroom]*

metal (*noun*) metal

metre, meter metre *[metreh]*; *see page 120*

midday: at midday öğleyin *[ur-layeen]*

middle: in the middle ortada; **in the middle of the road** yolun ortasında *[yoloon ortassuhnda]*

midnight: at midnight gece yarısı *[ghejeh yaruhssuh]*

might: I might want to stay another 3 days 3 gün daha kalmak isteyebilirim *[ewch ghewn daha kalmak eestayeh-beeleereem]*; **you might have warned me!** beni uyarabilirdiniz! *[benee ooyara-beeleerdeeneez]*

migraine migren *[meegren]*

mild (*taste*) hafif *[hafeef]*; (*weather*) ılımlı *[uhluhmluh]*

mile mil *[meel]*; **that's miles away!** orası çok uzak *[orassuh chok oozak]*; *see page 120*

mileometer kilometre saati *[keelometreh sa-atee]*

military (*adjective*) askeri *[askeree]*

milk süt *[sewt]*

milkshake milkşeyk *[meelk-shayk]*

millimetre, millimeter milimetre *[meeleemetreh]*

minaret minare *[meenareh]*

minced meat kıyma *[kuhy-ma]*

mind: I don't mind benim için farketmez *[beneem eecheen]*; **would you mind if I smoke/open the window?** sigara içmemin/pencereyi açmanın bir mahzuru var mı? *[seegara eechmemeen/penjerayee achmanuhn beer mahzooroo var muh]*; **never**

mind zarar yok; **I've changed my mind** fikrimi değiştirdim *[feekreemee deh-eeshteerdeem]*
mine: it's mine o benimdir *[beneemdeer]*; *see page 110*
mineral water maden suyu *[soo-yoo]*
minimum (*adjective*) asgari *[asgaree]*
mint (*sweet*) nane şekeri *[naneh shekeree]*
minus eksi *[eksee]*; **minus 3 degrees** eksi 3 derece *[ewch derejeh]*
minute dakika *[dakeeka]*; **in a minute** hemen şimdi *[hemen sheemdee]*; **just a minute** bir dakika *[beer]*
mirror ayna *['eye'-na]*
Miss Bayan *[b-'eye'-yan]*
miss: I miss you sizi özledim *[seezee urzledeem]*; **there's a ... missing** bir ... eksik *[beer ... ekseek]*; **we missed the bus** otobüsü kaçırdık *[otobewssew kachuhrduhk]*
mist sis *[seess]*
mistake hata; **I think there's a mistake here** sanırım bunda bir yanlışlık var *[sanuhruhm boonda beer yanluhshluhk var]*
misunderstanding yanlış anlama *[yanluhsh anlama]*
mixture karışım *[karuhshuhm]*
mix-up: there's been some sort of mix-up with ... ... ile bir sorun çıkmış *[eeleh beer soroon chuhkmuhsh]*
modern modern
modern art çağdaş sanat *[cha-dash]*
moisturizer nemlendirici krem *[nemlendeereejee]*
moment: I won't be a moment bir dakika sürmez *[dakeeka sewrmez]*
monastery manastır *[manastuhr]*
Monday Pazartesi *[pazartessee]*
money para; **I don't have any money** hiç param yok *[heech]*; **do you take English/American money?** İngiliz/Amerikan parası kabul ediyor musunuz? *[eengheeleez/amereekan parassuh kabool edeeyor moossoonooz]*
month ay *['eye']*
monument abide *[abeedeh]*
moon ay *['eye']*
moorings bağlama yeri *[ba-lama yeree]*
moped moped
more daha; **may I have some more?** biraz daha alabilir miyim? *[beeraz ... alabeeleer meeyeem]*; **more water, please** biraz daha su, lütfen *[soo lewtfen]*; **no more, thanks** başka istemem, teşekkür ederim *[bashka eestemem teshek-kewr edereem]*; **more expensive** daha pahalı *[pahaluh]*; **more than 50** 50-den fazla *[elleeden]*; **more than that** ondan daha fazla; **a lot more** çok daha fazla *[chok]*; **not any more** artık değil *[artuhk de-eel]*; **I don't stay there any more** artık orada kalmıyorum *[orada kalmuh-yoroom]*
morning sabah; **good morning** günaydın *[ghewn-'eye'-duhn]*; **this morning** bu sabah *[boo]*; **in the morning** sabahleyin *[sabahlayeen]*
Moslem Müslüman *[mewslewman]*
mosque cami *[jamee]*; **Blue Mosque** Sultan Ahmet Camisi *[sooltan ahmet jameessee]*
mosquito sivrisinek *[seevree-seenek]*
most: I like this one most en çok bunu beğeniyorum *[chok boonoo beh-eneeyoroom]*; **most of the time** çoğunlukla *[cho-oonlookla]*; **most hotels** otellerin çoğu *[otel-lereen cho-oo]*; **most Turks** Türklerin çoğu *[tewrklereen cho-oo]*
mother anne *[anneh]*; **my mother** annem *[annem]*
motif (*in pattern*) motif *[moteef]*
motor motor
motorbike motosiklet *[motoseeklet]*
motorboat motorbot
motorist otomobil sürücüsü *[otomobeel sewrew-jewssew]*
motorway ekspresyol *[ekspressyol]*
motor yacht motorlu yat *[motorloo]*
mountain dağ *[da]*; **up in the mountains** dağlarda *[da-larda]*; **a mountain village** bir dağ köyü *[beer ... kur-yew]*
mouse fare *[fareh]*
moustache bıyık *[buh-yuhk]*
mouth ağız *[a-uhz]*
move: he's moved to another hotel başka bir otele taşındı *[bashka beer oteleh tashuhnduh]*; **could you move your car?** arabanızı oradan alır mısınız? *[arabanuhzuh oradan aluhr muhsuhnuhz]*

movie filim *[feeleem]*; **let's go to the movies** hadi sinemaya gidelim *[hadee sinem-'eye'-ya gheedeleem]*
movie camera sinema kamerası *[seenema kamerassuh]*
movie theater sinema *[seenema]*
moving: a very moving tune çok duygulandırıcı bir melodi *[chok dooy-goo-landuhruhjuh beer melodee]*
Mr Bay *[b-'eye']*
Mrs Bayan *[b-'eye'-yan]*
Ms Bayan *[b-'eye'-yan]*
much çok *[chok]*; **much better** çok daha iyi *[daha eeyee]*; **much cooler** çok daha serin *[sereen]*; **not much** çok değil *[deh-eel]*; **not so much** o kadar değil *[kadar]*
muffler (*on car*) susturucu *[soostooroojoo]*
mug: I've been mugged saldırıya uğradım *[salduhruhya oo-raduhm]*
muggy sıkıntılı *[suhkuhntuhluh]*
mulberries dut *[doot]*
mule katır *[katuhr]*
mumps kabakulak *[kabakoolak]*
murals duvar resimleri *[doovar resseemleree]*
muscle kas *[kass]*
museum müze *[mewzeh]*
mushrooms mantar
music müzik *[mewzeek]*; **guitar music** gitar müziği *[gheetar mewzee-ee]*; **do you have the sheet music for ...?** sizde ...-nin notaları var mı? *[seezdeh ...-neen notalaruh var muh]*
musician müzisyen *[mewzeess-yen]*
mussels midye *[meed-yeh]*
must: I must ... ...-meliyim *[...-meleeyeem]*; **I must go back tonight** bu gece dönmeliyim *[ghejeh durnme-leeyeem]*; **I must make a phone call** telefon etmeliyim *[etmeleeyeem]*; **I mustn't drink ...** ...içmemem lazım *[eechmemem lazuhm]*; **you mustn't forget** sakın unutmayın *[sakuhn oonootm-'eye'-yuhn]*
mustache bıyık *[buh-yuhk]*
mustard hardal
my benim *[beneem]*; **my room** benim odam; *see page 108*
myself: I'll do it myself kendim yaparım *[kendeem yaparuhm]*

N

nail (*of finger*) tırnak *[tuhrnak]*; (*in wood*) çivi *[cheevee]*
nail clippers tırnak kesme aleti *[tuhrnak kessmeh aletee]*
nailfile tırnak törpüsü *[tuhrnak turpewssew]*
nail polish tırnak cilası *[tuhrnak jeelassuh]*
nail polish remover aseton *[asseton]*
nail scissors tırnak makası *[tuhrnak makassuh]*
naked çıplak *[chuhplak]*
name ad; **what's your name?** adınız nedir? *[aduhnuhz nedeer]*; **what's its name?** bunun adı nedir? *[boonoon aduh]*; **my name is ...** benim adım ... *[beneem aduhm]*
nap: he's having a nap biraz uzandı *[beeraz oozanduh]*
napkin (*serviette*) peçete *[pecheteh]*
nappy lastik don *[lasteek]*
nappy-liners çocuk bezi *[chojook bezee]*
narrow (*road*) dar
nasty (*taste, person, weather*) kötü *[kurtoo]*; (*cut*) fena
national ulusal *[ooloossal]*
nationality uyruk *[ooy-rook]*
natural doğal *[do-al]*
naturally (*of course*) tabii *[tabee-ee]*
nature (*trees etc*) doğa *[do-a]*
nausea mide bulantısı *[meedeh boolantuhssuh]*
near yakın *[yakuhn]*; **is it near here?** buraya yakın mı? *[boor-'eye'-ya ... muh]*; **near the window** pencerenin yakınında *[penjereneen yakuh-nuhnda]*; **do you go near ...?** ...-nin yakınından geçecek misiniz? *[...-neen yakuhnuhndan ghechejek mee-seeneez]*; **where is the nearest ...?** en yakın ... nerede? *[neredeh]*
nearby yakında *[yakuhnda]*
nearly hemen hemen

nearside wheel sağ tekerlek *[sa]*
neat (*room*) düzenli *[dewzenlee]*; (*drink*) su katılmamış *[soo katuhlmamuhsh]*
necessary gerekli *[ghereklee]*; **is it necessary to ...?** ... gerekli mi? *[mee]*; **it's not necessary** gerek yok *[gherek]*
neck boyun *[boyoon]*; (*dress, shirt*) yaka
necklace kolye *[kol-yeh]*
necktie kravat
need: I need a ... bir ...-e ihtiyacım var *[...-eh eehteeyajuhm var]*; **do I need a ...?** ... lazım mı? *[lazuhm muh]*; **it needs more salt** biraz daha tuz lazım *[beeraz daha tooz]*; **there's no need** gerek yok *[gherek]*; **there's no need to shout!** bağırmaya gerek yok *[ba-uhrm-'eye'-ya]*
needle iğne *[ee-neh]*
negative (*film*) negatif *[negateef]*
neighbo(u)r komşu *[komshoo]*
neighbo(u)rhood mahalle *[mahalleh]*
neither: neither of us ne sen ne de ben *[neh ... deh ...]*; **neither one** (*of them*) hiç biri *[heech beeree]*; **neither ... nor ...** ne ... ne ... ; **he doesn't speak Turkish - neither do I** o Türkçe bilmiyor - ben de bilmiyorum *[beelmeeyoroom]*; **she doesn't eat meat - neither do I** o et yemiyor - ben de yemiyorum *[yemeeyoroom]*
nephew yeğen *[yeh-en]*; **my nephew** yeğenim *[yeh-eneem]*
nervous sinirli *[seeneerlee]*
net (*fishing, tennis*) ağ *[a]*
nettle ısırgan otu *[uhsuhrgan otoo]*
neurotic sinir hastası *[seeneer hastassuh]*
neutral (*gear*) boş *[bosh]*
never asla *[assla]*
new yeni *[yenee]*
news haber; **is there any news?** bir haber var mı? *[beer var muh]*
newspaper gazete *[gazeteh]*; **do you have any English newspapers?** İngilizce gazete var mı? *[eengheeleezjeh ... var muh]*
newsstand gazete satıcısı *[gazeteh satuhjuhssuh]*
New Year Yeni Yıl *[yenee yuhl]*; **Happy New Year** Yeni Yılınız Kutlu Olsun *[yuhluhnuhz kootloo olsoon]*
New Year's Eve Yılbaşı *[yuhlbashuh]*
New Zealand Yeni Zelanda *[yenee]*
New Zealander Yeni Zelandalı *[yenee zelandaluh]*
next bir sonraki *[beer sonrakee]*; **it's at the next corner** bir sonraki köşede *[kurshedeh]*; **next week/Monday** gelecek hafta/Pazartesi *[pazartessee]*; **next to the post office** postanenin yanında *[postaneneen yanuhnda]*; **the one next to that** onun yanındaki *[onoon yanuhndakee]*
nextdoor kapı komşu *[kapuh komshoo]*
next of kin en yakın akraba *[yakuhn]*
nice (*person, town*) hoş *[hosh]*; (*meal, day*) güzel *[ghewzel]*; **that's very nice of you** çok naziksiniz *[chok nazeekseeneez]*; **a nice cold drink** güzel bir soğuk içecek *[beer so-ook eechejek]*
nickname takma ad
niece kız yeğen *[kuhz yeh-en]*; **my niece** kız yeğenim *[yeh-eneem]*
night gece *[ghejeh]*; **for one night** bir gece için *[beer ... eecheen]*; **for three nights** üç gece için *[ewch]*; **good night** iyi geceler *[eeyee ghejeler]*; **at night** geceleyin *[ghejelayeen]*
nightclub gece kulübü *[ghejeh koolewbew]*
nightdress gecelik *[ghejeleek]*
night flight gece seferi *[ghejeh seferee]*
nightie gecelik *[ghejeleek]*
night-life gece hayatı *[ghejeh h-'eye'-yatuh]*
nightmare karabasan *[karabassan]*
night porter gece nöbetçisi *[ghejeh nurbetcheessee]*
nits (*bugs in hair etc*) bit *[beet]*
no hayır *[h-'eye'-yuhr]*; **I've no money/matches** hiç param/kibritim yok *[heech param/keebreeteem]*; **there are no towels** havlu yok *[havloo]*; **there's no more** başka kalmadı *[bashka kalmaduh]*; **no more than ...** ...-den fazla değil *[...-den fazla deh-eel]*; **oh no!** (*upset*) tüh! *[tewh]*
nobody hiç kimse *[heech keemseh]*
noise gürültü *[ghewrewltew]*
noisy gürültülü *[ghewrewl-tewlew]*; **it's too noisy** fazla gürültülü
non-alcoholic alkolsüz *[alkolsewz]*

none hiç *[heech]*; **none of them** hiç biri *[beeree]*
nonsense saçma *[sachma]*
non-smoking (*compartment, section of plane*) sigara içmeyenlere mahsus *[seegara eechmayenlereh mahsooss]*
non-stop (*travel*) durmaksızın *[doormaksuhzuhn]*
no-one hiç kimse *[heech keemseh]*
nor: I don't smoke - nor do I ben sigara içmiyorum - ben de içmiyorum *[ben deh eechmeeyoroom]*
normal normal
north kuzey *[koozay]*; **to the north of ...** ...-in kuzeyinde *[...-een koozayeendeh]*; **in the north** kuzeyde *[koozaydeh]*
northeast kuzeydoğu *[koozay-do-oo]*; **to the northeast of ...** ...-in kuzeydoğusunda *[...een koozay-do-oossoonda]*; **in the northeast** kuzeydoğuda *[koozaydo-ooda]*
Northern Ireland Kuzey İrlanda *[koozay eerlanda]*
northwest kuzey batı *[koozay batuh]*; **to the northwest of ...** ...-in kuzeybatısında *[...-een koozaybatuhsuhnda]*; **in the northwest** kuzeybatıda
Norway Norveç *[norvech]*
nose burun *[booroon]*; **my nose is bleeding** burnum kanıyor *[boornoom kanuh-yor]*
not değil *[deh-eel]*; **it's not important** önemli değil *[urnemlee]*; **not that one** o değil; **not for me** benim için değil *[beneem eecheen]*; **I don't smoke** sigara içmem *[seegara eechmem]*; **he didn't say anything** hiç bir şey söylemedi *[heech beer shay surlemedee]*; **I have not seen him/that film** onu/o filmi görmedim *[onoo/o feelmee gurrmedeem]*; *see page 117*
note (*bank note*) banknot; (*written message etc*) not
notebook not defteri *[defteree]*
nothing hiç bir şey *[heech beer shay]*
November Kasım *[kassuhm]*
now şimdi *[sheemdee]*; **not now** şimdi değil *[deh-eel]*
nowhere hiç bir yerde *[heech beer yerdeh]*
nudist nüdist *[newdeest]*
nudist beach nüdistlere mahsus plaj *[newdeestlereh mahsoos plaJ]*
nuisance: he's being a nuisance bela oluyor *[bela oloo-yor]*
numb (*limb etc*) uyuşuk *[oo-yooshook]*
number (*figure*) sayı *[s-'eye'-yuh]*; **what number?** kaç numara? *[kach noomara]*
number plates plakalar
nurse hasta bakıcı *[hasta bakuhjuh]*
nursery (*at airport etc, for children*) çocuk odası *[chojook odassuh]*
nut fıstık *[fuhstuhk]*; (*for bolt*) somun *[somoon]*
nutter: he's a nutter kaçık *[kachuhk]*

O

oar kürek *[kewrek]*
obligatory mecburi *[mejbooree]*
oblige: much obliged (*thank you*) teşekkür ederim *[teshek-kewr edereem]*
obnoxious (*person*) tiksindirici *[teekseen-deereejee]*
obvious: that's obvious açıkça görülüyor *[achuhkcha ghewrewlew-yor]*
occasionally bazen
o'clock *see page 119*
October Ekim *[ekeem]*
octopus ahtapot
odd (*strange*) acayip *[aj-'eye'-yeep]*; (*number*) tek
odometer kilometre saati *[keelometreh sa-atee]*
of -in *[-een]*; **the name of the hotel** otelin adı *[oteleen aduh]*; **have one of mine** benimkilerden birini alın *[beneemkeelerden beereenee aluhn]*; *see page 106*
off: 20% off %20 indirim *[yewzdeh yeermee eendeereem]*; **the lights were off** ışıklar sönüktü *[uhshuhklar surnewktew]*; **just off the main road** ana yolun hemen yakınında *[ana yoloon hemen yakuhnuhnda]*
offend: don't be offended gü-

cenmeyin *[ghewjen-mayeen]*
office (*place of work*) büro *[bewro]*
officer (*said to policeman*) memur bey *[memoor bay]*
official (*noun*) görevli *[gurrevlee]*; **is that official?** bu resmi mi? *[boo resmee mee]*
off-season sezon dışı *[sezon duhshuh]*
off-side wheel sol tekerlek
often sık sık *[suhk suhk]*; **not often** nadiren *[nadeeren]*
oil (*for car, for salad*) yağ *[ya]*; **it's losing oil** yağ kaçırıyor *[kachuhruh-yor]*; **will you change the oil?** yağı değiştirir misiniz? *[ya-uh de-eeshteereer mee-seeneez]*; **the oil light's flashing** yağ göstergesi yanıp sönüyor *[gursterghessee yanuhp surnew-yor]*
oil painting yağlıboya resim *[ya-luhboya resseem]*
oil pressure yağ basıncı *[ya bassuhnjuh]*
ointment merhem
OK tamam; **are you OK?** iyi misin? *[eeyee meesseen]*; **that's OK thanks** tamam, teşekkür ederim *[teshek-kewr edereem]*; **that's OK by me** bana göre hava hoş *[bana gurreh hava hosh]*
old (*person*) yaşlı *[yashluh]*; (*thing*) eski *[eskee]*; **how old are you?** kaç yaşındasınız? *[kach yashuhnda-suhnuhz]*
old-age pensioner yaşlı emekli *[yashluh emeklee]*
old-fashioned eski moda *[eskee]*
old town (*old part of town*) eski şehir *[eskee sheheer]*
olive zeytin *[zayteen]*
olive oil zeytinyağı *[zayteenya-uh]*
omelet(te) omlet
on -de *[-deh]*; (*on top of*) üzerinde *[ewzereendeh]*; **on the roof** damın üzerinde *[damuhn]*; **on the beach** plajda *[plaJda]*; **on Friday** Cuma günü *[jooma ghewnew]*; **on television** televizyonda *[televeezyonda]*; **I don't have it on me** yanımda değil *[yanuhmda deh-eel]*; **this drink's on me** bu içki benden *[boo eechkee benden]*; **a book on Ankara** Ankara hakkında bir kitap *[ankara hak-kuhnda beer keetap]*; **the warning light comes on** uyarı lambası yandı *[oo-yaruh lambassuh yanduh]*; **the light was on** ışık yanıyordu *[uhshuhk yanuh-yordoo]*; **what's on in town?** şehirde eğlence olarak ne var *[sheheerdeh aylenjeh olarak neh var]*; **it's just not on!** (*not acceptable*) bu hiç olmaz! *[boo heech olmaz]*
once (*one time*) bir kere *[beer kereh]*; (*formerly*) bir keresinde *[keress-eendeh]*; **at once** (*immediately*) derhal
one bir *[beer]*; **that one** şu *[shoo]*; **only one** yalnız bir tane *[beer taneh]*; **the green one** yeşil olanı *[yesheel olanuh]*; **the one with the black skirt on** siyah eteklik giyeni *[seeyah etekleek gheeyenee]*; **the one in the blue shirt** mavi gömleklisi *[mavee gurmlekleessee]*
onion soğan *[so-an]*
only yalnız *[yalnuhz]*; **only one** yalnız bir tane *[beer taneh]*; **only once** yalnız bir kere *[kereh]*; **it's only 9 o'clock** saat daha dokuz *[sa-at daha dokooz]*; **I've only just arrived** ancak şimdi geldim *[anjak sheemdee gheldeem]*
open (*adjective*) açık *[achuhk]*; **when do you open?** saat kaçta açıyorsunuz? *[sa-at kachta achuh-yorsoonooz]*; **in the open** (*in open air*) açık havada; **it won't open** açılmıyor *[achuhlmuh-yor]*
opening times açılış ve kapanış saatleri *[achuhluhsh veh kapanuhsh sa-atleree]*
open top (*car*) üstü açılabilen spor araba *[ewstew achuhlabeelen]*
opera opera
operation (*medical*) ameliyat *[ameleeyat]*
operator (*telephone*) santral memuru *[santral memooroo]*
opportunity fırsat *[fuhrsat]*
opposite: opposite the mosque caminin karşısında *[jameeneen karshuhsuhnda]*; **it's directly opposite** tam karşıda *[karshuhda]*
oppressive (*heat*) boğucu *[bo-oojoo]*
optician gözlükçü *[gurzlewkchew]*
optimistic iyimser *[eeyeemser]*
optional isteğe göre *[eesteh-eh gurreh]*
or veya *[vaya]*
orange (*fruit*) portakal; (*colour*) turuncu *[tooroonjoo]*
orange juice (*fresh, fizzy, diluted*)

portakal suyu *[portakal sooyoo]*
orchestra orkestra
order: could we order now? (*in restaurant*) yemekleri şimdi ısmarlayabilir miyiz? *[yemekleree sheemdee uhsmarl-'eye'- yabeeleer meeyeez]*; **I've already ordered** ben ısmarladım *[uhsmarladuhm]*; **I didn't order that** ben bunu ısmarlamadım *[boonoo uhsmarlamaduhm]*; **it's out of order** (*lift etc*) arızalı *[aruhzaluh]*
ordinary olağan *[ola-an]*
organization (*company*) kuruluş *[koorooloosh]*
organize örgütlemek *[urrghewtlemek]*; **could you organize it?** bunu siz örgütleyebilir misiniz? *[boonoo seez urrghewtlayeh-beeleer mee-seeneez]*
original orijinal *[oreeJeenal]*; **is it an original?** bu orijinal midir? *[boo ... meedeer]*
ornament süsleme *[sewslemeh]*
ostentatious göz alıcı *[gurz aluhjuh]*
other diğer *[dee-er]*; **the other waiter** diğer garson; **the other one** öbürü *[urbewrew]*; **do you have any others?** başka var mı? *[bashka ... muh]*; **some other time, thanks** teşekkür ederim, başka bir zaman *[teshek-kewr edereem ... beer zaman]*
otherwise yoksa
ouch! of!
ought: he ought to be here soon biraz sonra gelmesi gerekir *[beeraz sonra ghelmessee gherekeer]*
ounce *see page 121*
our: our hotel bizim otel *[beezeem]*; **our suitcases** bizim bavullarımız *[bavool-laruhmuhz]*; *see page 108*
ours bizim *[beezeem]*; **that's ours** bunlar bizim *[boonlar]*; *see page 110*
out: he's out dışarı çıktı *[duhsharuh chuhktuh]*; **get out!** defol!; **I'm out of money** param kalmadı *[kalmaduh]*; **a few kilometres out of town** şehrin birkaç kilometre dışında *[shehreen beerkach keelometreh duhshuhnda]*; *see page 106*
outboard (*motor*) dıştan takma *[duhshtan takma]*
outdoors açık havada *[achuhk havada]*
outlet (*electric*) priz *[preez]*
outside dışarda *[duhsharda]*; **can we sit outside?** dışarda oturabilir miyiz? *[otoorabeeleer meeyeez]*
outskirts: on the outskirts of ... ...-in dış mahallelerinde *[...-een duhsh mahal-lelereendeh]*
oven fırın *[fuhruhn]*
over: over here burada *[boorada]*; **over there** orada; **over 100** 100-den fazla *[yewzden fazla]*; **I'm burnt all over** tüm vücudum yandı *[tewm vew-joodoom yanduh]*; **the holiday's over** tatil bitti *[tateel beet-tee]*
overcharge: you've overcharged me benden fazla para aldınız *[alduhnuhz]*
overcoat palto
overcooked fazla pişmiş *[peeshmeesh]*
overexposed (*photograph*) fazla ışık verilmiş *[fazla uhshuhk vereelmeesh]*
overheat: it's overheating (*car*) motor fazla ısınıyor *[uhsuhnuh-yor]*
overland kara yoluyla *[yolooy-la]*
overlook: overlooking the sea denize nazır *[deneezeh nazuhr]*
overnight (*travel*) geceleyin *[ghejelayeen]*
oversleep: I overslept fazla uyudum *[fazla ooyoodoom]*
overtake geçmek *[ghechmek]*
overweight (*person*) şişman *[sheeshman]*
owe: how much do I owe you? size borcum ne kadar? *[seezeh borjoom neh kadar]*
own: my own ... benim kendi ...-m *[beneem kendee]*; **are you on your own?** yalnız mısınız? *[yalnuhz muhsuhnuhz]*; **I'm on my own** yalnızım *[yalnuhzuhm]*
owner mal sahibi *[saheebee]*
oyster istiridye *[eesteereed-yeh]*

P

pack: a pack of cigarettes bir paket sigara *[paket seegara]*; **I'll go and pack** gidip eşyalarımı toplayacağım *[gheedeep eshyalaruhmuh topl-'eye'-yaja-uhm]*
package (*at post office*) koli *[kolee]*
package holiday paket tatil *[tateel]*
package tour paket tur *[toor]*
packed lunch kumanya *[koomanya]*
packed out: the place was packed out tıklım tıklım doluydu *[tuhkluhm ... dolooy-doo]*
packet paket; **a packet of cigarettes** bir paket sigara *[beer ... seegara]*
paddle (*noun*) padıl *[paduhl]*
padlock asma kilit *[assma keeleet]*
page (*of book*) sayfa *[s-'eye'-fa]*; **could you page Mr ...?** Bay ...-i çağırtır mısınız? *[b-'eye' ...-ee cha-uhrtuhr muhsuhnuhz]*
pain ağrı *[a-ruh]*; **I have a pain here** buram ağrıyor *[booram a-ruh-yor]*
painful can yakıcı *[jan yakuhjuh]*
painkillers ağrı giderici ilaçlar *[a-ruh gheedereejee eelachlar]*
paint (*noun*) boya; **I'm going to do some painting** (*artist*) biraz resim yapacağım *[beeraz resseem yapaja-uhm]*
paintbrush (*artist's*) fırça *[fuhrcha]*
painting resim *[resseem]*
pair: a pair of ... bir çift ... *[beer cheeft]*
pajamas pijama *[peejama]*
Pakistan Pakistan *[pakeestan]*
Pakistani Pakistanlı *[pakeestanluh]*
pal arkadaş *[arkadash]*
palace saray *[sar-'eye']*
pale solgun *[solgoon]*; **pale blue** açık mavi *[achuhk mavee]*
palm tree palmiye *[palmeeyeh]*
palpitations çarpıntı *[charpuntuh]*
pancake gözleme *[gurzlemeh]*
panic: don't panic telaşlanma *[telashlanma]*
panties külot *[kewlot]*
pants (*trousers*) pantalon; (*underpants*) don
panty girdle külotlu korse *[kewlotloo korseh]*
pantyhose külotlu çorap *[kewlotloo chorap]*
paper kâğıt *[ka-uht]*; (*newspaper*) gazete *[gazeteh]*; **a piece of paper** bir parça kâğıt *[beer parcha]*
paper handkerchiefs kâğıt mendil *[ka-uht mendeel]*
paraffin gazyağı *[gazya-uh]*
parallel: parallel to ... ...-e paralel *[...-eh paralel]*
parasol güneş şemsiyesi *[ghewnesh shemseeyessee]*
parcel paket
pardon (me)? (*didn't understand*) efendim? *[efendeem]*
parents anne ve baba *[anneh veh baba]*; **my parents** annem ve babam *[annem veh babam]*
parents-in-law kayınlarım *[k-'eye'-yuhnlaruhm]*
park (*noun*) park; **where can I park?** nerede park edebilirim? *[neredeh ... edebeeleereem]*; **there's nowhere to park** hiç park edecek yer yok *[heech ... edejek]*
parking lights park lambaları *[lambalaruh]*
parking lot otopark
parking place: there's a parking place! işte park edecek bir yer! *[eeshteh ... edejek beer]*
part (*noun*) parça *[parcha]*
partner (*boyfriend, girlfriend etc*) arkadaş *[arkadash]*; (*in business*) ortak
party (*group*) grup *[groop]*; (*celebration*) parti *[partee]*; **let's have a party** hadi kutlayalım *[hadee koot-l-'eye'-yaluhm]*
pass (*in mountains*) geçit *[ghecheet]*; (*verb: overtake*) geçmek *[ghechmek]*; **he passed out** kendinden geçti *[kendeenden ghechtee]*; **he made a pass at me** bana askıntı oldu *[bana askuhntuh oldoo]*
passable (*road*) geçilebilir *[ghecheeleh-beeleer]*
passenger yolcu *[yoljoo]*

passport pasaport *[passaport]*
past: in the past geçmişte *[ghechmeeshteh]*; **just past the bank** hemen bankayı geçince *[hemen bank-'eye'-yuh ghecheenjeh]*; *see page 119*
pastry (*dough*) hamur *[hamoor]*; (*small cake*) çörek *[churrek]*
patch: could you put a patch on this? bunu yamayabilir misiniz? *[boonoo yam-'eye'-yabeeleer meeseeneez]*
pâté pate *[pateh]*
path yol
patient: be patient sabırlı olun *[sabuhrluh oloon]*
patio teras *[terass]*
pattern örnek *[urnek]*; **a dress pattern** patron
paunch göbek *[gurbek]*
pavement (*sidewalk*) kaldırım *[kalduhruhm]*
pay (*verb*) ödemek *[urdemek]*; **can I pay, please?** lütfen, ben ödeyebilir miyim? *[lewtfen ben urdayeh-beeleer meeyeem]*; **it's already paid for** bunun bedeli ödendi *[boonoon bedelee urdendee]*; **I'll pay for this** bunun bedelini ben ödeyeceğim *[bedeleenee ben urdayejeh-eem]*
pay phone kumbaralı telefon *[koombaraluh telefon]*
peace and quiet sükunet *[sewkoonet]*
peach şeftali *[sheftalee]*
peanuts yerfıstığı *[yerfuhstuh-uh]*
pear armut *[armoot]*
pearl inci *[eenjee]*
peas bezelye *[bezelyeh]*
peculiar (*taste, custom*) garip *[gareep]*
pedal (*noun*) pedal
pedalo padılbot *[paduhlbot]*
pedestrian yaya *[y-'eye'-ya]*
pedestrian crossing yaya geçidi *[y-'eye'-ya ghecheedee]*
pedestrian precinct yayalara mahsus bölge *[y-'eye'-yalara mahsooss burlgheh]*
pee: I need to go for a pee çişim geldi *[cheesheem gheldee]*
peeping Tom röntgenci *[rurntghenjee]*
peg (*for washing*) mandal; (*for tent*) kazık *[kazuhk]*
pen mürekkepli kalem *[mewrekkeplee]*; **do you have a pen?** bir kaleminiz var mı? *[beer kalemeeneez var muh]*
pencil kurşun kalem *[koorshoon]*
penfriend mektup arkadaşı *[mektoop arkadashuh]*; **shall we be penfriends?** mektup arkadaşı olalım mı? *[olaluhm muh]*
penicillin penisilin *[peneesseeleen]*
penis penis *[pehneess]*
penknife çakı *[chakuh]*
pen pal mektup arkadaşı *[mektoop arkadashuh]*
pensioner emekli *[emeklee]*
people insanlar *[eensanlar]*; **a lot of people** bir sürü insan *[beer sewrew eensan]*; **the Turkish people** Türk halkı *[tewrk halkuh]*
pepper (*spice*) biber *[beeber]*; **green pepper** yeşil biber *[yesheel]*; **red pepper** kırmızı biber *[kuhrmuhzuh]*
peppermint (*sweet*) nane şekeri *[naneh shekeree]*
per: per night bir geceliği *[beer ghejelee-ee]*; **how much per hour?** saatte ne kadar? *[sa-at-teh neh kadar]*
per cent yüzde *[yewzdeh]*
perfect mükemmel *[mewkem-mel]*
perfume parfüm *[parfewm]*
perhaps belki *[belkee]*
period (*of time*) süre *[sewreh]*; (*menstruation*) aybaşı *['eye'-bashuh]*
perm perma
permit (*noun*) izin *[eezeen]*
person kişi *[keeshee]*
pessimistic karamsar
petrol benzin *[benzeen]*
petrol can benzin bidonu *[benzeen beedonoo]*
petrol station benzin istasyonu *[benzeen eestassyonoo]*
petrol tank (*in car*) yakıt deposu *[yakuht depossoo]*
pharmacy eczane *[ejzaneh]*
phone *see* **telephone**
photogenic fotojenik *[fotojeneek]*
photograph (*noun*) fotoğraf *[foto-raf]*; **would you take a photograph of us?** bir resmimizi çeker misiniz? *[beer ressmeemeezee cheker mee-seeneez]*
photographer fotoğrafçı *[fotorafchuh]*
phrase: a useful phrase yararlı bir deyim *[yararluh beer dayeem]*
phrasebook yabancı dil klavuzu *[yabanjuh deel klavoozoo]*

pianist piyanist *[peeyaneest]*
piano piyano *[peeyano]*
pickpocket yankeseci *[yankessejee]*
pick up: when can I pick them up? (*clothes from laundry etc*) ne zaman alabilirim? *[neh zaman alabeel-eereem]*; **will you come and pick me up?** lütfen gelip beni alır mısınız? *[lewtfen gheleep benee aluhr muhsuhnuhz]*
picnic (*noun*) piknik *[peekneek]*
picture resim *[resseem]*
pie (*meat*) etli börek *[etlee burrek]*; (*fruit*) meyvalı pay *[mayvaluh p-'eye']*
piece parça *[parcha]*; **a piece of ...** bir parça ... *[beer]*
pig domuz *[domooz]*
pigeon güvercin *[ghewverjeen]*
piles (*medical*) basur *[basoor]*
pile-up otomobil kazası *[otomobeel kazassuh]*
pill hap; **I'm on the pill** doğum kontrol hapı kullanıyorum *[do-oom kontrol hapuh koolanuh-yoroom]*
pillarbox mektup kutusu *[mektoop kootoossoo]*
pillow yastık *[yastuhk]*
pillow case yastık kılıfı *[yastuhk kuhluhfuh]*
pin (*noun*) toplu iğne *[toploo ee-neh]*
pineapple ananas *[ananass]*
pineapple juice ananas suyu *[ananass sooyoo]*
pink pembe *[pembeh]*
pint *see page 121*
pipe (*for smoking*) pipo *[peepo]*; (*for water*) boru *[boroo]*
pipe cleaner pipo temizleyici *[peepo temeezlayeejee]*
pipe tobacco pipo tütünü *[peepo tewtewnew]*
pistachio antep fıstığı *[fuhstuh-uh]*
pity: it's a pity yazık *[yazuhk]*
pizza pizza
place (*noun*) yer; **is this place taken?** bu yerin sahibi var mı? *[boo yereen saheebee ... muh]*; **would you keep my place for me?** lütfen yerimi tutar mısınız? *[lewtfen yereemee tootar muhsuhnuhz]*; **at my place** benim evde *[beneem evdeh]*
place mat şilte *[sheelteh]*
plain (*food*) sade *[sadeh]*; (*not patterned*) düz *[dewz]*
plane uçak *[oochak]*
plant bitki *[beetkee]*
plaster cast alçı *[alchuh]*
plastic plastik *[plasteek]*
plastic bag plastik çanta *[plasteek chanta]*
plate tabak
platform platform; **which platform, please?** kaçıncı platform? *[kachuhnjuh]*
play (*verb*) oynamak; (*noun: in theatre*) oyun *[oyoon]*
playboy hovarda
playground çocuk bahçesi *[chojook bahchessee]*
pleasant hoş *[hosh]*
please lütfen *[lewtfen]*; **yes please** evet, lütfen *[evet]*; **could you please ...?** lütfen ...-misiniz? *[...-meesseeneez]*
pleasure: with pleasure memnuniyetle *[memnooneeyetleh]*
plenty: plenty of ... bol bol ...; **that's plenty, thanks** teşekkür ederim, yeter *[teshek-kewr edereem, yeter]*
pleurisy zatülcenp *[zatewljenp]*
pliers kerpeten
plonk (*wine*) şarap *[sharap]*; (*cheap wine*) ucuz şarap *[oojooz]*
plug (*elec*) fiş *[feesh]*; (*for car*) buji *[boojee]*; (*in sink*) tıkaç *[tuhkach]*
plughole çıkış deliği *[chuhkuhsh delee-ee]*
plum erik *[ereek]*
plumber tesisatçı *[tessee-satchuh]*
plus artı *[artuh]*
pneumonia zatürree *[zatewr-reh-eh]*
poached egg suda yumurta *[sooda yoomoorta]*
pocket cep *[jep]*; **in my pocket** cebimde *[jebeemdeh]*
pocketbook (*woman's handbag*) el çantası *[chantassuh]*
pocketknife çakı *[chakuh]*
podiatrist ayak bakım uzmanı *['eye'-yak bakuhm oozmanuh]*
point: could you point to it? parmağınızla gösterebilir misiniz? *[parma-uhnuhzla gursterebeeleer mee-seeneez]*; **four point six** -dört virgül altı *[veerghewl]*; **there's no point** hiç anlamı yok *[heech anlamuh]*
points (*in car*) kesici platinler

[kesseejee plateenler]
poisonous zehirli *[zeheerlee]*
police polis *[poleess]*; **call the police!** polis çağırın! *[cha-uhruhn]*
policeman polis memuru *[poleess memooroo]*
police station polis karakolu *[poleess karakoloo]*
polish (*noun*) cila *[jeela]*; **will you polish my shoes?** ayakkaplarımı boyar mısınız? *['eye'-yak-kaplaruhmuh boyar muhsuhnuhz]*
polite nazik *[nazeek]*
politician politikacı *[poleeteekajuh]*
politics politika *[poleeteeka]*
polluted kirli *[keerlee]*
pond havuz *[havooz]*
pony midilli *[meedeel-lee]*
pool (*swimming*) havuz *[havooz]*; (*game*) delikli bilardo *[deleeklee beelardo]*
poor (*not rich*) fakir *[fakeer]*; (*quality*) kötü *[kurtew]*; **poor old Hasan!** zavallı Hasan! *[zaval-luh hassan]*
Pope Papa
pop music pop müziği *[mewzee-ee]*
popsicle eskimo *[eskeemo]*
pop singer pop şarkıcısı *[sharkuh-juhssuh]*
popular popüler *[popewler]*
population nüfus *[newfooss]*
pork domuz eti *[domooz etee]*
port (*for boats*) liman *[leeman]*; (*drink*) porto şarabı *[porto sharabuh]*
porter (*in hotel*) kapıcı *[kapuhjuh]*; (*at station etc*) hamal
portrait portre *[portreh]*
Portugal Portekiz *[portekeez]*
poser (*phoney person*) züppe *[zewp-peh]*
posh (*restaurant, people*) şık *[shuhk]*
possibility imkân *[eemkan]*
possible mümkün *[mewmkewn]*; **is it possible to ...?** ...-mek mümkün mü? *[-mek ... mew]*; **as ... as possible** mümkün olduğu kadar ... *[oldoo-oo]*
post (*noun: mail*) posta *[posta]*; **could you post this for me?** bunu benim için postalayabilir misiniz? *[boonoo beneem eecheen postal-'eye'-yabeeleer mee-seeneez]*
postbox posta kutusu *[posta kootoossoo]*
postcard kartpostal
poster afiş *[afeesh]*
poste restante postrestant
post office postane *[postaneh]*
pot kap; **a pot of tea for two** iki kişi için bir demlik çay *[eekee keeshee eecheen beer demleek ch-'eye']*; **pots and pans** kap kaçak *[kachak]*
potato patates *[patatess]*; **potato chips** patates kızartması *[patatess kuhzartmassuh]*; **potato salad** patates salatası *[patatess salatassuh]*
pottery (*objects*) çanak çömlek *[chanak churmlek]*; (*workshop*) çömlek imalathanesi *[imalat-hanessee]*
pound (*money*) sterlin *[sterleen]*; (*weight*) libre *[leebreh]*; *see page 121*
pour: it's pouring down bardaktan boşanırcasına yağıyor *[bardaktan boshanuhr-jassuhna ya-uh-yor]*
powder (*for face*) pudra *[poodra]*
powdered milk süt tozu *[sewt tozoo]*
power cut elektrik kesilmesi *[elektreek kesseelmessee]*
power point priz *[preez]*
power station elektrik santrali *[elektreek santralee]*
practise, practice: I need to practise egzersiz yapmam lazım *[egzerseez yapmam lazuhm]*
pram çocuk arabası *[chojook arabassuh]*
prawn cocktail karides kokteyli *[kareedess koktaylee]*
prawns karides *[kareedees]*
prefer: I prefer white wine beyaz şarabı tercih ederim *[bayaz sharabuh terjeeh edereem]*
preferably: preferably not tomorrow yarın olmamasını tercih ederim *[yaruhn olmamassuhnuh terjeeh edereem]*
pregnant gebe *[ghebeh]*
prescription (*for chemist*) reçete *[recheteh]*
present (*gift*) hediye *[hedeeyeh]*; **here's a present for you** size bir hediye *[seezeh beer]*; **at present** şu anda *[shoo anda]*
president (*of company*) başkan *[bashkan]*; (*of country*) cumhurbaşkanı *[joomhoor-bashkanuh]*
press: could you press these? bunları ütüler misiniz? *[boonlaruh ewtewler mee-seeneez]*
pretty güzel *[ghewzel]*; **it's pretty**

expensive oldukça pahalı *[oldookcha pahaluh]*
price fiyat *[feeyat]*
prickly heat isilik *[eesseeleek]*
priest rahip *[raheep]*
prime minister başbakan *[bashbakan]*
print (*noun: picture*) baskı *[basskuh]*
printed matter matbua *[matboo-a]*
priority (*in driving*) öncelik *[urnjeleek]*
prison hapishane *[hapeess-haneh]*
private özel *[urzel]*; **private bath** özel banyo
prize ödül *[urdewl]*
probably muhtemelen *[moohtemelen]*
problem sorun *[soroon]*; **I have a problem** bir sorunum var *[beer soroonoom]*; **no problem!** sorun değil! *[deh-eel]*
program(me) (*noun*) program
promise: I promise söz veriyorum *[surz vereeyoroom]*; **is that a promise?** söz mü? *[mew]*
pronounce: how do you pronounce this? bu nasıl telaffuz edilir? *[boo nassuhl telaffooz edeeleer]*; **I can't pronounce it** bu kelimeyi söyleyemiyorum *[boo keleemayee surlayemeeyoroom]*
properly doğru olarak *[do-roo olarak]*; **it's not repaired properly** doğru dürüst tamir edilmemiş *[do-roo dewrewst tameer edeelmemeesh]*
prostitute genel kadın *[ghenel kaduhn]*
protect korumak *[koroomak]*
protection factor koruma faktörü *[korooma fakturrew]*
protein remover (*for contact lenses*) protein giderici *[gheedereejee]*
Protestant Protestan
proud gururlu *[gooroorloo]*
prunes kuru erik *[kooroo ereek]*
public (*adjective*) halka açık *[achuhk]*
public convenience umumi helâ *[oomoomee hela]*
public holiday resmi tatil *[ressmee tateel]*
pudding puding
pull çekmek *[chekmek]*; **he pulled out without indicating** sinyal vermeden solladı *[seenyal vermeden sol-laduh]*
pullover kazak
pump (*noun*) pompa
punctual dakik *[dakeek]*
puncture (*noun*) patlak lastik *[lasteek]*
pure (*silk etc*) saf
purple mor
purse (*for money*) para çantası *[para chantassuh]*; (*handbag*) el çantası
push itmek *[eetmek]*; **don't push in!** itmeyin! *[eetmayeen]*
push-chair puset *[pooset]*
put koymak; **where did you put ...?** ...-i nereye koydunuz? *[...-ee nerayeh koydoonooz]*; **where can I put ...?** ...-i nereye koyabilirim? *[koyabeelee-reem]*; **could you put the lights on?** ışıkları yakar mısınız? *[uhshuhklar muhsuhnuhz]*; **will you put the light out?** ışığı söndürür müsünüz? *[uhshuh-uh surndewrewr mewssewnewz]*; **you've put the price up** fiyatı yükselttiniz *[feeyatuh yewkselt-teeneez]*; **could you put us up for the night?** bu gece burada konaklayabilir miyiz? *[boo ghejeh boorada konakl-'eye'-yabeeleer meeyeez]*
pyjamas pijama *[peejama]*

Q

quality kalite *[kaleeteh]*; **poor quality** kötü kalite *[kurtew]*; **good quality** iyi kalite *[eeyee]*
quarantine karantina *[karanteena]*
quart *see page 121*
quarter çeyrek *[chayrek]*; **quarter of an hour** çeyrek saat *[sa-at]*; *see page 119*
quay rıhtım *[ruhhtuhm]*
quayside: on the quayside rıhtımda *[ruhtuhmda]*
question soru *[soroo]*; **that's out of the question** söz konusu olamaz *[surz konoossoo olamaz]*
queue (*noun*) kuyruk *[kooy-rook]*; **there was a big queue** uzun bir

kuyruk vardı *[oozoon beer ... varduh]*
quick çabuk *[chabook]*; **that was quick** ne kadar çabuk *[neh kadar]*; **which is the quickest way?** en çabuk nasıl gidilir? *[nasuhl gheedeeleer]*
quickly hızla *[huhzla]*
quiet (*place, hotel*) sakin *[sakeen]*; **be quiet!** gürültü yapmayın! *[ghewrewltew yapm-'eye'-yuhn]*
quinine kinin *[keeneen]*
quite: quite a lot oldukça çok *[oldookcha chok]*; **it's quite different** oldukça farklı *[farkluh]*; **I'm not quite sure** pek emin değilim *[emeen deh-eeleem]*

R

rabbit tavşan *[tavshan]*
rabies kuduz *[koodooz]*
race (*for horses, cars*) yarış *[yaruhsh]*; **I'll race you there** seninle oraya kadar yarışırım *[seneenleh or-'eye'-ya kadar yaruhshuhruhm]*
racket (*sport*) raket
radiator radyatör *[radyaturr]*
radio radyo; **on the radio** radyoda
rag (*for cleaning*) bez
rail: by rail trenle *[trenleh]*
railroad, railway demiryolu *[demeer-yoloo]*
railroad crossing hemzemin geçit *[hemzemeen ghecheet]*
rain (*noun*) yağmur *[ya-moor]*; **in the rain** yağmurda *[ya-moorda]*; **it's raining** yağmur yağıyor *[ya-uh-yor]*
rain boots lastik çizme *[lasteek cheezmeh]*
raincoat yağmurluk *[ya-moorlook]*
rape (*noun*) ırza geçme *[uhrza ghechmeh]*
rare (*object etc*) nadide *[na-deedeh]*; (*steak*) az pişmiş *[peeshmeesh]*
rash (*on skin*) isilik *[eesseeleek]*
raspberry ahududu *[ahoo-doodoo]*
rat sıçan *[suhchan]*
rate (*for changing money*) kur *[koor]*; **what's the rate for the pound?** sterlinin kuru ne kadar? *[sterleeneen kooroo neh kadar]*; **what are your rates?** ne fiyat alıyorsunuz? *[feeyat aluh-yorsoonooz]*
rather: it's rather late/expensive oldukça geç/pahalı *[oldookcha ghech/pahaluh]*; **I'd rather ...** ...-i tercih ederim *[...-ee terjeeh edereem]*; **I'd rather have beer** ben bira tercih ederim *[beera]*
raw (*meat*) çiğ *[chee]*
razor (*dry*) ustura *[oostoora]*; (*electric*) elektrikli tıraş makinesi *[elektreeklee tuhrash makeenessee]*
razor blades jilet *[jeelet]*
reach: within easy reach yakında *[yakuhnda]*
read okumak *[okoomak]*; **I can't read it** okuyamıyorum *[okoo-yamuh-yoroom]*; **could you read it out?** yüksek sesle okur musunuz? *[yewksek sessleh okoor moossoonooz]*
ready hazır *[hazuhr]*; **when will it be ready?** ne zaman hazır olur? *[neh zaman ... oloor]*; **I'll go and get ready** gidip hazırlanayım *[gheedeep hazuhrlan-'eye'-yuhm]*; **I'm not ready yet** henüz hazır değilim *[henewz ... deh-eeleem]*
real gerçek *[gherchek]*
really gerçekten *[gherchekten]*; **I really must go** gerçekten gitmem gerekiyor *[gheetmem gherekeeyor]*; **is it really necessary?** gerçekten gerekli mi? *[ghereklee mee]*
realtor emlakçı *[emlakchuh]*
rear: at the rear arkada; **rear wheels** arka tekerlekler
rearview mirror dikiz aynası *[deekeez 'eye'-nassuh]*
reasonable (*prices etc*) makul *[makool]*; **be reasonable** makul olun *[oloon]*
receipt makbuz *[makbooz]*
recently kısa süre önce *[kuhssa sewreh urnjeh]*
reception resepsiyon *[ressepsseeyon]*; (*for guests*) kabul *[kabool]*
reception desk resepsiyon masası *[ressepsseeyon massassuh]*
receptionist resepsiyoncu

[ressepsseeyonjoo]
recipe yemek tarifi *[yemek tareefee]*; **can you give me the recipe for this?** bunun tarifini bana verir misiniz? *[boonoon tareefeenee bana vereer mee-seeneez]*
recognize tanımak *[tanuhmak]*; **I didn't recognize it** tanıyamadım *[tanuh-yamaduhm]*
recommend: could you recommend ...? ... tavsiye eder misiniz? *[tavseeyeh eder mee-seeneez]*
record (*music*) plak
record player pikap *[peekap]*
red kırmızı *[kuhrmuhzuh]*
reduction (*in price*) indirim *[eendeereem]*
red wine kırmızı şarap *[kuhrmuhzuh sharap]*
refreshing serinletici *[sereenleteejee]*
refrigerator buzdolabı *[booz-dolabuh]*
refund iade *[ee-adeh]*; **do I get a refund?** paramı geri alabilir miyim? *[paramuh gheree alabeeleer meeyeem]*
region bölge *[burlgheh]*
registered: by registered mail taahhütlü *[ta-ah-hewtlew]*
registration number kayıt numarasi *[k-'eye'-yuht noomarassuh]*
relative akraba; **my relatives** akrabalarım *[akrabalaruhm]*
relaxing: it's very relaxing çok dinlendirici *[chok deenlendeereejee]*
reliable güvenilir *[ghew-veneeleer]*
religion din *[deen]*
remains (*of old city etc*) harabeler
remember: I don't remember hatırlamıyorum *[hatuhrlamuh-yoroom]*; **I remember** hatırlıyorum *[hatuhrluh-yoroom]*; **do you remember?** hatırlıyor musunuz? *[hatuhrluh-yor moossoonooz]*
remote (*village etc*) ücra *[ewjra]*
rent (*noun: for apartment etc*) kira *[keera]*; (*verb: car etc*) kiralamak *[keeralamak]*; **I'd like to rent a bike/car** bir bisiklet/otomobil kiralamak istiyorum *[beer beesseeklet/ otomobeel ... eesteeyoroom]*
rental car kiralık otomobil *[keeraluhk otomobeel]*
repair (*verb*) tamir etmek *[tameer]*; **can you repair it?** tamir edebilir misiniz? *[edebeeleer mee-seeneez]*
repeat tekrarlamak; **could you repeat that?** tekrarlar mısınız? *[muhsuhnuhz]*
representative (*noun: of company*) temsilci *[temseeljee]*
request (*noun*) istek *[eestek]*
rescue (*verb*) kurtarmak *[koortarmak]*
reservation rezervasyon *[rezervassyon]*; **I have a reservation** rezervasyon yaptırdım *[yaptuhrduhm]*
reserve ayırtmak *['eye'-yuhrtmak]*; **I reserved a room in the name of ...** ... adına bir oda ayırttım *[aduhna beer oda 'eye'-yuhrt-tuhm]*; **can I reserve a table for tonight?** bu akşam için bir masa ayırtabilir miyim? *[boo aksham eecheen beer massa 'eye'-yuhrtabeeleer meeyeem]*
rest (*repose*) dinlenme *[deenlenmeh]*; (*remainder*) bakiye *[bakeeyeh]*; **I need a rest** dinlenmeye ihtiyacım var *[deenlenmayeh eehteeyajuhm]*; **the rest of the group** grubun geri kalan kısmı *[grooboon gheree kalan kuhssmuh]*
restaurant restoran
rest room tuvalet *[toovalet]*
retired: I'm retired ben emekliyim *[emekleeyeem]*
return: a return to Bursa Bursa'ya bir gidiş dönüş bileti *[boors-'eye'-ya beer gheedeesh durnewsh beeletee]* **I'll return it tomorrow** yarın geri veririm *[yaruhn gheree vereereem]*
returnable (*deposit*) iadeli *[ee-adelee]*
reverse charge call ihbarlı telefon konuşması *[eehbarluh telefon konooshmassuh]*
reverse gear geri vitesi *[gheree veetessee]*
revolting iğrenç *[ee-rench]*
rheumatism romatizma *[romateezma]*
Rhodes Rodos *[rodoss]*
rib kaburga *[kaboorga]*; **a cracked rib** çatlak kaburga kemiği *[chatlak ... kemee-ee]*
ribbon (*for hair*) şerit *[shereet]*
rice pirinç *[peereench]*; (*cooked*) pilav *[peelav]*
rich (*person*) zengin *[zengheen]*; (*food*) ağır *[a-uhr]*; **it's too rich** fazla ağır
ride: can you give me a ride into town? beni şehre bırakır mısınız? *[benee shehreh buhrakuhr muhsuhnuhz]*; **thanks for the ride**

beni arabanıza aldığınız için teşekkür ederim *[arabanuhza alduh-uhnuhz eecheen teshek-kewr edereem]*
ridiculous: that's ridiculous bu gülünç bir şey *[boo ghewlewnch beer shay]*
right (*correct*) doğru *[do-roo]*; (*not left*) sağ *[sa]*; **you're right** haklısınız *[hakluhsuhnuhz]*; **you were right** haklıymışsınız *[hakluhmuhsh-suhnuhz]*; **that's right** doğru; **that can't be right** bu doğru olamaz *[boo]*; **right!** tamam! **is this the right road for ...?** bu yol ...-e gidiyor mu? *[...-eh gheedeeyor moo]*; **on the right** sağda *[sa-da]*; **turn right** sağa dönün *[sa-a durnewn]*; **not right now** şimdi olmaz *[sheemdee]*
right-hand drive sağdan direksiyonlu *[sa-dan deereksseeyonloo]*
ring (*on finger*) yüzük *[yew-zewk]*; **I'll ring you** ben sizi telefonla ararım *[seezee telefonla araruhm]*
ring road çevre yolu *[chevreh yoloo]*
ripe (*fruit*) olgun *[olgoon]*
rip-off: it's a rip-off tam bir dalavere *[beer dalavereh]*; **rip-off prices** kazık fiyatlar *[kazuhk feeyatlar]*
risky rizikolu *[reezeekoloo]*; **it's too risky** rizikosu fazla *[reezeekossoo]*
river nehir *[neheer]*; **by the river** nehir kıyısında *[kuh-yuhsuhnda]*
road yol; **is this the road to ...?** bu ... yolu mudur? *[boo ... yoloo moodoor]*; **further down the road** yolun ilerisinde *[yoloon eelereesseendeh]*
road accident trafik kazası *[trafeek kazassuh]*
road hog bencil sürücü *[benjeel sewrewjew]*
road map karayolu haritası *[karayoloo hareetassuh]*
roadside: by the roadside yolun kenarında *[yoloon kenaruhnda]*
roadsign yol işareti *[eesharetee]*
roadwork(s) yol inşaatı *[eensha-atuh]*
roast beef rozbif *[rozbeef]*
rob: I've been robbed soyuldum *[soyooldoom]*
robe (*housecoat*) sabahlık *[sabahluhk]*
rock (*stone*) kaya *[k-'eye'-ya]*; **on the rocks** (*with ice*) buzlu *[boozloo]*
rocky (*coast etc*) kayalık *[k-'eye'-yaluhk]*
roll (*bread*) sandviç ekmeği *[sandveech ekme-ee]*
Roman Catholic Katolik *[katoleek]*
romance gönül macerası *[ghurnewl majerassuh]*
Rome: when in Rome ... Roma'da ... *[romada]*
roof dam; **on the roof** damda
roof rack üst bagaj yeri *[ewst bagaj yeree]*
room oda; **do you have a room?** bir odanız var mı? *[beer odanuhz ... muh]*; **a room for two people** iki kişilik bir oda *[eekee keesheeleek]*; **a room for three nights** üç gece için bir oda *[ewch ghejeh eecheen]*; **a room with a bathroom** banyolu bir oda *[banyoloo]*; **in my room** odamda; **there's no room** yer yok
room service oda servisi *[serveessee]*
rope ip *[eep]*
rose gül *[ghewl]*
rosé (*wine*) pembe şarap *[pembeh sharap]*
rotary (*for traffic*) dönel kavşak *[durnel kavshak]*
rough (*sea*) kaba dalgalı *[dalgaluh]*; **the engine sounds a bit rough** motor biraz ses yapıyor *[beeraz sess yapuh-yor]*; **I've been sleeping rough** açıkta yattım *[achuhkta yat-tuhm]*
roughly (*approximately*) kabataslak
roulette rulet *[roolet]*
round (*adjective*) yuvarlak *[yoovarlak]*; **it's my round** sıra bende *[suhra bendeh]*
roundabout (*for traffic*) dönel kavşak *[durnel kavshak]*
round-trip: a round-trip ticket to ... ...-e bir gidiş dönüş bileti *[...-eh beer gheedeesh durnewsh beeletee]*
route güzergah *[ghewzergah]*; **what's the best route?** en iyi hangi yoldan gidilir? *[eeyee hanghee yoldan gheedeeleer]*
rowboat, rowing boat kayık *[k-'eye'-yuhk]*
rubber (*material*) lastik *[lasteek]*; (*eraser*) silgi *[seelghee]*
rubber band lastik bant *[lasteek]*
rubbish (*waste*) çöp *[churp]*; (*poor quality goods*) süprüntü *[sewprewntew]*; **that's rubbish!** (*nonsense*) saçma!

[sachma]
rucksack sırt çantası *[suhrt chantassuh]*
rude terbiyesiz *[terbeeyesseez]*; **he was very rude** çok terbiyesizce davrandı *[chok ...-jeh davranduh]*
rug kilim *[keeleem]*; (*small blanket*) örtü *[urr-tew]*
ruins harabeler
rum rom; **rum and coke** rom ve koka kola *[veh]*
Rumania Romanya
run (*person*) koşmak *[koshmak]*; **I go running every morning** her sabah koşuyorum *[sabah koshoo-yoroom]*; **quick, run!** çabuk, koş! *[chabook, kosh]*; **how often do the buses run?** otobüslerin arası ne kadar? *[otobewsslereen arassuh neh kadar]*; **he's been run over** ezildi *[ezeeldee]*; **I've run out of gas/petrol** benzinim bitti *[benzeeneem beet-tee]*
rupture (*medical*) kırık *[kuhruhk]*
Russia Rusya *[roosya]*
Russian (*person, adjective*) Rus *[rooss]*

S

saccharine sakarin *[sakareen]*
sad üzgün *[ewzghewn]*
saddle (*for bike*) sele *[seleh]*; (*for horse*) eğer *[ay-er]*
safe (*not in danger*) emniyette *[emnee-yet-teh]*; (*not dangerous*) emniyetli *[emnee-yetlee]*; **will it be safe here?** burada emniyette midir? *[boorada ... meedeer]*; **is it safe to drink?** içilebilir mi? *[eecheeleh-beeleer mee]*; **is it a safe beach for swimming?** bu plajda emniyetle yüzülebilir mi? *[boo plajda emnee-yetleh yewzewleh-beeleer mee]*; **could you put this in your safe?** bunu kasanıza koyar mısınız? *[boonoo kassanuhza koyar muhsuhnuhz]*
safety pin çengelli iğne *[chenghel-lee eeneh]*
sail (*noun*) yelken; **can we go sailing?** yelkenliyle gezebilir miyiz? *[yelkenleeleh ghezebeeleer meeyeez]*
sailboard (*noun*) yelkenli sörf *[yelkenlee surrf]*; **I like sailboarding** yelkenli sörf yapmayı seviyorum *[yapm-'eye'-yuh seveeyoroom]*
sailor denizci *[deneez-jee]*
salad salata
salad cream mayonez *[m-'eye'-yonez]*
salad dressing salata sosu *[sossoo]*
sale: is it for sale? bu satılık mı? *[boo satuhluhk muh]*; **it's not for sale** o satılık değil *[deh-eel]*
sales clerk satıcı *[satuhjuh]*
salmon som balığı *[baluh-uh]*
salt tuz *[tooz]*
salty: it's too salty fazla tuzlu *[fazla toozloo]*
same ayni *[eye-nuh]*; **one the same as this** bunun aynısından *[boonoon 'eye'-nuhssuhndan]*; **the same again, please** bir tane daha, lütfen *[beer taneh daha lewtfen]*; **have a good time - same to you** iyi günler - size de *[seezeh deh]*; **it's all the same to me** benim için hepsi bir *[beneem eecheen hepssee beer]*; **thanks all the same** gene de teşekkür ederim *[gheneh deh teshek-kewr edereem]*
samovar semaver
sand kum *[koom]*
sandals sandal; **a pair of sandals** bir çift sandal *[beer cheeft]*
sandwich sandviç *[sandveech]*; **a chicken sandwich** tavuklu sandviç *[tavookloo]*
sandy kumlu *[koomloo]*; **a sandy beach** kumlu plaj *[plaJ]*
sanitary napkin/towel kadın bağı *[kaduhn ba-uh]*
sarcastic iğneleyici *[eenelayeejee]*
sardines sardayle *[sardalyeh]*
satisfactory tatminkâr *[tatmeenkar]*; **this is not satisfactory** bu tatminkâr değil *[boo ... deh-eel]*
Saturday Cumartesi *[joomartessee]*
sauce sos
saucepan tencere *[tenjereh]*
saucer fincan tabağı *[feenjan taba-uh]*
sauna sauna *[sa-oona]*

sausage sosis *[sosseess]*
sauté potatoes sote patates *[soteh patatess]*
save (*life*) kurtarmak *[koortarmak]*
savo(u)ry baharatlı *[baharatluh]*
say: how do you say ... in Turkish? Türkçe ... nasıl denir? *[tewrkcheh ... nassuhl deneer]*; **what did you say?** ne dediniz? *[neh dedeeneez]*; **what did he say?** ne dedi? *[dedee]*; **I said ...** ... dedim *[dedeem]*; **he said ...** ... dedi; **I wouldn't say no** hayır diyemem *[h-'eye'-yuhr deeyemem]*
scald: he's scalded himself kendini haşlamış *[kendeenee hashlamuhsh]*
scarf (*for neck*) atkı *[atkuh]*; (*for head*) eşarp *[esharp]*
scarlet kızıl *[kuhzuhl]*
scenery manzara
scent (*perfume*) parfüm *[parfewm]*
schedule tarife *[tareefeh]*
scheduled flight tarifeli sefer *[tareefelee sefer]*
school okul *[okool]*; (*university*) üniversite *[ewnee-verseeteh]*; **I'm still at school** hâlâ okula devam ediyorum *[hala okoola devam edeeyoroom]*
science bilim *[beeleem]*
scissors: a pair of scissors bir makas *[beer makass]*
scooter (*motor scooter*) küçük motosiklet *[kewchewk motosseeklet]*
scorching: it's really scorching (*weather*) kavurucu sıcak *[kavooroojoo suhjak]*
score: what's the score? kaç kaç? *[kach]*
scotch (*whisky*) İskoç viskisi *[eeskoch veeskeessee]*
Scotch tape (*tm*) seloteyp *[selotayp]*
Scotland İskoçya *[eeskochya]*
Scottish İskoç *[eeskoch]*
scrambled eggs karılmış sahanda yumurta *[karuhlmuhsh sahanda yoomoorta]*
scratch (*noun*) çizik *[cheezeek]*; **it's only a scratch** sadece hafif bir bere *[sadejeh hafeef beer bereh]*
scream (*verb*) çığlık atmak *[chuh-luhk]*
screw (*noun*) vida *[veeda]*
screwdriver tornavida *[tornaveeda]*
scrubbing brush (*for hands*) tırnak fırçası *[tuhrnak fuhrchassuh]*; (*for floors*) yer fırçası
scruffy süfli *[sewflee]*
scuba diving balık adamlık *[baluhk adamluhk]*
sea deniz *[deneez]*; **by the sea** deniz kıyısında *[kuh-yuhssuhnda]*
sea air deniz havası *[deneez havassuh]*
seafood deniz ürünleri *[deneez ewrewnleree]*
seafood restaurant balık lokantası *[baluhk lokantassuh]*
seafront sahil *[saheel]*; **on the seafront** sahilde *[saheeldeh]*
seagull martı *[martuh]*
search (*verb*) aramak; **I searched everywhere** her yeri aradım *[yeree araduhm]*
search party arama ekibi *[ekeebee]*
seashell deniz kabuğu *[deneez kaboo-oo]*
seasick: I feel seasick beni deniz tuttu *[benee deneez toot-too]*; **I get seasick** beni deniz tutar *[tootar]*
seaside: by the seaside plajda *[plaJda]*; **let's go to the seaside** hadi denize gidelim *[hadee deneezeh gheedeleem]*
season mevsim *[mevseem]*; **in the high season** yüksek sezonda *[yewksek sezonda]*; **in the low season** sezon dışında *[duhshuhnda]*
seasoning baharat
seat oturacak yer *[otoorajak]*; **is this anyone's seat?** bu yerin sahibi var mı? *[boo yereen saheebee var muh]*
seat belt emniyet kemeri *[emneeyet kemeree]*; **do you have to wear a seat belt?** emniyet kemeri takmak lazım mı? *[takmak lazuhm muh]*
sea urchin deniz kestanesi *[deneez kestanessee]*
seaweed deniz yosunu *[deneez yossoonoo]*
secluded mahfuz *[mahfooz]*
second (*adjective*) ikinci *[eekeenjee]*; (*of time*) saniye *[saneeyeh]*; **just a second!** bir saniye! *[beer]*; **can I have a second helping?** aynısından bir daha alabilir miyim? *['eye'-nuhssuhndan beer daha alabeeleer meeyeem]*
second class (*travel*) ikinci sınıf *[eekeenjee suhnuhf]*
second-hand elden düşme

[dewshmeh]
secret (*noun*) sır *[suhr]*
security check güvenlik kontrolü *[ghew-venleek kontrolew]*
sedative müsekkin *[mewsek-keen]*
see görmek *[ghurrmek]*; **I didn't see it** onu görmedim *[onoo gurrmedeem]*; **have you seen my husband/wife?** eşimi gördünüz mü? *[esheemee gurrdewnewz mew]*; **I saw him/her this morning** onu bu sabah gördüm *[boo sabah gurrdewm]*; **I would like to see the manager** şefinizle görüşmek istiyorum *[shefeeneezleh gurrewshmek eesteeyoroom]*; **see you tonight!** bu gece görüşmek üzere! *[ghejeh ... ewzereh]*; **can I see?** görebilir miyim? *[gurrebeeleer meeyeem]*; **oh, I see** (*I understand*) ha, anladım *[anladuhm]*; **will you see to it?** (*arrange it*) siz bunu halleder misiniz? *[seez boonoo hal-leder mee-seeneez]*
seldom nadiren *[nadeeren]*
self-service self servis *[serveess]*
sell satmak; **do you sell ...?** ... satıyor musunuz? *[satuh-yor moossoonooz]*; **will you sell it to me?** bunu bana satar mısınız? *[boonoo bana satar muhsuhnuhz]*
sellotape (*tm*) seloteyp *[selotayp]*
send göndermek *[gurndermek]*; **I want to send this to England** bunu İngiltere'ye göndermek istiyorum *[boonoo eegheelteryeh ... eesteeyoroom]*; **I'll have to send this food back** bu yemeği geri göndermem lazım *[boo yemeh-ee gheree gurndermem lazuhm]*
senior citizen yaşlı vatandaş *[yashluh vatandash]*
sensational (*holiday, experience etc*) heyecan verici *[hayejan vereejee]*
sense: I have no sense of direction hiç yön duygum yoktur *[heech yurn dooy-goom yoktoor]*; **it doesn't make sense** bunun anlamı yok *[boonoon anlamuh]*
sensible (*person, idea*) makul *[makool]*
sensitive (*person, skin*) hassas *[hassass]*
sentimental duygusal *[dooy-goossal]*
separate ayrı *['eye'-ruh]*; **can we have separate bills?** bizim hesaplarımızı ayrı hazırlar mısınız? *[beezeem hessaplaruhmuhzuh ... hazuhrlar muhsuhnuhz]*
separated: I'm separated eşimden ayrıldım *[esheemden 'eye'-ruhlduhm]*
separately ayrı ayrı *['eye'-ruh]*
September Eylül *[aylewl]*
septic mikroplu *[meekroploo]*
serious ciddi *[jeed-dee]*; **I'm serious** ciddiyim *[—yeem]*; **you can't be serious!** şaka ediyorsunuz! *[shaka edeeyorsoonooz]*; **is it serious, doctor?** ciddi mi, doktor?
seriously: seriously ill ağır hasta *[a-uhr hasta]*
service: the service was excellent servis mükemmeldi *[serveess mewkem-meldee]*; **could we have some service, please!** lütfen, bakar mısınız? *[lewtfen bakar muhsuhnuhz]*; **church service** kilise ayini *[keeleesseh 'eye'-yeenee]*; **the car needs a service** aracın servise ihtiyacı var *[arajuhn serveesseh eehteeyajuh]*
service charge servis ücreti *[serveess ewjretee]*
service station servis istasyonu *[serveess eestassyonoo]*
serviette peçete *[pecheteh]*
sesame seed roll simit *[seemeet]*
set: it's time we were setting off şimdi yola çıkmamız lazım *[sheemdee yola chuhkmamuhz lazuhm]*
set menu tabldot
settle up: can we settle up now? şimdi hesap görebilir miyiz? *[sheemdee hessap gurrebeeleer meeyeez]*
several birkaç *[beerkach]*
sew dikmek *[deekmek]*; **could you sew this back on?** bunu yerine dikebilir misiniz? *[boonoo yereeneh deekebeeleer mee-seeneez]*
sex (*sexual intercourse*) seks
sexist (*noun*) seksist *[sekseest]*
sexy cazibeli *[jazeebelee]*
shade: in the shade gölgede *[gurlghedeh]*
shadow gölge *[gurlgheh]*
shake: let's shake hands tokalaşalım *[tokalashaluhm]*
shallow (*water*) sığ *[suh]*
shame: what a shame! ne yazık! *[neh yazuhk]*
shampoo (*noun*) şampuan *[shampoo-an]*; **can I have a shampoo and set?**

şampuan ve mizanpli yapar mısınız? *[veh meezanplee yapar muhsuhnuhz]*
shandy, shandy-gaff limonatalı bira *[leemonataluh beera]*
share (*verb: room, table etc*) paylaşmak *[p-'eye'-lashmak]*; **let's share the cost** masrafları bölüşelim *[masraflaruh burlewsheleem]*
shark köpek balığı *[kurpek baluh-uh]*
sharp (*knife, taste*) keskin *[kesskeen]*; (*pain*) şiddetli *[sheed-detlee]*
shattered: I'm shattered (*very tired*) elim ayağım tutmuyor *[eleem 'eye'-ya-uhm tootmoo-yor]*
shave: I need a shave tıraş olman lazım *[tuhrash olmam lazuhm]*; **can you give me a shave?** sakal tıraşı yapar mısınız? *[sakal tuhrashuh yapar muhsuhnuhz]*
shaver tıraş makinesi *[tuhrash makeenessee]*
shaving brush tıraş fırçası *[tuhrash fuhrchassuh]*
shaving foam tıraş köpüğü *[tuhrash kurpew-ew]*
shaving point tıraş makinesi prizi *[tuhrash makeenessee preezee]*
shaving soap tıraş sabunu *[tuhrash saboonoo]*
shawl şal *[shal]*
she o; **is she here?** o burada mı? *[boorada muh]*; **where does she live?** nerede oturuyor? *[neredeh otoorooyor]*; *see page 110*
sheep koyun *[koyoon]*
sheet (*for bed*) çarşaf *[charshaf]*
shelf raf
shell deniz kabuğu *[deneez kaboo-oo]*
shellfish kabuklu deniz ürünleri *[kabookloo deneez ewrewnleree]*
shingles zona
ship gemi *[ghemee]*; **by ship** gemiyle *[—leh]*
shirt gömlek *[gurmlek]*
shit! hay anasını! *[h-'eye' annassuhnuh]*
shock (*surprise*) şok *[shok]*; **I got an electric shock from the ...** ...-den elektrik çarptı *[...-den elektreek charptuh]*
shock-absorber amortisör *[amorteesurr]*
shocking korkunç *[korkoonch]*
shoe ayakkabı *['eye'-yak-kabuh]*; **my shoes** benim ayakkabılarım *[beneem 'eye'-yak-kabuhlaruhm]*; **a pair of shoes** bir çift ayakkabı *[beer cheeft]*
shoelaces ayakkabı bağı *['eye'-yak-kabuh ba-uh]*
shoe polish ayakkabı cilası *['eye'-yak-kabuh jeelassuh]*
shoe repairer kundura tamircisi *[koondoora tameerjeessee]*
shop dükkân *[dewk-kan]*
shopping: I'm going shopping ben çarşıya çıkıyorum *[charshuh-ya chuhkuh-yoroom]*
shop window vitrin *[veetreen]*
shore (*of sea, lake*) sahil *[saheel]*
short kısa *[kuhssa]*; **it's only a short distance** fazla uzak değil *[oozak deh-eel]*
short-change: you've short-changed me üstünü eksik verdiniz *[ewstewnew ekseek verdeeneez]*
short circuit kısa devre *[kuhssa devreh]*
shortcut kestirme *[kessteermeh]*
shorts şort *[short]*; (*underpants*) külot *[kewlot]*
should: what should I do? ne yapmam lazım? *[neh yapmam lazuhm]*; **he shouldn't be long** birazdan gelir *[beerazdan gheleer]*; **you should have told me** bana söylemeliydiniz *[bana surlemelee-deeneez]*
shoulder omuz *[omooz]*
shoulder blade kürek kemiği *[kewrek kemee-ee]*
shout (*verb*) bağırmak *[ba-uhrmak]*
show: could you show me? bana gösterebilir misiniz? *[bana gursterebeeleer mee-seeneez]*; **does it show?** görünüyor mu? *[ghewrew-new-yor moo]*; **we'd like to go to a show** bir şova gitmek istiyoruz *[beer shova gheetmek eesteeyorooz]*
shower (*in bathroom*) duş *[doosh]*; **with shower** duşlu *[dooshloo]*
showercap bone *[boneh]*
show-off: don't be a show-off gösteriş yapma *[ghurstereesh yapma]*
shrimps karides *[kareedess]*
shrine kutsal yer *[kootsal]*; (*grave of holy person*) yatır *[yatuhr]*
shrink: it's shrunk çekti *[chektee]*
shut (*verb*) kapatmak; **when do you shut?** ne zaman kapatıyorsunuz?

[neh zaman kapatuh-yorsoonooz]; **when do they shut?** ne zaman kapatıyorlar? *[kapatuh-yorlar]*; **it was shut** kapalıydı *[kapaluhduh]*; **I've shut myself out** anahtarı içerde unuttum *[anahtaruh eecherdeh onoot-toom]*; **shut up!** sus! *[sooss]*
shutter (*on camera*) obdüratör *[obdewraturr]*; (*on window*) kepenk
shutter release deklanşör *[deklanshurr]*
shy çekingen *[chekeenghen]*
sick (*ill*) hasta; **I think I'm going to be sick** (*vomit*) kusacağım galiba *[koossaja-uhm galeeba]*
side yan; (*in game*) taraf; **at the side of the road** yolun kenarında *[yoloon kenaruhnda]*; **the other side of town** şehrin öbür tarafında *[shehreen urbewr tarafuhnda]*
side lights park lambaları *[lambalaruh]*
side salad garnitür salata *[garneetewr]*
side street kenar sokak
sidewalk yaya kaldırımı *[y-'eye'-ya kalduhruhmuh]*
sidewalk café kaldırım kahvesi *[kalduhruhm kahvessee]*
siesta öğle uykusu *[ur-leh ooy-koossoo]*
sight: the sights of ... ...-nin görmeye değer yerleri *[...neen gurrmayeh deh-er yerleree]*
sightseeing: sightseeing tour şehir turu *[sheheer tooroo]*; **we're going sightseeing** biz gezmeye çıkıyoruz *[beez gezmayeh chuhkuh-yorooz]*
sign (*roadsign etc*) trafik işareti *[trafeek eesharetee]*; **where do I sign?** nereyi imzalayayım? *[nerayee eemzal-'eye'-y-'eye'-yuhm]*
signal: he didn't give a signal (*driver*) işaret vermedi *[eesharet vermedee]*
signature imza
signpost işaret levhası *[eesharet levhassuh]*
silence sessizlik *[sess-seezleek]*
silencer susturucu *[sooss-tooroojoo]*
silk ipek
silly (*person*) sersem; (*thing to do etc*) saçma *[sachma]*; **that's silly!** saçma!
silver gümüş *[ghewmewsh]*
silver foil gümüş yaprak *[ghewmewsh]*
similar benzer
simple (*easy*) basit *[basseet]*
since: since yesterday dünden beri *[dewnden beree]*; **since we got here** buraya geldiğimizden beri *[boor-'eye'-ya gheldee-eemeezden beree]*
sincere içten *[eechten]*
sing şarkı söylemek *[sharkuh surlemek]*
singer şarkıcı *[sharkuhjuh]*
single: a single room tek kişilik bir oda *[keesheeleek beer oda]*; **a single to ...** ...-e bir gidiş bileti *[...-eh beer gheedeesh beeletee]*; **I'm single** bekârım *[bekaruhm]*
sink (*in kitchen*) bulaşık teknesi *[boolashuhk teknessee]*; **it sank** battı *[bat-tuh]*
sir beyefendi *[bayefendee]*; **excuse me, sir** affedersiniz, beyefendi *[af-federseeneez]*
sirloin sığır filetosu *[suh-uhr feeletossoo]*
sister kız kardeş *[kuhz kardesh]*; (*elder sister*) abla; **my sister** kız kardeşim *[kuhz kardesheem]*
sister-in-law (*wife's sister*) baldız *[balduhz]*; (*husband's sister*) görümce *[gurrewmjeh]*; (*brother's wife*) yenge *[yengheh]*
sit: may I sit here? burada oturabilir miyim? *[boorada otoorabeeleer mee-yeem]*; **is anyone sitting here?** burada oturan var mı? *[otooran var muh]*
sitting: the second sitting for lunch ikinci yemek grubu *[eekeenjee yemek grooboo]*
situation durum *[dooroom]*
size büyüklük *[bew-yewklewk]*; **do you have any other sizes?** başka boyları da var mı? *[bashka boylaruh da var muh]*
sketch (*noun*) taslak *[tasslak]*
ski (*noun*) kayak *[k-'eye'-yak]*; (*verb*) kayak yapmak; **a pair of skis** bir çift kayak *[beer cheeft]*
skid: I skidded kaydım *[k-'eye'-duhm]*
skiing kayak sporu *[k-'eye'-yak sporoo]*; **we're going skiing** kayak yapmaya gidiyoruz *[yapm-'eye'-ya gheedeeyorooz]*
skin cilt *[jeelt]*
skin-diving balık adamlık *[baluhk adamluhk]*; **I'm going skin-diving**

ben dalmaya gidiyorum *[dalm-'eye'-ya gheedeeyoroom]*
skinny sıska *[suhska]*
skirt etek
skull kafatası *[kafatassuh]*
sky gök *[gurk]*
sleep (*noun*) uyku *[ooy-koo]*; **I can't sleep** uyuyamıyorum *[oo-yooyamuh-yoroom]*; **did you sleep well?** iyi uyudunuz mu? *[eeyee oo-yoodoonooz moo]*; **I need a good sleep** iyi bir uykuya ihtiyacım var *[beer ooy-kooya eehteeyajuhm]*
sleeper (*rail*) yataklı vagon *[yatakluh]*
sleeping bag uyku tulumu *[ooy-koo tooloomoo]*
sleeping car (*rail*) yataklı vagon *[yatakluh vagon]*
sleeping pill uyku ilacı *[ooy-koo eelajuh]*
sleepy (*person*) uykulu *[ooy-kooloo]*; (*weather, day*) bunaltıcı *[boonaltuh-juh]*; (*town*) sakin *[sakeen]*; **I'm feeling sleepy** uykum geldi *[ooy-koom gheldee]*
sleeve yen
slice (*noun*) dilim *[deeleem]*
slide (*phot*) diyapozitif *[deeyapozee-teef]*
slim (*adjective*) zayıf *[z-'eye'-yuhf]*; **I'm slimming** zayıflamaya çalışıyorum *[z-'eye'-yuhflam-'eye'-ya chaluhshuh-yoroom]*
slip (*under dress*) kombinezon *[kombeenezon]*; **I slipped** (*on pavement etc*) ayağım kaydı *['eye'-ya-uhm k-'eye'-duh]*
slipped disc disk kayması *[deesk k-'eye'-massuh]*
slipper terlik *[terleek]*
slippery kaygan *[k'eye'-gan]*; **it's slippery** (*road*) yollar kaygan *[yol-lar k-'eye'-gan]*
slow yavaş *[yavash]*; **slow down!** (*driving, speaking*) yavaş!
slowly yavaşça *[yavash-cha]*; **could you say it slowly?** biraz daha yavaş söyler misiniz? *[beeraz daha yavash surler mee-seeneez]*; **very slowly** çok yavaş *[chok]*
small küçük *[kewchewk]*
small change bozuk para *[bozook]*
smallpox çiçek hastalığı *[cheechek hastaluh-uh]*
smart (*clothes*) şık *[shuhk]*
smashing şahane *[shahaneh]*
smell: there's a funny smell garip bir koku var *[gareep beer kokoo]*; **what a lovely smell!** ne güzel kokuyor! *[neh ghewzel kokoo-yor]*; **it smells** (*smells bad*) kötü kokuyor *[kurtew]*
smile (*verb*) gülümseme *[ghewlewm-semeh]*
smoke (*noun*) duman *[dooman]*; **do you smoke?** sigara kullanıyor musunuz? *[seegara kullanuh-yor moossoonooz]*; **do you mind if I smoke?** sigara içebilir miyim? *[eechebeeleer meeyeem]*; **I don't smoke** ben sigara kullanmıyorum *[kool-lanmuh-yoroom]*
smooth (*surface*) düzgün *[dewzghewn]*
snack: I'd just like a snack yalnız hafif bir şey istiyorum *[yalnuhz hafeef beer shay eesteeyoroom]*
snackbar büfe *[bewfeh]*
snake yılan *[yuhlan]*
sneakers spor ayakkabısı *['eye'-yak-kabuhssuh]*
sneeze hapşirmak *[hapshuhrmak]*
snob züppe *[zewp-peh]*
snorkel şnorkel *[shnorkel]*
snow (*noun*) kar
so: it's so hot ne kadar sıcak *[neh kadar suhjak]*; **it was so beautiful!** ne kadar güzeldi! *[ghewzeldee]*; **not so fast** daha yavaş *[yavash]*; **thank you so much** çok teşekkür ederim *[chok teshek-kewr edereem]*; **so am I** ben de *[deh]*; **so do I** ben de; **how was it? - so-so** nasıldı? - şöyle böyle *[nassuhlduh - shurleh burleh]*
soaked: I'm soaked sırıl sıklam ıslandım *[suhruhl suhklam uhsslanduhm]*
soaking solution (*for contact lenses*) koruyucu sıvı *[koroo-yoojoo suhvuh]*
soap sabun *[saboon]*
soap-powder sabun tozu *[saboon tozoo]*
sober ayık *['eye'-yuhk]*
soccer futbol *[footbol]*
sock çorap *[chorap]*
socket (*elec*) priz *[preez]*
soda (water) soda
sofa sedir *[sedeer]*
soft yumuşak *[yoomooshak]*
soft drink alkolsüz içki *[alkolsewz*

eechkee]
soft lenses yumuşak kontak lensleri *[yoomooshak kontak lenssleree]*
soldier asker
sole (*of shoe, of foot*) taban; **could you put new soles on these?** bunlara yeni pençe yapar mısınız? *[boonlara yenee pencheh yapar muhsuhnuhz]*
solid katı *[katuh]*
some: may I have some water? biraz su verir misiniz? *[beeraz soo vereer mee-seeneez]* **do you have some matches?** kibritiniz var mı? *[keebreeteeneez var muh]*; **that's some drink!** ama ne içki! *[neh eechkee]*; **some of them** bazıları *[bazuhlaruh]*; **can I have some?** biraz alabilir miyim? *[beeraz alabeeleer meeyeem]*
somebody, someone birisi *[beereessee]*
something bir şey *[beer shay]*; **something to drink** içecek bir şey *[eechejek]*
sometime: sometime this afternoon öğleden sonra bir ara *[urleden sonra beer ara]*
sometimes bazen
somewhere bir yerde *[beer yerdeh]*
son oğul *[o-ool]*; **my son** oğlum *[o-loom]*
song şarkı *[sharkuh]*
son-in-law damat; **my son-in-law** damadım *[damaduhm]*
soon yakında *[yakuhnda]*; **I'll be back soon** hemen gelirim *[hemen gheleereem]*; **as soon as you can** mümkün olduğu kadar çabuk *[mewmkewn oldoo-oo kadar chabook]*
sore: it's sore dokununca acıyor *[dokoonoonja ajuh-yor]*
sore throat: I have a sore throat boğazım ağrıyor *[bo-azuhm a-ruh-yor]*
sorry: (I'm) sorry özür dilerim *[urzewr deeleereem]*; **sorry?** (*didn't understand*) efendim? *[efendeem]*
sort: what sort of ...? ne tür ...? *[neh tewr]*; **a different sort of ...** farklı türden bir ... *[farkluh tewrden beer]*; **will you sort it out?** siz halledebilir misiniz? *[seez hal-ledebeeleer mee-seeneez]*
soup çorba *[chorba]*
sour (*taste*) ekşi *[ekshee]*
south güney *[ghewnay]*; **to the south of ...** ... -in güneyinde *[-een ghewnayeendeh]*; **in the south** güneyde *[ghewnaydeh]*
South Africa Güney Afrika *[ghewnay afreeka]*
South African (*man, woman*) Güney Afrikalı *[ghewnay afreekaluh]*
southeast güney doğu *[ghewnay do-oo]*; **to the southeast of ...** ...-in güney doğusunda *[-een ghewnay do-ossoonda]*; **in the southeast** güney doğuda *[do-ooda]*
southwest güney batı *[ghewnay batuh]*; **to the southwest of ...** ...-in güney batısında *[-een ghewnay batuhssuhnda]*; **in the southwest** güney batıda *[batuhda]*
souvenir hatıra *[hatuhra]*
spa (*for bathing*) kaplıca *[kapluhja]*; (*for waters to drink*) içmeler *[eechmeler]*
space heater soba
spade bel
Spain İspanya *[eespanya]*
spanner somun anahtarı *[somoon anahtaruh]*
spare part yedek parça *[parcha]*
spare tyre/tire yedek lastik *[lasteek]*
spark(ing) plug buji *[booᴊee]*
speak: do you speak English? İngilizce biliyor musunuz? *[eenghee-leezjeh beeleeyor moossoonooz]*; **I don't speak ...** ... bilmiyorum *[beelmeeyoroom]*; **can I speak to ...?** ... ile görüşebilir miyim? *[eeleh gurrew-shebeeleer meeyeem]*; **speaking** (*on telephone*) benim *[beneem]*
special özel *[urzel]*; **nothing special** olağanüstü bir şey değil *[ola-anewstew beer shay deh-eel]*
specialist uzman *[oozman]*
special(i)ty uzmanlık *[oozmanluhk]*; **the special(i)ty of the house** lokantanın spesiyalitesi *[lokantanuhn spesseeya-leetessee]*
spectacles gözlük *[gurzlewk]*
speed hız *[huhz]*; **he was speeding** fazla sürat yapıyordu *[sewrat yapuh-yordoo]*
speedboat sürat motoru *[sewrat motoroo]*
speed limit sürat tahdidi *[sewrat tahdeedee]*

speedometer kilometre saati *[keelometreh sa-atee]*
spell: how do you spell it? nasıl yazılıyor? *[nassuhl yazuhluh-yor]*
spend harcamak *[harjamak]*; **I've spent all my money** bütün paramı harcadım *[bewtewn paramuh harjaduhm]*
spice baharat
spicy: it's very spicy çok baharatlı *[chok bahartluh]*
spider örümcek *[urrewmjek]*
spin-dryer santrifüjlü kurutma makinesi *[santreefewJlew koorootma makeenessee]*
splendid mükemmel *[mewkem-mel]*
splint (*for broken limb*) süyek *[sew-yek]*
splinter (*in finger*) kıymık *[kuhymuhk]*
splitting: I've got a splitting headache korkunç başım ağrıyor *[korkoonch bashuhm a-ruh-yor]*
sponge sünger *[sewngher]*
spoon kaşık *[kashuhk]*
sport spor
sport(s) jacket spor ceket *[jeket]*
spot (*on face etc*) sivilce *[seeveeljeh]*; **will they do it on the spot?** hemen orada yaparlar mı? *[muh]*
sprain: I've sprained my ... ...-ı burktum *[...-uh boorktoom]*
spray (*for hair*) sprey *[spray]*
spring (*season*) ilkbahar *[eelkbahar]*; (*of car, seat*) yay *[y-'eye']*
square (*in town*) meydan *[maydan]*; **ten square meters** on metre kare *[metreh kareh]*
stain (*noun: on clothes*) leke *[lekeh]*
stairs merdiven *[merdeeven]*
stale (*bread, taste*) bayat *[b-'eye'-yat]*
stall: the engine keeps stalling motor normal çalışırken duruyor *[motor normal chaluhshuhrken dooroo-yor]*
stalls (*in theatre*) koltuk *[koltook]*
stamp (*noun*) pul *[pool]*; **a stamp for England, please** lütfen, İngiltere için bir pul *[lewtfen eengheeltereh eecheen beer]*
stand: I can't stand ... (*can't tolerate*) ...-i hiç çekemem *[...-ee heech chekemem]*
standard (*adjective*) standart
standby yedek
star (*also in movies*) yıldız *[yuhlduhz]*
start (*noun*) başlangıç *[bashlanghuhch]*; **when does the film start?** filim ne zaman başlıyor? *[feeleem neh zaman bashluh-yor]*; **the car won't start** araba çalışmıyor *[chaluhshmuh-yor]*
starter (*of car*) marş *[marsh]*; (*food*) ordövr *[ordurvr]*
starving: I'm starving çok acıktım *[chok ajuhktuhm]*
state (*in country*) devlet; **the States** (*USA*) Birleşik Devletler *[beerlesheek devletler]*
station istasyon *[eestass-yon]*; **at the station** istasyonda *[eestass-yonda]*
statue heykel *[haykel]*
stay: we enjoyed our stay ziyaretimiz çok iyi geçti *[zee-yareteemeez chok eeyee ghechtee]*; **where are you staying?** nerede kalıyorsunuz? *[neredeh kaluh-yorsoonooz]*; **I'm staying at ...** ...-de kalıyorum *[...-deh kaluhyoroom]*; **I'd like to stay another week** bir hafta daha kalmak istiyorum *[eesteeyoroom]*; **I'm staying in tonight** bu akşam dışarı çıkmayacağım *[boo aksham duhsharuh chuhkm-'eye'-yaja-uhm]*
steak biftek *[beeftek]*
steal çalmak *[chalmak]*; **my bag has been stolen** çantam çalındı *[chantam chaluhnduh]*
steep (*hill*) dik *[deek]*
steering direksiyon sistemi *[deerekseeyon seestemee]*; **the steering is slack** direksiyonda fazla boşluk var *[deereksseeyonda fazla boshlook]*
steering wheel direksiyon *[deereksseeyon]*
step (*in front of house etc*) basamak
stereo stereo
sterling sterlin
stew haşlama *[hashlama]*
steward (*on plane*) kabin memuru *[kabeen memooroo]*
stewardess hostes
sticking plaster yapıştırıcı plaster *[yapuhsh-tuhruhjuh plaster]*
sticky: it's sticky yapışkan *[yapuhshkan]*
sticky tape yapışkan bant *[yapuhshkan]*
still: I'm still waiting hâlâ bekliyorum *[hala bekleeyoroom]*; **will you still be open?** o saatte hâlâ açık mı-

sınız? *[sa-at-teh ... achuhk muhsuhnuhz]*; **it's still not right** hâlâ doğru değil *[do-roo deh-eel]*; **that's still better** bu daha da iyi *[boo daha da eeyee]*; **keep still!** kımıldamayın! *[kuhmuhldam-'eye'-yuhn]*

sting: a bee sting arı sokması *[aruh sokmassuh]*; **I've been stung** beni böcek soktu *[benee burjek soktoo]*

stink pis kokmak *[peess]*; **it stinks** pis kokuyor *[kokoo-yor]*

stockings çoraplar *[choraplar]*

stolen çalınmış *[chaluhnmuhsh]*; **my wallet's been stolen** para cüzdanım çalındı *[jewzdanuhm chaluhnduh]*

stomach mide *[meedeh]*; **do you have something for an upset stomach?** mide bozulmasına karşı bir ilaç var mı? *[bozoolmassuhna karshuh beer eelach var muh]*

stomach-ache karın ağrısı *[karuhn a-ruhssuh]*

stone (*rock*) taş *[tash]*; *see page 121*

stop (*bus stop*) durak *[doorak]*; **which is the stop for ...?** ...-e gitmek için durak nerede? *[...-eh gheetmek eecheen ... neredeh]*; **please, stop here** (*to taxi driver etc*) lütfen, burada durun *[lewtfen boorada dooroon]*; **do you stop near ...?** ... yakınında duruyor musunuz? *[yakuhnuhnda dooroo-yor moo-soonooz]*; **stop doing that!** öyle yapmayın! *[urleh yapm-'eye'-yuhn]*

stopover ara durak *[ara doorak]*

store (*shop*) dükkân *[dewk-kan]*

stor(e)y (*of building*) kat

storm fırtına *[fuhrtuhna]*

story (*tale*) hikâye *[heek-'eye'-yeh]*

stove ocak *[ojak]*

straight (*road etc*) düz *[dewz]*; **it's straight ahead** dümdüz ilerde *[dewmdewz eelerdeh]*; **straight away** hemen şimdi *[hemen sheemdee]*; **a straight whisky** sek viski *[veeskee]*

straighten: can you straighten things out? (*sort things out*) meseleyi halledebilir misiniz? *[messelayee halledebeeleer mee-seeneez]*

strange (*odd*) acayip *[aj-'eye'-yeep]*; (*unknown*) yabancı *[yabanjuh]*

stranger yabancı *[yabanjuh]*; **I'm a stranger here** buranın yabancısıyım *[booranuhn yabanjuhsuh-yuhm]*

strap (*on watch, on suitcase*) kayış *[k-'eye'-yuhsh]*; (*on dress*) kemer

strawberry çilek *[cheelek]*

streak: could you put streaks in? (*in hair*) meç yapar mısınız? *[mech yapar muhsuhnuhz]*

stream dere *[dereh]*

street sokak; **on the street** sokakta

street café sokak kahvesi *[kahvessee]*

streetcar tramvay

streetmap şehir planı *[sheheer planuh]*

strep throat boğaz ağrısı *[bo-az a-ruhssuh]*

strike: they're on strike grevdeler

string ip *[eep]*; **have you got some string?** biraz ip var mı? *[beeraz ... muh]*

striped yollu *[yol-loo]*

striptease striptiz *[streepteez]*

stroke: he's had a stroke felç oldu *[felch oldoo]*

stroll: let's go for a stroll yürüyüşe çıkalım *[yewrew-yewsheh chuhk-aluhm]*

stroller (*for babies*) puset *[pooset]*

strong (*person, drink*) güçlü *[ghewchlew]*

stroppy (*official, waiter*) aksi *[aksee]*

stuck: the key's stuck anahtar sıkıştı *[anahtar suhkuhshtuh]*

student öğrenci *[ur-renjee]*

stupid aptal; **that's stupid** saçma *[sachma]*

sty(e) (*in eye*) arpacık *[arpajuhk]*

subtitles altyazılar *[altyazuhlar]*

suburb banliyö *[banliyur]*

subway (*underground*) metro

successful: were you successful? başardınız mı? *[basharduhnuhz muh]*

suddenly aniden *[aneeden]*

sue: I intend to sue dava açmak niyetindeyim *[achmak neeyeteendayeem]*

suede süet *[sewet]*

sugar şeker *[sheker]*; **no sugar thanks** şeker istemem, teşekkür ederim *[eestemem teshek-kewr edereem]*

suggest: what do you suggest? ne önerirsiniz? *[neh urnereer-seeneez]*

suit (*noun*) kostüm *[kostewm]*; **it doesn't suit me** (*clothes etc*) bana yakışmıyor *[yakuhshmuhyor]*; **it suits you** (*clothes etc*) size yakışıyor *[seezeh yakuhshuh-yor]*; **that suits me fine**

(*arrangements etc*) benim için uygundur *[beneem eecheen ooygoondoor]*
suitable (*time, place*) uygun *[ooy-goon]*
suitcase bavul *[bavool]*
sulk: he's sulking surat asıyor *[soorat assuh-yor]*
sultry (*weather*) bunaltıcı *[boonaltuhjuh]*
summer yaz; **in the summer** yazın *[yazuhn]*
sun güneş *[ghewnesh]*; **in the sun** güneş altında *[altuhnda]*; **out of the sun** gölgede *[gurlghedeh]*; **I've had too much sun** fazla güneşte kaldım *[fazla ghewneshteh kalduhm]*
sunbathe güneş banyosu yapmak *[ghewnesh banyossoo yapmak]*
sunblock (*cream*) güneş merhemi *[ghewnesh merhemee]*
sunburn güneş yanığı *[ghewnesh yanuh-uh]*
sunburnt güneşte yanmış *[ghewneshteh yanmuhsh]*
Sunday Pazar
sunglasses güneş gözlüğü *[ghewnesh ghurzlew-ew]*
sun lounger (*chair*) şezlong *[shezlong]*
sunny: if it's sunny eğer hava güneşli olursa *[eh-er hava ghewneshlee oloorsa]*; **a sunny day** güneşli bir gün *[beer ghewn]*
sunrise gündoğumu *[ghewndo-oomoo]*
sun roof (*in car*) açılır tavan *[achuhluhr tavan]*
sunset günbatımı *[ghewn-batuhmuh]*
sunshade güneşlik *[ghewneshleek]*
sunshine güneş ışığı *[ghewnesh uhshuh-uh]*
sunstroke güneş çarpması *[ghewnesh charpmassuh]*
suntan bronz ten
suntan lotion güneş losyonu *[ghewnesh lossyonoo]*
suntanned bronzlaşmış *[bronzlashmuhsh]*
suntan oil güneş yağı *[ghewnesh yauh]*
super fevkalade *[fevkaladeh]*; **super!** mükemmel! *[mewkem-mel]*
superb nefis *[nefeess]*
supermarket süpermarket *[sewpermarket]*
supper akşam yemeği *[aksham yemeh-ee]*
supplement (*extra*) ek ücret *[ewjret]*
suppose: I suppose so sanırım öyle *[sanuhruhm urleh]*
suppository supozituvar *[soopozeetoovar]*
sure: I'm sure eminim *[emeeneem]*; **are you sure?** emin misiniz? *[emeen mee-seeneez]*; **he's sure** emin; **sure!** tabii! *[tabee-ee]*
surname soyadı *[soyaduh]*
surprise (*noun*) sürpriz *[sewrpreez]*
surprising: that's not surprising bunda şaşılacak bir şey yok *[boonda shashuhlajak beer shay]*
suspension (*of car*) süspansiyon *[sewspansseeyon]*
swallow (*verb*) yutmak *[yootmak]*
swearword küfür *[kewfewr]*
sweat terlemek; (*noun*) ter; **covered in sweat** kan ter içinde *[eecheendeh]*
sweater kazak
sweatshirt svetşört *[svetshurrt]*
Sweden İsveç *[eesvech]*
sweet tatlı *[tatluh]*; (*noun: dessert*) tatlı
sweets şeker *[sheker]*
swelling şişlik *[sheeshleek]*
sweltering: it's sweltering boğucu sıcak *[bo-oojoo suhjak]*
swerve: I had to swerve (*when driving*) direksiyonu hızla kırmak zorunda kaldım *[deereksseeyonoo huhzla kuhrmak zoroonda kalduhm]*
swim (*verb*) yüzmek *[yewzmek]*; **I'm going for a swim** yüzmeye gidiyorum *[yewzmayeh gheedeeyoroom]*; **do you want to go for a swim?** yüzmeye gitmek ister misiniz? *[gheetmek eester mee-seeneez]*; **I can't swim** yüzmeyi bilmiyorum *[yewzmayee beelmeeyoroom]*
swimming yüzme *[yewzmeh]*; **I like swimming** yüzmeyi severim *[yewzmayee severeem]*
swimming costume mayo *[m-'eye'-yo]*
swimming pool yüzme havuzu *[yewzmeh havoozoo]*
swimming trunks mayo *[m-'eye'-yo]*
Swiss İsviçreli *[eesveechrelee]*
switch (*noun*) anahtar; **could you switch it on?** açar mısınız? *[achar muhsuhnuhz]*; **could you switch it off?** kapatır mısınız? *[kapatuhr]*

Switzerland İsviçre *[eesveechreh]*
swollen şişmiş *[sheeshmeesh]*
swollen glands şişmiş guddeler *[sheeshmeesh good-deler]*
sympathy anlayış *[anl-'eye'-yuhsh]*
synagogue sinagog *[seenagog]*
synthetic sentetik *[senteteek]*
Syria Suriye *[sooreeyeh]*

T

table masa *[massa]*; **a table for two** iki kişilik bir masa *[eekee keesheeleek beer]*; **at our usual table** her zamanki masamızda *[zamankee massamuhzda]*
tablecloth masa örtüsü *[massa urrtewssew]*
table tennis masatopu *[massa-topoo]*
table wine sofra şarabı *[sharabuh]*
tactful (*person*) ince *[eenjeh]*
tailback (*of traffic*) taşıt kuyruğu *[tashuht kooy-roo-oo]*
tailor terzi *[terzee]*
take almak; **will you take this to room 12?** bunu 12 numaralı odaya götürür müsünüz? *[boonoo on eekee noomaraluh od-'eye'-ya gurtewrewr mewssewnewz]*; **will you take me to the airport?** beni hava limanına götürür müsünüz? *[benee hava leemanuhna]*; **do you take credit cards?** kredi kartı kabul ediyor musunuz? *[kredee kartuh kabool edeeyor moossoonooz]*; **OK, I'll take it** tamam, bunu alıyorum *[tamam boonoo aluh-yoroom]*; **how long does it take?** ne kadar sürer? *[neh kadar sewrer]*; **it'll take 2 hours** iki saat sürer *[eekee sa-at]*; **is this seat taken?** bu yerin sahibi var mı? *[boo yereen saheebee var muh]*; **I can't take too much sun** uzun süre güneşte kalamıyorum *[oozoon sewreh ghewnesteh kalamuh-yoroom]*; **to take away** (*hamburger etc*) dışarıya götürmek *[duhsharuhya gurtewrmek]*; **will you take this back, it's broken** bunu lütfen geri alır mısınız, kırıkmış *[lewtfen gheree aluhr muhsuhnuhz kuhruhkmuhsh]*; **could you take it in at the side?** (*dress, jacket*) yandan biraz içeri alabilir misiniz? *[yandan beeraz eecheree alabeeleer mes-eeneez]*; **when does the plane take off?** uçak kaçta kalkıyor? *[oochak kachta kalkuh-yor]*; **can you take a little off the top?** (*to hairdresser*) üstten biraz kısaltır mısınız? *[ewst-ten beeraz kuhssaltuhr muhssuhnuhz]*
talcum powder talk pudrası *[poodrassuh]*
talk (*verb*) konuşmak *[konooshmak]*
tall (*person*) uzun boylu *[oozoon boyloo]*; (*building*) yüksek *[yewksek]*
tampax (*tm*) tampax
tampons tampon
tan (*noun*) bronz ten; **I want to get a good tan** iyice bronzlaşmak istiyorum *[eeyeejeh bronzlashmak eesteeyoroom]*
tank (*of car*) yakıt deposu *[yakuht depossoo]*
tap musluk *[mooslook]*
tape (*for cassette*) teyp *[tayp]*; (*sticky*) yapışkan bant *[yapuhshkan]*
tape measure mezür *[mezewr]*
tape recorder ses alma cihazı *[sess alma jeehazuh]*
taste (*noun*) tat; **can I taste it?** tadına bakabilir miyim? *[taduhna bakabeeleer meeyeem]*; **it has a peculiar taste** garip bir tadı var *[gareep beer taduh]*; **it tastes very nice** tadı çok güzel *[chok ghewzel]*; **it tastes revolting** iğrenç bir tadı var *[eerench]*
taxi taksi *[taksee]*; (*Turkish shared taxi*) dolmuş *[dolmoosh]*; **will you get me a taxi?** bana bir taksi bulur musunuz? *[bana beer ... booloor moossoonooz]*
taxi-driver taksi şoförü *[taksee shofurrew]*
taxi rank, taxi stand taksi durağı *[taksee doora-uh]*
tea (*drink*) çay *[ch-'eye']*; **tea for two please** iki kişilik çay, lütfen *[eekee*

keesheeleek ... lewtfen]; **a glass of tea** bir bardak çay *[beer bardak]*; **could I have a cup of tea?** bir fincan çay rica ediyorum *[feenjan ... reeja edeyoroom]*

teabag çay şasesi *[ch-'eye' shassessee]*

teach: could you teach me? bana öğretir misiniz? *[urreteer meeseeneez]*; **could you teach me Turkish?** bana Türkçe öğretir misiniz? *[tewrkcheh]*

teacher öğretmen *[urretmen]*

team (*sport*) takım *[takuhm]*; (*group*) ekip *[ekeep]*

teapot demlik *[demleek]*

teetotal: he's teetotal o hiç içki içmez *[heech eechkee eechmez]*

telegram telgraf; **I want to send a telegram** bir telgraf göndermek istiyorum *[gurndermek eesteeyoroom]*

telephone telefon; **can I make a telephone call?** bir telefon edebilir miyim? *[edebeeleer meeyeem]*; **could you talk to him for me on the telephone?** benim yerime telefonda onunla siz konuşur musunuz? *[beeneem yereemeh telefonda onoonla seez konooshoor moossoonooz]*

telephone box/booth telefon kulübesi *[koolewbessee]*

telephone directory telefon rehberi *[rehberee]*

telephone number telefon numarası *[noomarassuh]*; **what's your telephone number?** telefon numaranız kaç? *[noomaranuhz kach]*

telephoto lens teleobjektif *[telehobjekteef]*

television televizyon *[televeez-yon]*; **I'd like to watch television** televizyon seyretmek istiyorum *[sayretmek eesteeyoroom]*; **is the match on television?** televizyon maçı verecek mi? *[machuh verejek mee]*

tell: could you tell him ...? ona ...-i söyler misiniz? *[...-ee surler meeseeneez]*

temperature (*weather*) sıcaklık *[suhjakluhk]*; (*fever*) ateş *[atesh]*; **he has a temperature** ateşi var *[ateshee]*

temple (*religious*) tapınak *[tapuhnak]*

temporary geçici *[ghecheejee]*

tenant (*of aparment*) kiracı *[keerajuh]*

tennis tenis *[teneess]*

tennis ball tenis topu *[teneess topoo]*

tennis court tenis kortu *[teneess kortoo]*; **can we use the tennis court?** tenis kortunu kullanabilir miyiz? *[teneess kortoonoo koollanabeeleer meeyeez]*

tennis racket tenis raketi *[teneess raketee]*

tent çadır *[chaduhr]*

term sömestr *[surmestr]*

terminus (*rail*) son istasyon *[eestassyon]*

terrace teras; **on the terrace** terasta *[terassta]*

terrible berbat

terrific müthiş *[mewt-heesh]*

testicle husye *[hoos-yeh]*

than -den; **smaller than ...** ...-den küçük *[kewchewk]*; *see page 109*

thanks, thank you teşekkür ederim *[teshek-kewr edereem]*; **thank you very much** çok teşekkür ederim *[chok]*; **thank you for everything** her şey için teşekkürler *[shay eecheen teshek-kewrler]*; **no thanks** hayir, teşekkür ederim *[h-'eye'-yuhr]*

that: that woman şu kadın *[shoo kaduhn]*; **that man** şu adam; **that one** şu; **I hope that ...** umarım ki ... *[oomaruhm kee]*; **that's perfect** bu mükemmel *[boo mewkem-mel]*; **that's strange** bu acayip *[aj-'eye'-yeep]*; **is that ...?** ... mı? *[muh]*; **that's it** (*that's right*) tamam; **is it that expensive?** o kadar pahalı mı? *[kadar pahaluh muh]*

the *see page 106*

theater, theatre tiyatro *[teeyatro]*

their onların *[onlaruhn]*; **their house** onların evi *[evee]*; *see page 108*

theirs onlarınki *[onlaruhnkee]*; *see page 110*

them onları *[onlaruh]*; **I saw them** onları gördüm *[gurrdewm]*; **for them** onlar için *[onlar eecheen]*; **with them** onlarla; **I gave it to them** onlara verdim *[verdeem]*; **who? - them** kim? - onlar *[keem]*; *see page 110*

then (*at that time*) o zaman; (*after that*) ondan sonra

there orası *[orassuh]*; **over there** şurada *[shoorada]*; **up there** yukarıda *[yookaruhda]*; **is there ...?** ... var mı? *[muh]*; **are there ...?** ... var mı?;

there is ... ...var; **there are ...** ... var; **there you are** (*giving something*) buyrun *[booy-roon]*
thermal spring kaplıca *[kapluhja]*
thermometer termometre
thermos flask termos
thermostat (*in car*) thermostat
these bunlar *[boonlar]*; **can I have these?** bunları alabilir miyim? *[boonlaruh alabeeleer meeyeem]*
they onlar; **are they ready?** hazırlar mı? *[hazuhrlar muh]*; **are they coming?** geliyorlar mı? *[gheleeyorlar muh]*; *see page 110*
thick kalın *[kahluhn]*; (*stupid*) mankafa
thief hırsız *[huhrsuhz]*
thigh but *[boot]*
thin ince *[eenjeh]*
thing şey *[shay]*; **have you seen my things?** benim şeylerimi gördünüz mü? *[beneem shaylereemee gurrdewnewz mew]*; **first thing in the morning** sabah ilk iş *[sabah eelk eesh]*
think düşünmek *[dewshewnmek]*; **what do you think?** ne düşünüyorsunuz? *[neh dewshewnew-yorsoonooz]*; **I think so** bence öyle *[benjeh urleh]*; **I don't think so** bence öyle değil *[urleh deh-eel]*; **I'll think about it** düşüneceğim *[dewshewnejeh-eem]*
third-class üçüncü sınıf *[ewchewnjew suhnuhf]*
third party insurance mecburi trafik sigortası *[mejbooree trafeek seegor-tassuh]*
thirsty: I'm thirsty susadım *[soossa-duhm]*
this: this hotel bu otel *[boo]*; **this street** bu sokak; **this one** bu; **this is my wife/husband** bu benim eşim *[beneem esheem]*; **this is my favo(u)rite café** bu benim en sevdiğim kahvedir *[sevdee-eem kahvedeer]*; **is this yours?** bu sizin mi? *[seezeen mee]*
those şunlar *[shoonlar]*; **not these, those** bunlar değil, şunlar *[boonlar deh-eel]*
thread (*noun*) iplik *[eepleek]*
throat boğaz *[bo-az]*
throat lozenges boğaz pastilleri *[bo-az pasteel-leree]*
throttle (*on motorbike*) gaz
through içinden *[eecheenden]*; **does it go through Istanbul?** İstanbul'un içinden geçiyor mu? *[eestanbooloon ... ghecheeyor moo]*; **Monday through Friday** Pazartesiden Cumaya kadar *[pazartesseeden joom-'eye'-ya kadar]*; **straight through the city centre** tam şehir merkezinden *[sheheer merkezeenden]*
through train direkt tren *[deerekt]*
throw (*verb*) atmak; **don't throw it away** onu atmayın *[onoo atm-'eye'-yuhn]*; **I'm going to throw up** kusacağım *[koosaja-uhm]*
thumb başparmak *[bashparmak]*
thumbtack raptiye *[rapteeyeh]*
thunder (*noun*) gök gürültüsü *[gurk ghewrewl-tewssew]*
thunderstorm gök gürültülü fırtına *[gurk ghewrewl-tewlew fuhrtuhna]*
Thursday Perşembe *[pershembeh]*
ticket bilet *[beelet]*
ticket office bilet gişesi *[beelet gheeshessee]*
tie (*noun: around neck*) kravat
tight (*clothes etc*) dar; **the waist is too tight** beli fazla dar *[belee fazla]*
tights külotlu çorap *[kewlotloo chorap]*
time zaman; **what's the time?** saat kaç *[sa-at kach]*; **at what time do you close?** saat kaçta kapatıyorsunuz? *[kachta kapatuh-yorsoonooz]*; **there's not much time** fazla zaman kalmadı *[fazla ... kalmaduh]*; **for the time being** şimdilik *[sheemdeeleek]*; **from time to time** zaman zaman; **right on time** tam zamanında *[zamanuhnda]*; **this time** bu kez *[boo]*; **last time** son defasında *[defassuhnda]*; **next time** bir daha sefere *[beer daha sefereh]*; **four times** dört kere *[durrt kereh]*; **have a good time!** iyi eğlenceler! *[eeyee e-lenjeler]*; *see page 119*
timetable tarife *[tareefeh]*
tin (*can*) teneke kutu *[tenekeh kootoo]*
tinfoil alüminyum folyo *[alewmeen-yoom fol-yo]*
tin-opener konserve açacağı *[konserveh achaja-uh]*
tint (*verb: hair*) ton vermek
tiny minik *[meeneek]*
tip (*to waiter etc*) bahşiş *[bahsheesh]*;

does that include the tip? bahşiş dahil mi? *[daheel mee]*
tire (*for car*) lastik *[lasteek]*
tired yorgun *[yorgoon]*; **I'm tired** yorgunum *[—oom]*
tiring yorucu *[yoroojoo]*
tissues kâğıt mendil *[ka-uht mendeel]*
to: to Antalya/England Antalya'ya/İngiltere'ye *[antaly-'eye'-ya/eengheelter-'eye'-yeh]*; **to London** Londra'ya *[londr-'eye'-ya]*; **to the airport** hava limanına *[hava leemanuhna]*; **here's to you!** (*toast*) şerefinize! *[sherefeeneezeh]*; *see pages 106, 119*
toast (*bread*) kızarmış ekmek *[kuhzarmuhsh ekmek]*; (*drinking*) kadeh kaldırma *[kadeh kalduhrma]*
tobacco tütün *[tewtewn]*
tobacconist, tobacco store sigaracı *[seegarajuh]*
today bugün *[booghewn]*; **today week** bu hafta *[boo hafta]*
toe ayak parmağı *['eye'-yak parma-uh]*
toffee karamela
together beraber; **we're together** beraberiz *[—eez]*; **can we pay together?** hesabı birlikte ödeyebilir miyiz? *[hessabuh beerleekteh urdayebeeleer meeyeez]*
toilet tuvalet *[toovalet]*; **where's the toilet?** tuvalet nerede? *[neredeh]*; **I have to go to the toilet** tuvalete gitmem lazım *[toovaleteh gheetmem lazuhm]*; **she's in the toilet** o tuvalette *[toovalet-teh]*
toilet paper tuvalet kâğıdı *[toovalet ka-uhduh]*
toilet water kolonya
toll (*for motorway, bridge etc*) geçiş parası *[ghecheesh parassuh]*
tomato domates
tomato juice domates suyu *[domatess soo-yoo]*
tomato ketchup ketçap *[ketchap]*
tomorrow yarın *[yaruhn]*; **tomorrow morning** yarın sabah; **tomorrow afternoon** yarın öğleden sonra *[urleden sonra]*; **tomorrow evening** yarın akşam *[aksham]*; **the day after tomorrow** öbür gün *[urbewr ghewn]*; **see you tomorrow** yarın görüşmek üzere *[ghewrewshmek ewzereh]*
ton ton; *see page 120*
toner (*cosmetic*) yüz losyonu *[yewz lossyonoo]*
tongue dil *[deel]*
tonic (*water*) tonik *[toneek]*
tonight bu gece *[boo ghejeh]*; **not tonight** bu gece değil *[deh-eel]*
tonsillitis bademcik iltihabı *[bademjeek eelteehabuh]*
tonsils bademcikler *[bademjeekler]*
too (*excessively*) fazla; (*also*) de *[deh]*; **too much** çok fazla *[chok]*; **me too** ben de; **I'm not feeling too good** kendimi pek iyi hissetmiyorum *[kendeemee pek eeyee heess-setmeeyoroom]*; *see page 118*
tooth diş *[deesh]*
toothache diş ağrısı *[deesh a-ruhssuh]*
toothbrush diş fırçası *[deesh fuhrchassuh]*
toothpaste diş macunu *[deesh majoonoo]*
top: on top of ... ...-in üstünde *[...-een ewstewndeh]*; **on top of the car** arabanın üstünde *[arabanuhn]*; **on the top floor** üst katta *[ewst katta]*; **at the top** üstte *[ewst-teh]*; **at the top of the hill** tepenin üstünde *[tepeneen]*; **top quality** en iyi kalite *[eeyee kaleeteh]*; **bikini top** bikini üstü *[beekeenee ewstew]*
topless göğüsleri açık *[gur-ewssleree achuhk]*; **topless beach** göğsü açık olarak gezilen plaj *[gur-ssew ... olarak ghezeelen plaJ]*
torch el feneri *[feneree]*
total (*noun*) toplam
touch (*verb*) dokunmak *[dokoonmak]*; **let's keep in touch** haberleşelim *[haberlesheleem]*
tough (*meat*) sert; **tough luck!** vah vah!
tour tur *[toor]*; **is there a tour of ...?** ...-e tur var mı? *[...-eh ... muh]*
tour guide tur rehberi *[toor rehberee]*
tourist turist *[tooreest]*
tourist information office turist danışma bürosu *[tooreest danuhshma bewrossoo]*
tourist police turizm zabıtası *[tooreezm zabuhtassuh]*
touristy turistlere yönelik *[toor-eestlereh yurneleek]*; **somewhere not so touristy** fazla turist olmayan bir yer *[fazla tooreest olm-'eye'-yan beer]*

tour operator tur organizatörü *[toor organeezaturew]*
tow: can you give me a tow? arabamı yedekte çeker misiniz? *[arabamuh yedekteh cheker mee-seeneez]*
toward(s) -e doğru *[—eh do-roo]*; **toward(s) Ankara** Ankara'ya doğru *[ankar-'eye'-ya]*
towel havlu *[havloo]*
town şehir *[sheheer]*; **in town** şehirde *[sheheerdeh]*; **which bus goes into town?** şehre hangi otobüs gidiyor? *[shehreh hanghee otobewss gheedeeyor]*; **we're staying just out of town** şehrin hemen dışında kalıyoruz *[shehreen hemen duhshuhnda kaluhyorooz]*
town hall belediye sarayı *[beledeeyeh sar-'eye'-yuh]*
tow rope yedek halatı *[yedek halatuh]*
toy oyuncak *[oyoonjak]*
track suit eşofman *[eshofman]*
traditional geleneksel *[gheleneksel]*; **a traditional Turkish meal** geleneksel Türk yemeği *[tewrk yemeh-ee]*
traffic trafik *[trafeek]*
traffic circle dönel kavşak *[durnel kavshak]*
traffic cop trafik polisi *[trafeek poleessee]*
traffic jam trafik tıkanıklığı *[trafeek tuhkanuhkluh-uh]*
traffic light(s) trafik lambaları *[trafeek lambalaruh]*
trailer (*for carrying tent etc*) römork *[rurmork]*; (*caravan*) treyler *[trayler]*
train tren; **when's the next train to ...?** ...-e ilk tren saat kaçta? *[...-eh eelk ... sa-at kachta]*; **by train** trenle *[trenleh]*
trainers (*shoes*) spor ayakkabısı *['eye'-yak-kabuhsuh]*
train station tren istasyonu *[eestass-yonoo]*
tram tramvay
tramp (*person*) berduş *[berdoosh]*
tranquillizers müsekkin *[mewsek-keen]*
transformer (*electric*) transformatör *[transformaturr]*
transistor (*radio*) transistörlü radyo *[transeesturrlew radyo]*
transit lounge (*at airport*) transit yolcu salonu *[transeet yoljoo salonoo]*
translate tercüme etmek *[terjewmeh etmek]*; **could you translate that?** bunu tercüme edebilir misiniz? *[boonoo ... edebeeleer mee-seeneez]*
translation tercüme *[terjewmeh]*
translator tercüman *[terjewman]*
transmission (*of car*) transmisyon *[transmiss-yon]*
travel seyahat *[sayahat]*; **we're travel(l)ing around** geziyoruz *[ghezeeyorooz]*
travel agent seyahat acentesi *[sayahat ajentessee]*
travel(l)er yolcu *[yoljoo]*
traveller's cheque, traveler's check seyahat çeki *[sayahat chekee]*
tray tepsi *[tepssee]*
tree ağaç *[a-ach]*
tremendous muazzam *[moo-az-zam]*
trendy (*clothes*) son moda; (*person*) şık *[shuhk]*
tricky (*difficult*) zor
trim: just a trim please (*to hairdresser*) lütfen yalnız uçlarından alın *[lewtfen yalnuhz uchlaruhndan aluhn]*
trip (*journey*) yolculuk *[yoljoolook]*; **I'd like to go on a trip to ...** ...-e seyahat etmek istiyorum *[...-eh sayahat etmek eesteeyoroom]*; **have a good trip** yolunuz açık olsun *[yoloonooz achuhk olsoon]*
tripod (*for camera*) sehpa
tropical tropikal *[tropeekal]*
trouble (*noun*) dert; **I'm having trouble with ...** ... ile başım dertte *[eeleh bashuhm dert-teh]*; **sorry to trouble you** rahatsız ettiğim için özür dilerim *[rahatsuh et-tee-eem eecheen urzewr deeleereem]*
trousers pantalon
trouser suit pantalonlu elbise *[pantalonloo elbeesseh]*
trout alabalık *[alabaluhk]*
truck kamyon
truck driver kamyon şoförü *[kamyon shofurrew]*
true gerçek *[gherchek]*; **that's not true** bu doğru değil *[boo do-roo deh-eel]*
trunk (*of car*) bagaj *[bagaJ]*; (*for belongings: big case*) sandık *[sanduhk]*
trunks (*swimming*) mayo *[m-'eye'-yo]*
truth gerçek *[gherchek]*; **it's the truth** gerçek budur *[boodoor]*

try denemek; **please try** lütfen deneyin *[lewtfen denayeen]*; **will you try for me?** deneyebilir misiniz *[denayebeeleer mee-seeneez]*; **I've never tried it** hiç denemedim *[heech denemedeem]*; **can I have a try?** deneyebilir miyim? *[denayebeeleer meeyeem]*; **may I try it on?** (*clothes*) üstümde deneyebilir miyim? *[ewstewmdeh]*
T-shirt tişört *[teeshurrt]*
tube (*for tyre*) iç lastik *[eech lasteek]*
Tuesday Salı *[saluh]*
tuition: I'd like tuition özel ders almak istiyorum *[urzel derss almak eesteeyoroom]*
tulip lâle *[laleh]*
tuna fish ton balığı *[baluh-uh]*
tune (*noun*) ezgi *[ezghee]*
tunnel tünel *[tewnel]*
Turk Türk *[tewrk]*
Turkey Türkiye *[tewrkeeyeh]*; **in Turkey** Türkiye'de *[tewrkeeyedeh]*; **Turkey's climate** Türkiye'nin iklimi *[tewrkeeyeneen eekleemee]*; **made in Turkey** Türkiye imalatı *[eemalatuh]*; **when we come back to Turkey** tekrar Türkiye'ye geldiğimiz zaman *[tewrkeeyeyeh gheldee-eemeez]*
Turkish (*adjective*) Türk *[tewrk]*; (*language*) Türkçe *[tewrkcheh]*; **what's the Turkish for ...?** ...-in Türkçesi nedir? *[...-een tewrkchessee nedeer]*
Turkish bath Hamam
Turkish coffee Türk kahvesi *[tewrk kahvessee]*
Turkish Cypriot (*man, woman*) Kıbrıslı *[kuhbruhsluh]*
Turkish delight lokum *[lokoom]*
Turkish wrestling yağlı güreş *[ya-luh ghewresh]*
turn: it's my turn now şimdi sıra bende *[sheemdee suhra bendeh]*; **turn left** sola dönün *[sola dewnewn]*; **where do we turn off?** nereden sapacağız? *[nereden sapaja-uhz]*; **can you turn the air-conditioning on?** klima cihazını çalıştırır mısınız? *[kleema jeehazuhnuh chaluhsh-tuhruhr muhsuhnuhz]*; **can you turn the air-conditioning off?** klima cihazını kapatır mısınız? *[kapatuhr]*; **he didn't turn up** gelmedi *[ghelmedee]*
turning (*in road*) sapak
TV TV *[teveh]*
tweezers cımbız *[juhmbuhz]*
twice iki kere *[eekee kereh]*; **twice as much** iki misli *[meesslee]*
twin beds tek kişilik iki yatak *[keesheeleek eekee yatak]*
twin room çift yataklı oda *[cheeft yatakluh oda]*
twins ikizler *[eekeezler]*
twist: I've twisted my ankle ayak bileğimi burktum *['eye'-yak beeleh-eemee boorktoom]*
type tip *[teep]*; **a different type of ...** başka tip bir ... *[bashka ... beer]*
typewriter yazı makinesi *[yazuh makeeneessee]*
typhoid tifo *[teefo]*
typical (*dish etc*) tipik *[teepeek]*; **that's typical!** al işte! *[eeshteh]*
tyre lastik *[lasteek]*

U

ugly çirkin *[cheerkeen]*
ulcer ülser *[ewlser]*
Ulster Kuzey İrlanda *[koozay eerlanda]*
umbrella şemsiye *[shemseeyeh]*
uncle amca *[amja]*; **my uncle** amcam *[amjam]*
uncomfortable (*chair etc*) rahatsız *[rahatsuhz]*
unconscious baygın *[b-'eye'-guhn]*
under (*spatially*) altında *[altuhnda]*; (*less than*) -den az; **under the table** masanın altında *[massanuhn altuhnda]* **under 500 liras** 500 liradan az *[besh yewz leeradan]*
underdone az pişmiş *[peeshmeesh]*
underground (*rail*) metro
underpants don
undershirt fanila *[faneela]*
understand: I don't understand anla-

mıyorum *[anlamuh-yoroom]*; **I understand** anlıyorum *[anluh-yoroom]*; **do you understand?** anlıyor musunuz? *[anluhyor moossoonooz]*
underwear iç çamaşırı *[eech chamashuhruh]*
undo (*clothes*) açmak *[achmak]*
uneatable: it's uneatable yenecek gibi değil *[yenejek gheebee deh-eel]*
unemployed işsiz *[eesh-seez]*
unfair: that's unfair bu haksızlıktır *[boo haksuhzluhktuhr]*
unfortunately ne yazık ki *[neh yazuhk kee]*
unfriendly soğuk *[so-ook]*
unhappy mutsuz *[mootsooz]*
unhealthy sağlıksız *[sa-luhksuhz]*
United States Birleşik Amerika *[beerlesheek amereeka]*; **in the United States** Birleşik Amerika'da *[amereekada]*
university üniversite *[ewnee-verseeteh]*
unlimited mileage (*on hire car*) kilometre kısıtlaması yok *[keelometreh kuhsuhtlamassuh]*
unlock kilidi açmak *[keeleedee achmak]*; **the door was unlocked** kapı kilitli değildi *[kapuh keeleetlee deh-eeldee]*
unpack eşyaları bavuldan çıkarmak *[eshyalaruh bavooldan chuhkarmak]*
unpleasant nahoş *[nahosh]*
unpronounceable: it's unpronounceable söylenmesi mümkün değil *[surlenmessee mewmkewn deh-eel]*
untie çözmek *[churzmek]*
until: until ... ...-e kadar *[...-eh kadar]*; **until we meet again** (*parting words*) tekrar görüşmek üzere *[tekrar gurrewshmek ewzereh]*; **not until Wednesday** en erken Çarşamba günü *[erken charshamba ghewnew]*
unusual alışılmamış *[aluhshuhl-mamuhsh]*
up yukarı *[yookaruh]*; **up there** yukarıda *[yookaruhda]*; **further up the road** yolun biraz ilerisinde *[yoloon beeraz eeleereesseendeh]*; **he's not up yet** (*not out of bed*) henüz kalkmadı *[henewz kalkmaduh]*; **what's up?** (*what's wrong?*) ne oldu? *[neh oldoo]*
upmarket (*restaurant, hotel, goods etc*) sükseli *[sewkselee]*
upset stomach mide bozukluğu *[meedeh bozookloo-oo]*
upside down baş aşağı *[bash asha-uh]*
upstairs üst katta *[ewst kat-ta]*
urgent acil *[ajeel]*; **it's very urgent** çok acildir *[chok ajeeldeer]*
urinary tract infection idrar yolu iltihabı *[eedrar yoloo eelteehabuh]*
us biz *[beez]*; **with us** bizimle *[beezeemleh]*; **for us** bizim için *[beezeem eecheen]*; *see page 110*
use (*verb*) kullanmak *[kool-lanmak]*; **may I use ...?** ...-i kullanabilir miyim? *[...-ee kool-lanabeeleer meeyeem]*
used: I used to swim a lot eskiden çok yüzerdim *[eskeeden chok yewzerdeem]*; **when I get used to the heat** sıcağa alışınca *[suhja-a aluhshuhnja]*
useful yararlı *[yaraluh]*
usual olağan *[ola-an]*; **as usual** her zamanki gibi *[zamankee gheebee]*
usually genellikle *[ghenel-leekleh]*
U-turn geriye dönüş *[ghereeyeh durnewsh]*

V

vacancy: do you have any vacancies? (*hotel*) boş odanız var mı? *[bosh odanuhz var muh]*
vacation tatil *[tateel]*; **we're here on vacation** buraya tatile geldik *[boor-'eye'-ya tateeleh gheldeek]*
vaccination aşılama *[ashuhlama]*
vacuum cleaner elektrik süpürgesi *[elektreek sewpewr-ghessee]*
vacuum flask termos
vagina dölyolu *[durl-yoloo]*
valid (*ticket etc*) geçerli *[ghecherlee]*; **how long is it valid for?** ne zamana kadar geçerli? *[neh zamana kadar]*

valley vadi *[vadee]*
valuable (*adjective*) değerli *[deh-erlee]*; **can I leave my valuables here?** değerli eşyalarımı burada bırakabilir miyim? *[eshyalaruhmuh boorada buhraka-beeleer meeyeem]*
value (*noun*) değer *[deh-er]*
van kamyonet
vanilla vanilya *[vaneel-ya]*; **a vanilla ice cream** vanilyalı dondurma *[vaneel-yaluh dondoorma]*
varicose veins varis *[vareess]*
variety show varyete *[var-yeteh]*
vary: it varies değişir *[deh-eesheer]*
vase vazo
vaudeville vodvil *[vodveel]*
VD zührevi hastalık *[zewhrevee hastaluhk]*
veal dana eti *[dana etee]*
vegetables sebze
vegetarian vejeteryen *[vejeteryen]*; **I'm a vegetarian** ben vejeteryenim *[vejeteryeneem]*
velvet kadife *[kadeefeh]*
vending machine otomat
ventilator vantilatör *[vanteelaturr]*
very çok *[chok]*; **very much** çok çok; **not very much** fazla değil *[fazla deh-eel]*; **just a very little for me** bana yalnız birazcık *[bana yalnuhz beerazjuhk]*; **I like it very much** çok beğeniyorum *[bayeneeyoroom]*
vest (*under shirt*) fanila *[faneela]*; (*waistcoat*) yelek
via üzerinden *[ewzereenden]*; **via Ankara** Ankara üzerinden
video video
view manzara; **what a superb view!** nefis bir manzara! *[nefeess beer]*
viewfinder (*of camera*) vizör *[veezurr]*
villa villa
village köy *[kur-y]*
vine asma
vinegar sirke *[seerkeh]*
vine-growing area şaraplık üzüm bölgesi *[sharapluhk ewzewm burlghessee]*
vineyard bağ *[ba]*
vintage (*of wine*) yıl *[yuhl]*; **vintage wine** yıllanmış şarap *[yuhl-lanmuhsh sharap]*
visa vize *[veezeh]*
visibility (*for driving etc*) görüş uzaklığı *[gurrewsh oozakluh-uh]*
visit (*verb*) ziyaret *[zeeyaret]*; **I'd like to visit ...** ...-i ziyaret etmek isterim *[...-ee ... etmek eestereem]*; **come and visit us** bize de buyrun *[beezeh deh booy-roon]*
vital: it's vital that ... ... çok önemlidir *[chok urnemleedeer]*
vitamins vitaminler *[veetameenler]*
vodka votka
voice ses
voltage gerilim *[ghereeleem]*
vomit kusmak *[koosmak]*

wafer (*with ice cream*) kâğıt helvası *[ka-uht helvassuh]*
waist bel
waistcoat yelek
wait beklemek; **wait for me** beni bekleyin *[benee beklayeen]*; **don't wait for me** beni beklemeyin *[beklemayeen]*; **it was worth waiting for** beklediğimize değdi *[bekledeeeemeezeh daydee]*; **I'll wait until my wife/husband comes** eşim gelinceye kadar bekleyeceğim *[esheem gheleenjayeh kadar beklayejeh-eem]*; **I'm waiting for someone** birisini bekliyorum *[beereesseenee bekleeyoroom]*; **I'll wait a little longer** biraz daha bekleyeceğim *[beeraz]*; **can you do it while I wait?** beklerken yapabilir misiniz? *[yapabeeleer meeseeneez]*
waiter garson; **waiter!** garson!
waiting room bekleme salonu *[beklemeh salonoo]*
waitress garson; **waitress!** garson!
wake: will you wake me up at 6.30? beni 6.30'da uyandırır mısınız? *[benee altuh otoozda oo-yanduhruhr muhsuhnuhz]*
Wales Galler Ülkesi *[gal-ler ewlkessee]*
walk: let's walk there oraya kadar

yürüyelim *[or-'eye'-ya kadar yewrew-yeleem]*; **is it possible to walk there?** oraya yayan gidilebilir mi? *[y-'eye'-yan gheedeeleh-beeleer mee]*; **I'll walk back** ben yürüyerek geri döneceğim *[yewrew-yerek ghereee durnejeh-eem]*; **is it a long walk?** yürüyerek uzak mıdır? *[oozak muhduhr]*; **it's only a short walk** yürüyerek kısa bir masafededir *[kuhssa beer messafededeer]*; **I'm going out for a walk** ben yürüyüşe çıkıyorum *[yewrew-yewsheh chuhkuh-yoroom]*; **let's take a walk around town** yürüyerek şehri dolaşalım *[shehree dolashaluhm]*

walking: I want to do some walking biraz yürümek istiyorum *[beeraz yewrewmek eesteeyoroom]*

walking boots yürüyüş ayakkabıları *[yewyrew-yewsh 'eye'-yak-kabuhlaruh]*

walking stick baston

walkman (*tm*) walkman

wall duvar *[doovar]*

wallet para cüzdanı *[para jewzdanuh]*

wander: I like just wandering around başıboş dolaşmayı severim *[bashuhbosh dolashm-'eye'-yuh severeem]*

want: I want a ... bir ... istiyorum *[beer ... eesteeyoroom]*; **I don't want any ...** ... istemiyorum *[eestemeeyoroom]*; **I want to go home** eve dönmek istiyorum *[eveh durnmek]*; **I don't want to** istemiyorum; **he wants to ...** ... istiyor *[eesteeyor]*; **what do you want?** ne istiyorsunuz? *[neh eesteeyorsoonooz]*

war savaş *[savash]*

ward (*in hospital*) koğuş *[ko-oosh]*

warm sıcak *[suhjak]*; **it's so warm today** bugün hava ne kadar sıcak *[booghewn hava neh kadar]*; **I'm so warm** beni sıcak bastı *[benee ... basstuh]*

warning (*noun*) uyarı *[oo-yaruh]*

was: it was ... ...-di *[...-dee]*; *see page 115*

wash (*verb*) yıkamak *[yuhkamak]*; (*oneself*) yıkanmak *[yuhkanmak]*; **I need a wash** yıkanmam lazım *[yuhkanmam lazuhm]*; **can you wash the car?** arabayı yıkayabilir misiniz? *[arab-'eye'-yuh yuhk-'eye'-ya-beeleer mee-seeneez]*; **can you wash these?** bunları yıkayabilir misiniz? *[boonlaruh]*; **it'll wash off** yıkanınca çıkar *[yuhkanuhnja chuhkar]*

washcloth sabun bezi *[saboon bezee]*

washer (*for bolt etc*) rondela

washhand basin el yıkama yeri *[yuhkama yeree]*

washing (*clothes*) çamaşır *[chamashuhr]*; **where can I hang my washing?** çamaşırımı nereye asabilirim? *[chama-shuhruhmuh nerayeh asabeeleereem]*; **can you do my washing for me?** çamaşırımı yıkayabilir misiniz? *[yuhk-'eye'-ya-beeleer mee-seeneez]*

washing machine çamaşır makinesi *[chamashuhr makeenessee]*

washing powder deterjan *[deterJan]*

washing-up: I'll do the washing-up bulaşıkları ben yıkayacağım *[boolash-uhklaruh ben yuhk-'eye'-yaja-uhm]*

washing-up liquid bulaşık deterjanı *[boolashuhk deterJanuh]*

wasp yabanarısı *[yaban-aruhssuh]*

wasteful: that's wasteful bu israftır *[boo eesraftuhr]*

wastepaper basket çöp sepeti *[churp sepetee]*

watch (*wrist-*) saat *[sa-at]*; **will you watch my things for me?** eşyalarıma göz kulak olur musunuz? *[eshyalar-uhma gurz koolak oloor moos-soonooz]*; **I'll just watch** ben sadece seyredeceğim *[sadeje sayredejeh-eem]*; **watch out!** dikkat! *[deek-kat]*

watch strap saat kayışı *[sa-at k-'eye'-yuhshuh]*

water su *[soo]*; **may I have some water?** biraz su verir misiniz? *[beeraz soo vereer mee-seeneeez]*

watercolo(u)r suluboya *[sooloo-boya]*

waterproof (*adjective*) su geçirmez *[soo ghecheermez]*

waterski: I'd like to learn to waterski su kayağı yapmayı öğrenmek istiyorum *[soo k-'eye'-ya-uh yap-m-'eye'-yuh urrenmek eesteeyoroom]*

waterskiing sukayağı *[sook-'eye'-ya-uh]*

water sports su sporları *[soo sporlaruh]*

water wings yüzme yastıkları *[yewzmeh yastuhklaruh]*

wave (*in sea*) dalga
way: which way is it? nereden gidilir? *[nereden gheedeeleer]*; **it's this way** bu tarafta *[boo tarafta]*; **it's that way** o tarafta; **could you tell me the way to ...?** ...-e nereden gidilir? *[...-eh]*; **is it on the way to Istanbul?** İstanbul yolu üzerinde midir? *[eestanbool yoloo ewzereendeh meedeer]*; **you're blocking the way** yolu kapatıyorsunuz *[yoloo kapatuh-yorsoonooz]*; **is it a long way to ...?** ... buraya uzak mı? *[boor-'eye'-ya oozak muh]*; **would you show me the way to do it?** nasıl yapılacağını bana gösterir misiniz? *[nassuhl yapuhlaja-uhnuh bana gurstereer mee-seeneez]*; **do it this way** böyle yapın *[burleh yapuhn]*; **no way!** asla olmaz!
we biz *[beez]*; *see page 110*
weak (*person*) zayıf *[z-'eye'-yuhf]*; (*drink*) hafif *[hafeef]*
wealthy zengin *[zengheen]*
weather hava; **what foul weather!** ne berbat hava!; **what beautiful weather!** ne güzel hava! *[ghewzel]*
weather forecast hava tahmini *[hava tahmeenee]*
wedding düğün *[dew-ewn]*
wedding anniversary evlenme yıldönümü *[evlenmeh yuhldurnewmew]*
wedding ring alyans
Wednesday Çarşamba *[charshamba]*
week hafta; **a week (from) today** haftaya bugün *[haft-'eye'-ya booghewn]*; **a week (from) tomorrow** haftaya yarın *[yaruhn]*; **Monday week** haftaya Pazartesi *[pazartessee]*
weekend hafta sonu *[sonoo]*; **at/on the weekend** hafta sonunda *[sonoonda]*
weight ağırlık *[a-uhrluhk]*; **I want to lose weight** kilo vermek istiyorum *[keelo vermek eesteeyoroom]*
weight limit ağırlık tahdidi *[a-uhrluhk tahdeedee]*
weird tuhaf *[toohaf]*
welcome: welcome to ... ...-e hoş geldiniz *[...-eh hosh gheldeeneez]*; **you're welcome** (*don't mention it*) bir şey değil *[beer shay deh-eel]*
well: I don't feel well kendimi iyi hissetmiyorum *[kendeemee eeyee heess-setmeeyorom]*; **I haven't been very well** pek iyi değildim *[deh-eeldeem]*; **she's not well** iyi değil *[deh-eel]*; **how are you - very well, thanks** nasılsınız - çok iyiyim, teşekkür ederim *[chok eeyeeyeem, teshek-kewr edereem]*; **you speak English very well** çok iyi İngilizce konuşuyorsunuz *[eengheeleezjeh konooshoo-yorsoonooz]*; **me as well** ben de; **well done!** aferin! *[afereen]*; **well well!** (*surprise*) hayret! *[h-'eye'-ret]*
well-done (*meat*) iyi pişmiş *[eeyee peeshmeesh]*
wellingtons lastik çizmeler *[lasteek cheezmeler]*
Welsh Galli *[gal-lee]*
were *see page 115*
west batı *[batuh]*; **to the west of ...** ...-in batısında *[...-een batuhssuhnda]*; **in the west** batıda
West Indian Antilli *[anteel-lee]*; (*adjective*) Batı Hint *[batuh heent]*
West Indies Batı Hint Adaları *[batuh heent adalaruh]*
wet ıslak *[uhsslak]*; **it's all wet** tamamen ıslak; **it's been wet all week** bütün hafta yağdı *[bewtewn hafta ya-duh]*
wet suit (*for diving etc*) lastik bağımsız dalgıç elbisesi *[lasteek ba-uhmsuhz dalguhch elbeessessee]*
what? ne?; **what's that?** o nedir? *[nedeer]*; **what is he saying?** ne diyor? *[deeyor]*; **I don't know what to do** ne yapacağımı bilmiyorum *[yapaja-uhmuh beelmeeyoroom]*; **what a view!** ne manzara!
wheel tekerlek
wheelchair tekerlekli sandalye *[tekerleklee sandalyeh]*
when? ne zaman? *[neh]*; **when do we go?** ne zaman gidiyoruz? *[gheedee-yorooz]*; **when we get back** dönünce *[deewnewnjeh]*; **when we got back** döndüğümüz zaman *[dewndew-ewmewz]*
where? nerede? *[neredeh]*; **where is ...?** ... nerede?; **I don't know where he is** nerede olduğunu bilmiyorum *[oldoo-oonoo beelmeeyoroom]*; **that's where I left it** işte buraya bırakmıştım *[eeshteh boor-'eye'-ya*

buhrakmuhshtuhm]
which: which bus? hangi otobüs *[hanghee otobewss]*; **which one?** hangisi? *[hangheessee]*; **which is yours?** sizinki hangisi? *[seezeenkee]*; **I forget which it was** hangisi olduğunu unuttum *[oldoo-oonoo oonoot-toom]*; **the one which ...** ... olanı *[olanuh]*
while -iken *[-eeken]*; **while I'm here** ben buradayken *[boorad-'eye'-ken]*
whipped cream krem şantiye *[shanteeyeh]*
whisky viski *[veeskee]*
whisper fısıldamak *[fuhssuhldamak]*
white beyaz *[bayaz]*
white wine beyaz şarap *[bayaz sharap]*
who? kim? *[keem]*; **who was that?** o kimdi? *[keemdee]*; **the man who ...** ... adam
whole: the whole week bütün hafta *[bewtewn]*; **two whole days/weeks** tam iki gün/hafta *[eekee ghewn]*; **the whole lot** hepsi *[hepssee]*
whooping cough boğmaca *[bo-maja]*
whose: whose is this? bu kimin? *[boo keemeen]*
why? niçin *[neecheen]*; **why not?** niçin değil? *[deh-eel]*; **that's why it's not working** bu nedenle çalışmıyor *[boo nedenleh chaluhshmuh-yor]*
wide geniş *[gheneesh]*
wide-angle lens geniş açılı objektif *[gheneesh achuhluh objekteef]*
widow/widower dul *[dool]*
wife karı *[karuh]*; **my wife** karım *[karuhm]*
wig perük *[perewk]*
will: will you ask him ona sorar mısınız? *[muhsuhnuhz]*; *see page 113*
win (*verb*) kazanmak; **who won?** kim kazandı? *[keem kazanduh]*
wind (*noun*) rüzgar *[rewzgar]*
windmill yel değirmeni *[deh-eermenee]*
window pencere *[penjereh]*; **near the window** pencerenin yakınında *[penjereneen yakuhnuhnda]*; **in the window** (*shop*) vitrinde *[veetreendeh]*
window seat pencere yanı *[penjere yanuh]*
windscreen, windshield ön cam *[urn jam]*
windscreen wipers, windshield wipers silecekler *[seelejekler]*
windsurf: I'd like to windsurf yelkenli sörf yapmak istiyorum *[yelkenlee surrf yapmak eesteeyoroom]*
windsurfing yelkenli sörf *[yelkenlee surrf]*
windy rüzgarlı *[rewzgarluh]*; **it's so windy** ne kadar rüzgarlı
wine şarap *[sharap]*; **can we have some more wine?** bize biraz daha şarap verir misiniz? *[beezeh beeraz daha ... vereer mee-seeneez]*
wine glass şarap kadehi *[sharap kadehee]*
wine list şarap listesi *[sharap leestessee]*
wing (*of plane, bird*) kanat; (*of car*) çamurluk *[chamoorlook]*
wing mirror yan ayna *['eye'-na]*
winter kış *[kuhsh]*; **in the winter** kışın *[kuhshuhn]*
winter holiday kış tatili *[kuhsh tateelee]*
wire tel; (*electric*) kablo
wireless radyo
wiring elektrik tesisatı *[elektreek tesseessatuh]*
wish: wishing you were here burada olabilmenizi dilerdim *[boorada olabeelmeneezee deelerdeem]*; **best wishes** en iyi dileklerimle *[eeyee deeleklereemleh]*
with ile *[eeleh]*; **I'm staying with ...** ... ile kalıyorum *[kaluh-yoroom]*; **coffee with cream/milk** kremalı/sütlü kahve *[kremaluh/sewtlew kahveh]*; **I agree with you/him** sizinle/onunla aynı fikirdeyim *[seezeenleh/onoonla 'eye'-nuh feekeerday-eem]*
without -siz *[-seez]*; **without doubt** şüphesiz *[shewp-hesseez]*; **tea without sugar** şekersiz çay *[shekerseez ch-'eye']*
witness tanık *[tanuhk]*; **will you be a witness for me?** benim için tanıklık eder misiniz? *[beneem eecheen tanuhkluhk eder mee-seeneez]*
witty şakacı *[shakajuh]*
wobble: it wobbles (*wheel*) yalpa yapıyor *[yapuh-yor]*
woman kadın *[kaduhn]*
women kadınlar *[kaduhnlar]*

wonderful harikulade *[hareekooladeh]*
won't: it won't start çalışmıyor *[chaluhshmuh-yor]*; *see pages 113, 117*
wood (*material*) tahta
woods (*forest*) orman
wool yün *[yewn]*
word kelime *[keleemeh]*; **you have my word** söz veriyorum *[surz vereeyoroom]*
work (*verb*) çalışmak *[chaluhshmak]*; (*noun*) iş *[eesh]*; **how does it work?** nasıl işliyor? *[nassuhl eeshleeyor]*; **it's not working** çalışmıyor *[chaluhshmuh-yor]*; **I work in an office** bir büroda çalışıyorum *[beer bewroda chaluhshuh-yoroom]*; **do you have any work for me?** bana verebileceğiniz bir iş var mı? *[bana verebeelejeh-eeneez beer eesh var muh]*; **when do you finish work?** işten kaçta çıkıyorsunuz? *[eeshten kachta chuhkuh-yorsunuz]*
work permit çalışma izni *[chaluhsma eeznee]*
world dünya *[dewnya]*; **all over the world** bütün dünyada *[bewtewn dewnyada]*
worn-out (*person*) bitkin *[beetkeen]*; (*shoes, clothes*) partal
worry: I'm worried about her onun için üzülüyorum *[onoon eecheen ewzewlew-yoroom]*; **don't worry** merak etme *[etmeh]*
worry beads tespih *[tespeeh]*
worse: it's worse daha beter; **it's getting worse** gitgide kötüleşiyor *[gheetgheedeh kurtewlesheeyor]*
worst en kötü *[kurtew]*
worth: it's not worth 5000 liras bu 5000 lira etmez *[boo besh been leera etmez]*; **it's worth more than that** bu daha fazla eder; **is it worth a visit?** ziyaret etmeye değer mi? *[zeeyaret etmayeh deh-er mee]*
would: would you give this to ...? bunu ...-e verir misiniz? *[boonoo ...-eh vereer mee-seeneez]*; **what would you do?** ne yapardınız? *[neh yaparduhnuhz]*
wrap: could you wrap it up? paket yapar mısınız? *[muhsuhnuhz]*
wrapping ambalaj *[ambalaJ]*
wrapping paper ambalaj kâğıdı *[ambalaJ ka-uhduh]*
wrench (*tool*) İngiliz anahtarı *[eengheeleez anahtaruh]*
wrist bilek *[beelek]*
write yazmak; **could you write it down?** yazar mısınız? *[yazar muhsuhnuhz]*; **how do you write it?** nasıl yazılır? *[nassuhl yazuhluhr]*; **I'll write to you** size mektup yazarım *[seezeh mektoop yazaruhm]*; **I wrote to you last month** geçen ay size yazdım *[ghechen 'eye' ... yazduhm]*
write-off: it's a write-off tam hasar
writer yazar
writing yazı *[yazuh]*
writing paper yazı kâğıdı *[yazuh ka-uhduh]*
wrong: you're wrong yanlışınız var *[yanluhshuhnuhz]*; **the bill's wrong** bu hesap yanlış *[boo hessap yanluhsh]*; **sorry, wrong number** affedersiniz, yanlış numara *[affederseeneez ... noomara]*; **I'm on the wrong train** yanlış trendeyim *[trendayeem]*; **I went to the wrong room** yanlış odaya gittim *[do-'eye'-ya gheet-teem]*; **that's the wrong key** o yanlış anahtar; **there's something wrong with ...** ...-de bir sorun var *[...-deh beer soroon]*; **what's wrong?** ne oldu? *[neh oldoo]*; **what's wrong with it?** nesi var? *[nessee]*

X-ray röntgen *[rurntghen]*

Y

yacht yat
yacht club yat klübü *[klewbew]*
yard: in the yard avluda *[avlooda]*; *see page 120*
year yıl *[yuhl]*
yellow sarı *[saruh]*
yellow pages meslekler rehberi *[messlekler rehberee]*
yes evet
yesterday dün *[dewn]*; **yesterday morning** dün sabah; **yesterday afternoon** dün öğleden sonra *[urleden sonra]*; **the day before yesterday** evvelsi gün *[ev-velsee ghewn]*
yet: has it arrived yet? geldi mi? *[gheldee mee]*; **not yet** henüz değil *[henewz deh-eel]*
yobbo kopuk *[kopook]*
yog(h)urt yoğurt *[yo-oort]*
you siz *[seez]*; (*familiar singular*) sen; **this is for you** bu sizin için *[boo seezeen eecheen]*; **with you** sizinle *[seezeenleh]*; *see page 110*
young genç *[ghench]*
young people gençler *[ghenchler]*
your sizin *[seezeen]*; (*familiar singular*) senin *[seneen]*; **your camera** sizin fotoğraf makineniz *[foto-raf makeeneneez]*; *see page 108*
yours sizinki *[seezeenkee]*; (*familiar singular*) seninki *[seneenkee]*; *see page 110*
youth hostel hostel
Yugoslavia Yugoslavya *[yoogoslavya]*

Z

zero sıfır *[suhfuhr]*
zip, zipper fermuar *[fermoo-ar]*; **could you put a new zip on?** yeni fermuar takabilir misiniz? *[yenee ... takabeeleer mee-seeneez]*
zoo hayvanat bahçesi *[h-'eye'-vanat bahchessee]*
zoom lens değişken odaklı objektif *[deh-eeshken odakluh obJekteef]*

Turkish-English

A

abone kartı season ticket
abonman book of bus tickets
acele urgent
acil vaka emergency
açık open
açık hava tiyatrosu open air theatre/theater
açılış: 1.nci/2.nci açılış first/second collection
açılış saatleri opening times; collection times
açma *[achma]* bun
ada(lar) island(s)
adaçayı *[adach-'eye'-yuh]* sage tea
Adana kebabı *[adana kebabuh]* spicy hot meatballs
adı name
adres address
affedersiniz *[af-federseeneez]* excuse me
afiyet olsun! *[afeeyet olsoon]* hope you enjoyed your meal/drink
Ağustos August
ahize receiver; handset
ahududu *[ahoodoodoo]* raspberries
aile gazinosu family night club
ailesiz girilmez entry only for families
aileye mahsus only for family groups
Akdeniz Mediterranean
akide şekeri *[akeedeh shekeree]* sugar candy
akşam yemeği dinner, evening meal
aktarma connection (*travel*)
aktör actor
aktris actress
alabalık *[alabaluhk]* trout
alabalık ızgarası *[alabaluhk uhzgarassuh]* grilled trout
alkolsüz içkiler *[alkolsewz eechkeeler]* non-alcoholic drinks
allahaısmarladık *[al-laha-uhsmarladuhk]* goodbye (*said by person leaving*)
Allah belanı versin! *[allah belanuh verseen]* damn you!
Allah kahretsin! *[allah kahretseen]* damn!
Allah korusun *[allah koroossoon]* may God protect you; God forbid
Alman German
Almanya Germany
alo hello (*on telephone*)
alo, ben ... hello, this is ... speaking
ameliyat operation
Amerikalı American
Anadolu Anatolia
anahtar key
ananas *[ananas]* pineapple
anasını sattığım *[anassuhnuh sat-tuhuhm]* damned
ana yol main road
ana yol ilerde main road ahead
ançüez *[anchew-ez]* anchovies
ançüez ezmesi *[anchew-ez ezmessee]* anchovy purée
anıt monument
antep fıstığı *[antep fuhstuh-uh]* pistachio
antep fıstık ezmesi *[antep fuhstuhk ezmessee]* sweet made with crushed pistachio nuts
aptesane toilet, rest room
ara interval
araba car
araba vapuru car ferry
Aralık December
Arap Arab
arıza breakdown
arkada at the back
arkadan inilir exit at the back
armut *[armoot]* pears
Arnavut ciğeri *[arnavoot jee-eree]* Albanian spicy fried liver with onions
Arnavut kaldırımı cobblestone pavement
asansör lift, elevator
AŞ (Anonim Şirket) joint stock company
aşağı down
aşure *[ashooreh]* Noah's pudding — a

dessert with wheat grains, nuts and dried fruit
atınız insert
Atina Athens
avanak *[avanak]* idiot
avlu courtyard
Avrupa Europe
Avrupalı European
ay month
ayakkabıcı shoe shop/store
Aya Sofya Saint Sophia
ay çöreği *['eye'-churreh-ee]* moon-shaped cake
ayı *['eye'-yuh]* yobbo (*literally: bear*)
aylık kart season ticket
ayran *['eye'-ran]* yoghurt drink
ayşekadın *['eye'-shehkaduhn]* string beans, green beans
ayva *['eye'-va]* quince
ayva laabı *['eye'-va la-abuh]* quince jelly
ayva reçeli *['eye'-va rechelee]* quince jam
azami ağırlık weight limit
azami genişlik maximum width
azami hız/sürat speed limit
azami yükseklik maximum height
az pişmiş *[peeshmeesh]* rare
az şekerli kahve *[shekerlee kahveh]* slightly sweetened Turkish coffee

B

badem *[badem]* almonds
badem ezmesi *[badem ezmessee]* marzipan
badem kurabiyesi *[badem koorabee-yessee]* almond cakes
badempare *[bademparch]* almond cakes in syrup
badem şekeri *[badem shekeree]* sugared almonds
badem tatlısı *[badem tatluhssuh]* almond cakes
bagaj luggage
bagaj alma yeri baggage claim
bagaj fişi baggage receipt
bagaj kaydı check-in
bagaj kayıt masası check-in desk
bagaj kontrolü baggage check
bağlantı connection (*travel*)
baharat *[baharat]* spices
bahçıvan kebabı *[bahchuhvan kebabuh]* casseroled kebab
bakkal grocer
bakla *[bakla]* broad beans
baklava *[baklava]* pastry filled with nuts and syrup
bal honey
balık *[baluhk]* fish
balık buğulaması *[baluhk boo-oolamassuh]* fish baked with tomatoes
balıkçı fishmonger
balık çorbası *[baluhk chorbassuh]* fish and lemon soup
balık kızartması *[baluhk kuhzart-massuh]* fried fish
balık köftesi *[baluhk kurftessee]* fish balls
balık pazarı fish market
balkon balcony; circle
balkonlu with balcony
balsam conditioner
bamya *[bamya]* okra, ladies' fingers
banka bank
banket hard shoulder
banliyö suburbs
banliyö gişesi ticket office for suburban trains
banyo bath
banyolu with bath
barbunya *[barboonya]* red mullet
barbunya pilakisi *[barboonya peelakeessee]* dried beans cooked in olive oil and served hot or cold
barbunya tava *[barboonya tava]* fried red mullet
bardakla *[bardakla]* by the glass
basınız press
başkent capital
baş üstüne *[bash ewstewneh]* with pleasure
batı west
bayan iç çamaşırı ladies' underwear
bayan konfeksiyon ladies' wear
bayanlar ladies, ladies' room
baylar gents, men's room
baypas by-pass

bayram festival
bazlama *[bazlama]* flat bread cooked on a hot-plate
bedesten vaulted and fireproof part of market for valuable goods
beğendili kebap *[beh-endeelee kebap]* roast meat with aubergine/eggplant purée
beklemek yasaktır no waiting
bekleme salonu waiting room
bekleyiniz wait
belediye sarayı town hall
benzin petrol, gas
benzin istasyonu petrol/gas station
benzin pompası petrol/gas pump
berber men's hairdresser
beyazlar white
beyaz peynir *[bayaz payneer]* white cheese
beyaz peynirli makarna *[bayaz payneerlee makarna]* noodles with white cheese
beyaz şarap *[bayaz sharap]* white wine
beyin salatası *[bayeen salatassuh]* brain salad
beyin tava *[bayeen tava]* fried brains
bezelye *[bezelyeh]* green peas
bezelye çorbası *[bezelyeh chorbassuh]* pea soup
bıldırcın *[buhlduhrjuhn]* quail
bıyık moustache
biber *[beeber]* peppers
biber dolması *[beeber dolmassuh]* stuffed green peppers
biftek *[beeftek]* steak
bijuteri jewel(le)ry
bilet ticket
biletçi conductor
bilet gişesi ticket office
binilir get on here
biniş kartı boarding card
bira *[beera]* beer
birinci kat (*UK*) first floor; (*US*) second floor
birinci sınıf first class
bir şey değil *[beer shay deh-eel]* not at all, you're welcome
bisküvi *[beeskew-vee]* biscuits, cookies
Bizans Byzantine
bodrum kat basement
boğaz straits
Boğaziçi Bosp(h)orus
bombok *[bombok]* shitty
bonfile *[bonfeeleh]* fillet steak
boş vacant; empty
boyar not colo(u)r fast
boza *[boza]* thick fermented grain drink
bozuk out of order; broken
bozuk para small change
böbrek *[burbrek]* kidneys
böbrek ızgara *[burbrek uhzgara]* grilled kidneys
böbrek sote *[burbrek soteh]* sautéed kidneys
bölge region; district
börek *[burrek]* layered pastry with cheese/meat/spinach filling
buğulama *[boo-oolama]* steamed, poached
Bulgar Bulgarian
Bulgaristan Bulgaria
bulgur pilavı *[boolgoor peelavuh]* cracked wheat cooked with tomatoes
bulvar boulevard
Bursa kebabı *[boorsa kebabuh]* grilled lamb on pitta bread with tomato sauce and yoghurt
buyurun *[boo-yooroon]* can I help you?; yes?; this way
buz *[booz]* ice
buzlu *[boozloo]* with ice
büfe buffet
bülbül yuvası *[bewlbewl yoovassuh]* dessert with nuts and syrup
büyük big
büyükler adults

C

cacık *[jajuhk]* chopped cucumber in garlic-flavo(u)red yoghurt
cadde street
camı kırınız break the glass
cami mosque
cankurtaran ambulance
can yeleği koltuğunuzun altındadır life jacket is under your seat
can yelekleri life jackets
can yelekleri tavandadır life jackets up above
ceviz *[jeveez]* walnuts
cevizli baklava *[jeveezlee baklava]* pastry with walnuts and syrup
cezerye *[jezereh]* candy made with carrots, sugar and nuts
cızbız köfte *[juhzbuhz kurfteh]* grilled meat rissoles
ciğer *[jee-er]* liver
ciğer sarması *[jee-er sarmassuh]* minced liver wrapped in lamb's fat
ciğer tava *[jee-er tava]* fried liver
cin *[jeen]* gin
cinsi type
cinsiyeti sex
cintonik *[jeentoneek]* gin and tonic
cirit oyunu javelin game played on horseback
Cuma Friday
Cumartesi Saturday

Ç

çağır call (*lift, elevator*)
çağlayan waterfall
çalışma saatleri working hours
çam fıstığı *[cham fuhstuh-uh]* pine nuts
Çanakkale Boğazı Dardanelles
çarşaf bed linen
Çarşamba Wednesday
çarşı market
çavdar ekmeği *[chavdar ekmeh-ee]* rye bread
çay *[ch-'eye']* tea; stream
çay bahçesi tea garden
çayevi tea house, tea shop
çek cheques, checks
çeker will shrink
çek-in check-in
çekiniz pull
çek kabul edilir cheques/checks accepted
çekmez non-shrink
Çerkez tavuğu *[cherkez tavoo-oo]* 'Circassian' cold chicken in walnut sauce with garlic
çeşitli *[chesheetlee]* assorted
çeşme fountain
çeviriniz dial
çevir sesi/tonu dial(ling) tone
çevre yolu ring road
çeyizlik trousseau goods
çıkılır exit
çıkılmaz no exit
çıkış exit
çıkış kapısı gate
çıkmaz sokak cul-de-sac, dead end
çıkmaz yol dead end
çılbır *[chuhlbuhr]* poached eggs with yoghurt
çiçekçi, çiçekevi florist
çift yataklı oda twin room
çiğ köfte *[chee kurfteh]* a dish made of minced meat/ground beef, pounded wheat and chilli powder
çiğnemek için for chewing
çikolata *[cheekolata]* chocolate
çikolatalı *[cheekolataluh]* with chocolate
çikolatalı dondurma *[cheekolataluh dondoorma]* chocolate ice cream
çikolatalı pasta *[cheekolataluh pasta]* chocolate cake
çilek *[cheelek]* strawberries
çilekli dondurma *[cheeleklee dondoorma]* strawberry ice cream

---

çilek reçeli *[cheelek rechelee]* strawberry jam
çimenlere basmayınız keep off the grass
çini tiles
çips *[cheeps]* crisps, potato chips
çiroz *[cheeroz]* salted dried mackerel
çoban salatası *[choban salatassuh]* mixed tomatoes, peppers, cucumbers and onion salad
çocuk doktoru p(a)ediatrician
çocuk konfeksiyon children's wear
çocuklar children
çok pişmiş *[chok peesmeesh]* well-done
çok şekerli kahve *[chok shekerlee kahveh]* very sweet Turkish coffee
çorba *[chorba]* soup
çöp rubbish
çöp kebabı *[churp kebabuh]* small pieces of lamb on wooden spits
çörek *[churrek]* kind of bun
çulluk *[chool-look]* woodcock

D

D (dolmuş) taxi stop (*for shared taxis*)
dağ mountain
dahili extension
dahiliye internal medicine
dahiliyeci internist
dana eti *[dana etee]* veal
dana rozbif *[dana rozbeef]* roast veal
danışma information
daralan kaplama road narrows
darüşşifa old hospital
dayanıklı süt *[d-'eye'-yanuhkluh sewt]* long life milk
debriyaj clutch
değil mi? *[deh-eel mee]* isn't it?; doesn't it?
deniz sea
deniz otobüsü sea bus
deniz ürünleri *[deneez ewrewnleree]* seafood
dere valley; stream
dereotu *[dereh-otoo]* dill
deri mamulleri leather goods
devamlı virajlar series of bends
deve camel
deve güreşi camel wrestling
dışarı sarkmayınız do not lean out
Dicle River Tigris
Didim Didyma (*historical ruins*)
dikkat caution
dil *[deel]* ox tongue, lamb's tongue
dil balığı *[deel baluh-uh]* sole
dilber dudağı *[deelber dooda-uh]* lip-shaped sweet pastry with nut filling
dil peyniri *[deel payneeree]* cheese made in long strips
din religion
direksiyon steering wheel
dispanser out-patients' clinic
dişçi dentist
diş hekimi/tabibi dentist
doğu east
doğum tarihi date of birth
doğum yeri place of birth
dokunmayınız do not touch
dolma *[dolma]* stuffed vegetables (with or without meat)
dolmuş shared taxi
dolmuş bindirme yeri shared taxi set-down point
dolmuş indirme yeri shared taxi pick-up point
dolu full
doluyuz we're full
domates *[domatess]* tomatoes
domatesli *[domatesslee]* with tomatoes
domatesli pilav *[domatesslee peelav]* rice cooked with tomatoes
domatesli pirinç çorbası *[domatesslee peereech chorbassuh]* rice and tomato soup
domates salatası *[domatess salatassuh]* tomato salad
domates salçalı patlıcan kızartması *[domatess salchaluh patluhjan kuhzartmassuh]* fried aubergines/eggplants with tomato and garlic sauce
domates salçası *[domatess salchassuh]* tomato sauce
domates suyu *[domatess soo-yoo]* tomato juice
domuz eti *[domooz etee]* pork

dondurma *[dondoorma]* ice cream
dondurmalı rokoko *[dondoormaluh rokoko]* ice-cream cake
dozaj dosage
dönel kavşak roundabout, rotary
döner kebab *[durner kebab]* lamb grilled on a spit and cut into thin slices, usually with rice and salad
dönerli sandviç *[durnerlee sandveech]* roll with thin slices of grilled lamb
dönüş return
dört yol ağzı crossroads, intersection
döşemelik furniture
döviz foreign currency
döviz alım belgesi document for purchase of foreign currency
döviz alınır foreign money exchanged
döviz kuru exchange rate
draje coated pill
dur stop
duracak the bus is going to stop
duracak yer standing room
durak stop
durmak yasaktır no stopping
durulmaz no stopping
duş shower
duşlu with shower
dut *[doot]* mulberries
düğmeye basınız press the button
düğün çorbası *[dew-ewn chorbassuh]* 'wedding' soup made of meat stock, yoghurt and egg
dükkân shop

E

eczane chemist, pharmacy
efendim? *[efendeem]* I beg your pardon; sir/madam
Efes Ephesus
Ege Aegean
Ekim October
ekmek *[ekmek]* bread
ekmek kadayıfı *[ekmek kad-'eye'-yuhfuh]* sweet pastry
ekspresyol motorway, highway
ekspresyol kavşağı motorway/highway junction
ekspresyolun sonu end of motorway/highway
ekşi *[ekshee]* sour
el bagajı hand baggage
elbette *[elbet-teh]* certainly
elçilik embassy
elde yıkanabilir can be hand washed
elle yıkayınız wash by hand
elma *[elma]* apples
elma çayı *[elma ch-'eye'-yuh]* apple tea
elma suyu *[elma soo-yoo]* apple juice
elma tatlısı *[elma tatluhssuh]* dessert made with apples
emanet left luggage, baggage checkroom
emanet fişi left luggage receipt, baggage checkroom ticket
emniyet kemerlerinizi bağlayınız fasten seat belts
enformasyon information
enginar *[engheenar]* artichokes
erik *[ereek]* plums
erişkinler adults
erişte *[ereeshteh]* homemade noodles
erkek gömleği men's shirts
erkek iç çamaşırı men's underwear
erkek konfeksiyon menswear
erkekler men, men's room
Ermeni Armenian
esans *[esans]* essence
estağfurullah *[esta-foorool-lah]* don't mention it
eşşoğlueşşek *[esh-sho-loo-esh-shek]* ass; lout
et meat
etli *[etlee]* with meat
etli ayşekadın *[etlee 'eye'-sheh-kaduhn]* meat with green beans
etli bezelye *[etlee bezelyeh]* pea and meat stew
etli biber dolması *[etlee beeber dolmassuh]* peppers stuffed with rice and meat
etli börek *[etlee burrek]* pastry filled with minced meat/ground beef
etli bulgur pilavı *[etlee boolgoor peelavuh]* cracked wheat with meat
etli domates dolması *[etlee domatess dolmassuh]* tomatoes stuffed with

meat and rice
etli ekmek *[etlee ekmek]* flat bread baked with minced meat/ground beef and tomatoes
etli kabak dolması *[etlee kabak dolmassuh]* marrows stuffed with meat and rice
etli kapuska *[etlee kapooska]* cabbage stew with meat
etli kuru fasulye *[etlee kooroo fassoolyeh]* lamb and haricot beans in tomato sauce
etli lahana dolması *[etlee lahana dolmassuh]* cabbage leaves stuffed with meat and rice
etli nohut *[etlee nohoot]* chickpea and meat stew
etli yaprak dolması *[etlee yaprak dolmassuh]* vine leaves stuffed with rice and meat
et pazarı meat market
et suyu *[soo-yoo]* meat stock
evet *[evet]* yes
Eylül September
ezan Moslem call to prayer
ezme(si) *[ezme(see)]* purée
ezo gelin çorbası *[ezo gheleen chorbassuh]* rice soup

F

faiz interest
fasulye *[fassoolyeh]* beans
fasulye pilaki *[fassoolyeh peelakee]* beans in olive oil
fasulye piyazı *[fassoolyeh peeyazuh]* bean and onion salad
fava *[fava]* broad bean purée
feribot ferryboat
fes fez
fiçıdan *[fuhchuhdan]* on tap
fındık *[fuhnduhk]* hazelnuts
Fırat River Euphrates
fırın *[fuhruhn]* baked, oven-roasted; baker
fırında *[fuhruhnda]* baked, oven-roasted
fırın sütlaç *[fuhruhn sewtlach]* baked rice pudding
fıstık *[fuhstuhk]* pistachio nuts
fıstıklı *[fuhstuhkluh]* with pistachio nuts
fıstıklı muhallebi *[fuhstuhkluh moohal-lebee]* rice flour and rosewater pudding with pistachio nuts
filim film, movie
fiş receipt
fiyatlarımıza K.D.V. dahildir VAT included
fiyat listesi *[fee-at listessee]* price list
formüler form
fön blow dry
francala *[franjala]* French bread
Fransa France
Fransızca French
fren brakes
fuar fair
füme *[fewmeh]* smoked

G

galeri upper circle
gar terminus
garaj garage
gazi Moslem warrior
gazino night club
gazoz *[gazoz]* fizzy drink
gece night
gece klubü nightclub
geçme yasağı no overtaking/passing
geçmiş olsun! *[ghechmeesh olsoon]* get well soon!
geldiği ülke country of departure
Gelibolu Gallipoli
geliş arrival
geliş nedeni purpose of visit
gemi boat
geri dönülmez no U-turns
gevşek malzeme loose chippings

gevşek şev falling rocks
gezi trip
gezinti trip, outing
gıda *[guhda]* food
gıda pazarı food store
gideceği yer destination
giden yolcular salonu departure lounge
gidilecek yol route
gidiş single
gidiş bileti single/one-way ticket
gidiş dönüş bileti return/round-trip ticket
girilir entrance
girilmez no entry
giriş entrance
giriş holü foyer
Girit Crete
girmek yasaktır no admittance
girmeyiniz do not enter
gişe ticket counter; token counter
göl lake
gölgede kurutunuz dry away from direct sunlight
gönderen sender
göz doktoru optician
greyfurut *[grayfooroot]* grapefruit
güle güle *[ghewleh]* goodbye (*said by person remaining behind*)
güllaç *[ghewl-lach]* rice wafers stuffed with nuts, cooked in rose-flavo(u)red milky syrup
güllü dondurma *[ghewl-lew dondoorma]* rose-flavo(u)red ice cream
gümrük customs
gümrük beyannamesi customs declaration
gümüş *[ghew-mewsh]* silverware; silverfish
gün day
günde per day
günde bir/iki/üç defa once/twice/three times a day
günde üç defa ikişer tablet alınız take two tablets three times a day
gündüz daytime
güney south
günün çorbası *[ghewnewn chorbassuh]* soup of the day
güveç *[ghew-vech]* meat and vegetable stew
güvercin *[ghew-verjeen]* pigeon

H

hafif müzik light music
hafif yemek *[hafeef yemek]* snack
halıcı carpet seller
Haliç Golden Horn (*an area in Istanbul*)
haliç inlet; bay; estuary
halk müziği folk music
halk oyunları folk dances
hamal porter
hamam Turkish bath
hamsi *[hamsee]* anchovy
han inn; caravansaray
hanım parmağı *[hanuhm parma-uh]* 'Lady's Fingers' — finger-shaped pastry sticks in syrup
hap pills
hardal *[hardal]* mustard
hareket departure(s)
hareket saati time of departure
harem women's apartments
harita map
hastalık sigortası health insurance
hastane hospital
haşlama *[hashlama]* boiled, stewed
haşlanmış yumurta *[hashlanmuhsh yoomoorta]* boiled egg
hat route
havaalanı airport
hava basıncı air pressure
havale money order
havalimanı airport
havayolu airline
havuç *[havooch]* carrots
havuç salatası *[havooch salatassuh]* shredded carrot salad
havyar *[havyar]* caviar
hayır *[h-'eye'-yuhr]* no
hayırlı yolculuklar have a good journey
hayvanlara yiyecek vermeyiniz do not feed the animals
hazır yemek *[hazuhr yemek]* ready-to-eat food
Haziran June

hekim doctor
hela toilet, rest room
helva *[helva]* general name for various sweets made from cereals, nuts, sesame oil and honey
hemzemin geçit level crossing, railroad crossing
her gün every day
hesap bill; account
heybe embroidered bag
heykel statue
hırdavatçı ironmonger, hardware store
Hıristiyan Christian
hıyar *[huh-yar]* cucumber; lout
hindi *[heendee]* turkey
hindiba *[heendeeba]* wild chicory
hindi dolması *[heendee dolmassuh]* stuffed turkey
hindistan cevizi *[heendeestan jeveezee]* coconut
Hititler Hittites
hostel youth hostel
hostes hostess
hoşaf *[hoshaf]* stewed fruit
hoş bulduk! *[hosh booldook]* it's nice to be here! (*said by person welcomed*)
hoş geldiniz! *[hosh gheldeeneez]* welcome!
hurma *[hoorma]* dates
hünkar beğendi *[hewnkar beh-endee]* 'Sultan's Delight' — lamb served with aubergine/eggplant purée

I

ıhlamur *[uhhlamoor]* lime blossom tea
ılık ütü warm iron
Iraklı Iraki
ırmak river
ıspanak *[uhspanak]* spinach
ıspanaklı börek *[uhspanakluh burrek]* spinach wrapped in thin pastry
ıspanaklı yumurta *[uhspanakluh yoomoorta]* eggs with spinach
ızgara *[uhzgara]* grilled

iadeli taahhütlü recorded with advice of delivery
içecek(ler) *[eechejek(ler)]* beverage(s)
içilmez not for drinking
iç kale citadel
içki *[eechkee]* alcoholic drink
içli köfte *[eechlee kurfteh]* meatballs stuffed with cracked wheat
içme suyu drinking water
iç pilav *[eech peelav]* rice with currants, pine nuts and onions
iki kişilik oda double room
ikinci kat (*UK*) second floor, (*US*) third floor
ikinci sınıf second class
iki yönlü trafik two-way traffic
ilaç medicine
ilave additional, extra
ilave bir yatak an extra bed
ilerleyelim lütfen! *[eelerlayeleem lewtfen]* please move forward!
ilk hareket first train
ilk yardım first aid
imam bayıldı *[eemam b-'eye'-yuhlduh]* split aubergine/eggplant with tomatoes and onions, eaten cold with olive oil
imdat emergency
imdat çıkışı emergency exit
imdat freni emergency brake
incir *[eenjeer]* figs
indirimli reduced
inek *[eenek]* idiot (*literally: cow*)
İngiliz British
İngiliz sterlini pound sterling
İngiltere UK
inilir get off here
inşallah *[eenshal-lah]* God willing; I hope so
ipek silk

İranlı Iranian
irmik helvası *[eermeek helvassuh]* semolina helva
iskele quay; boarding/landing pier
İskender kebabı *[eeskender kebabuh]* grilled lamb on pitta bread with tomato sauce and yoghurt
İslami Islamic
islim kebabı *[eesleem kebabuh]* steamed kebab
istakoz *[eestakoz]* lobster
İstanbul Boğazı Bosp(h)orus
istasyon station
İstiklal Harbi the Turkish War of Independence after the First World War culminating in the establishment of the Republic of Turkey
istiridye *[eesteereedyeh]* oyster
iş günü weekdays
işhanı office block
işkembe çorbası *[eeshkembeh chorbassuh]* tripe soup
işkembe salonu tripe shop
işleme günleri days of operation
itfaiye fire brigade
itiniz push
iyi *[ee-yee]* good; well
iyi pişmiş *[ee-yee peeshmeesh]* well-done, well-cooked

J

jambon *[jambon]* ham
jambonlu *[jambonloo]* with ham
jarse jersey cloth
jeton telephone token; token for turnstiles to board ferries and sea buses
jinekolog gyn(a)ecologist
jöle *[jurleh]* jelly

K

kabak *[kabak]* courgettes/zucchinis, pumpkin, marrow
kabak dolması *[kabak dolmassuh]* stuffed courgettes/zucchinis
kabak kızartması *[kabak kuh-zartmassuh]* fried marrows
kabak reçeli *[kabak reechelee]* marrow jam
kabak tatlısı *[kabak tatluhssuh]* pumpkin with syrup and walnuts
kabin memuru steward
kadın budu köfte *[kaduhn boodoo kurfteh]* 'Lady's Thighs' — meat and rice croquettes
kadın göbeği *[kaduhn gurbeh-ee]* 'Lady's Navel' — a ring-shaped syrupy pastry
kadınlar women, ladies' room
kadran dial
kafeterya cafeteria
kağıt kebabı *[ka-uht kebabuh]* lamb and vegetables in paper
kağıtta barbunya *[ka-uht-ta bar-boonya]* red mullet grilled in paper wrapping
kağıtta pişmiş *[ka-uht-ta peeshmeesh]* baked in paper
kahvaltı breakfast
kahvaltı dahil breakfast included
kahve *[kahveh]* coffee; coffee shop (*usually men only*)
kakao *[kaka-o]* cocoa
kakaolu dondurma *[kaka-oloo dondoorma]* chocolate ice cream
kaldırınız lift (the receiver)
kale castle
kalkan *[kalkan]* turbot
kalkış departure
kalkış saati departure time(s)
kalorifer central heating
kambiyo exchange
kanyak *[kanyak]* brandy
Kapadokya Cappadocia
kapalı closed
kapı gate
kaplıca thermal spring

---

kara biber *[kara beeber]* black pepper
Karadeniz Black Sea
karadut *[karadoot]* black mulberries
Karagöz main character in Punch and Judy style shadow play
karagöz *[karagurz]* black bream
karakol police station
karayolu motorway, highway
kara zeytin *[kara zayteen]* black olives
karışık *[karuhshuhk]* mixed
karışık ızgara *[karuhshuhk uhzgara]* mixed grill
karışık kebap *[karuhshuhk kebap]* mixed roast meats
karides *[kareedess]* prawns
karides tavası *[kareedess tavassuh]* prawns fried in batter
karnıbahar *[karnuh-bahar]* cauliflower
karnıbahar tavası *[karnuh-bahar tavassuh]* fried cauliflower
karnıyarık *[karnuhyaruhk]* split aubergine/eggplant with meat filling
karpuz *[karpooz]* water melon
kasa cash desk
kasaba small town
kasap butcher
Kasım November
kasis uneven road surface
kaşar peyniri *[kashar payneeree]* mild yellow cheese
kaşar peynirli makarna *[kashar payneerlee makarna]* noodles with 'kaşar' cheese
kat floor, storey
katedral cathedral
katkısızdır no additives
kavun *[kavoon]* honeydew melon
kavurma *[kavoorma]* meat braised in its own fat
kaygan yol slippery road
kayık boat
kayısı *[k-'eye'-yuhssuh]* apricots
kayısı reçeli *[k-'eye'-yuhssuh rechelee]* apricot jam
kayısı suyu *[k-'eye'-yuhssuh soo-yoo]* apricot juice
kaymak *[k-'eye'-mak]* clotted cream
kaymaklı *[k-'eye'-makluh]* with clotted cream
kaymaklı dondurma *[k-'eye'-makluh dondoorma]* dairy ice cream
kaz goose
kaza accident
kazan dibi *[kazan deebee]* pudding with a caramel base
KDV (Katma Değer Vergisi) VAT, sales tax
kebabçı meat restaurant
kebap *[kebap]* roast meat
kefal *[kefal]* grey mullet
kefal pilakisi *[kefal peelakeessee]* mullet in olive oil with vegetables
kek cake
keklik *[kekleek]* partridge
kemençe small violin
kent town
kereviz *[kereveez]* celery
kervansaray caravansaray, inn
kestane *[kestaneh]* chestnuts
kestane şekeri *[kestaneh shekeree]* marrons glacés, candied chestnuts
keşkek *[keshkek]* lamb with wheat
keşkül *[keshkewl]* almond pudding
keten linen
Kıbrıs Cyprus
Kıbrıslı Cypriot
kılıç (balığı) *[kuhluhch (baluh-uh)]* swordfish
kılıç şiş *[kuhluhch sheesh]* swordfish on skewers
kırmızı biber *[kuhrmuhzuh beeber]* paprika
kırmızı mercimek çorbası *[kuhrmuhzuh merjeemek chorbassuh]* red lentil soup
kırmızı şarap *[kuhrmuhzuh sharap]* red wine
kırtasiye stationery
kırtasiyeci stationer
kısır *[kuhsuhr]* cracked wheat and paprika
kış türlüsü *[kuhsh tewrlewssew]* stewed winter vegetables
kıyma *[kuhy-ma]* minced meat, ground beef
kıymalı *[kuhy-maluh]* with mince meat/ground beef
kıymalı bamya *[kuhy-maluh bamya]* okra with minced meat/ground beef
kıymalı ıspanak *[kuhy-maluh uhspanak]* spinach with minced meat/ground beef
kıymalı makarna *[kuhy-maluh makarna]* noodles with minced meat/ground beef
kıymalı pide *[kuhy-maluh peedeh]* pitta bread with meat filling
kızarmış ekmek *[kuhzarmuhsh*

ekmek] toast
kızartma *[kuhzartma]* fried, broiled
Kızılay Red Cross
kilise Church
kimyon *[keemyon]* cummin
kiralık for hire, to rent
kiraz *[keeraz]* cherries
kitabevi bookshop, bookstore
kitaplık library
KKTC (Kuzey Kıbrıs Türk Cumhuriyeti) Turkish Republic of Northern Cyprus
Klasik Batı müziği Western classical music
klima air conditioning
koç yumurtası *[koch yoomoortassuh]* 'ram's eggs' — a delicacy made from ram's testicles
kokoreç *[kokorech]* lamb's intestines grilled on a spit
kokteyl *[koktayl]* cocktail
koli parcels
koltuk seat; stalls
kompartıman compartment
komple kahvaltı full breakfast
komposto *[komposto]* cold stewed fruit
konfeksiyon women's fashions
konser concert
konserve *[konserveh]* jam
konsolosluk consulate
konuk guest
koy bay
koyun eti *[koyoon etee]* mutton
köfte *[kurfteh]* meatballs or patties
köprü bridge
köpüklü şarap *[kurpewklew sharap]* sparkling wine
körfez gulf; bay
köşk kiosk; lodge
köy village
köy yolu country road
kredi kartı credit card
kredi kartı kabul edilmez credit cards not accepted
krema *[krema]* cream
kremalı pasta *[kremaluh pasta]* cream cake
kuaför women's hairdresser
kubbe dome
kule tower
kumbara ticket box
kundura shoes
kunduracı shoeshop, shoestore
kurabiye *[koorabee-yeh]* cake with almonds or nuts
Kurban Bayramı Moslem festival of sacrifice
kuru *[kooroo]* dried
kuru fasulye *[kooroo fasoolyeh]* haricot beans in tomato sauce
kurukahveci coffee seller
kuru köfte *[kooroo kurfteh]* fried meatballs
kuru pasta *[kooroo pasta]* dry cake
kuru temizleme dry clean
kuru üzüm *[kooroo ewzewm]* raisins
kuru yemiş *[kooroo yemeesh]* dried fruit and nuts
kuru yemişçi dried fruit seller
kuskus pilavı *[kooskooss peelavuh]* cous-cous — cooked semolina, usually served with meat
kusura bakmayın *[koossoora bak-m-'eye'-yuhn]* pardon me
kuşbaşı *[koosh-bashuh]* small pieces of casseroled meat
kuşet couchette
kuşkonmaz *[kooshkonmaz]* asparagus
kuyu well
kuzey north
kuzu eti *[koozoo etee]* lamb
kuzu fırında *[koozoo fuhruhnda]* roast leg of lamb
kuzu kapama *[koozoo kapama]* lamb with lettuce
kuzu pirzolası *[koozoo peerzolassuh]* grilled lamb chops
kuzu şiş kebabı *[koozoo sheesh kebabuh]* lamb roasted on a skewer
küçük small
küçükler children
külliye complex of buildings attached to a mosque
kültür merkezi cultural centre/center
Kültür ve Turizm Bakanlığı Ministry of Culture and Tourism
küpür bilet book of bus tickets
Kürt Kurdish
kütüphane library

L

lahana *[lahana]* cabbage
lahana dolması *[lahana dolmassuh]* stuffed cabbage leaves
lahana turşusu *[lahana toorshoossoo]* pickled cabbage
lahmacun *[lahmajoon]* pancakes with spicy meat topping
lakerda *[lakerda]* salted tunny
lastik tyre, tire
lastik basıncı tyre/tire pressure
lavabo washbasin
leblebi *[leblebee]* small chickpeas
Lefkoşa Nicosia
levrek *[levrek]* sea bass
likör *[leekurr]* liqueur
liman port
limon *[leemon]* lemon
limonata *[leemonata]* still lemon drink
lise high school
lokanta restaurant
lokum *[lokoom]* Turkish Delight
lop yumurta *[yoomoorta]* soft-boiled egg
lüfer *[lewfer]* bluefish
lütfen *[lewtfen]* please
lütfen bozuk para veriniz small change please

M

maalesef *[ma-alessef]* I'm sorry ...
maden sodası *[maden sodassuh]* mineral water (*carbonated*)
maden suyu *[maden soo-yoo]* mineral water
mağara cave
mağaza store
Magosa Famagusta
mahalle quarter; area of city
makarna *[makarna]* macaroni, noodles
makbuz receipt
manav greengrocer
mandalina *[mandaleena]* tangerines
manifatura haberdashery, notions
mantar *[mantar]* mushrooms
mantı *[mantuh]* type of ravioli
marbre kek *[marbreh]* dry cake with chocolate or fruit
Marmara Denizi Sea of Marmara
marmelat *[marmelat]* jam
Mart March
marul *[marool]* lettuce
marul göbeği *[marool gurbeh-ee]* cos lettuce hearts
maşallah *[mashal-lah]* isn't he/she/it etc lovely! (*said in order to avert the evil eye*)
matbua printed matter
matine matinée
mavi tren blue train (*Ankara-Istanbul train*)
maydanoz *[m-'eye'-danoz]* parsley
Mayıs May
mayonez *[m-'eye'-yonez]* mayonnaise
mayonezli balık *[m-'eye'-yonezlee baluhk]* fish with mayonnaise
mecburi iniş emergency landing
meç highlights
medeni hali marital status
medrese theological school
mefruşat fabrics and furnishings
mehter takımı Ottoman military band
mektup atma yeri postbox
memleket country
memnun oldum *[memnoon oldoom]* pleased to meet you
menba suyu *[menba soo-yoo]* spring water
menemen *[menemen]* omelet(te) with tomatoes and peppers
mercan *[merjan]* bream
mercimek *[merjeemek]* lentils
mercimek corbası *[merjeemek chorbassuh]* lentil soup
merhem ointment

merkez centre, center
mersin balığı *[merseen baluh-uh]* sturgeon
Meryem Ana Virgin Mary
mesaj message
mescid small mosque
mesleği occupation
meslekler rehberi yellow pages
meşgul engaged, occupied
meşrubat *[meshroobat]* soft drinks
metro underground
Mevlevi whirling dervish
mevsim meyvaları *[mevseem may-valaruh]* fruit in season
meydan square
meyva salatası *[mayva salatassuh]* fruit salad
meyva suyu *[mayva soo-yoo]* fruit juice
mezarlık cemetery
meze *[mezeh]* hors d'oeuvres
mısır *[muhssuhr]* corn
Mışır çarşısı spice bazaar
mısır gevreği *[muhssuhr gevreh-ee]* cornflakes
midye *[meed-yeh]* mussels
midye dolması *[meed-yeh dolmassuh]* stuffed mussels
midyeli pilav *[meed-yelee peelav]* rice with mussels
midye pilakisi *[meed-yeh peela-keessee]* mussels in oil with vegetables
midye tavası *[meed-yeh tavassuh]* fried mussels
mihrap prayer niche
miktar amount
milletlerarası international
milli park national park
mimber pulpit in mosque
minare minaret
misafir guest
mobilya furniture
motor engine; motorboat
mozaik mosaic
mönü *[murnew]* menu
muavin driver's assistant on inter-city coaches
muayene examination
muayenehane surgery, doctor's office
muhallebi *[moohal-lebee]* rice flour and rosewater pudding
muhallebici pudding shop
musakka *[moossak-ka]* moussaka
muska böreği *[mooska burreh-ee]* triangles of pastry filled with cheese, parsley etc
muz *[mooz]* banana
mücver *[mewjver]* vegetable patties
müdür manager
müezzin one who calls Moslems to prayer
Müslüman Moslem
mütehassıs specialist
müze museum

N

nakit cash
nane *[naneh]* mint
nar pomegranate
nargile water pipe
Nasrettin Hoca 13th century humorist and sage from Akşehir
nehir river
nemse böreği *[nemseh burreh-ee]* meat pie with puff pastry
neskafe *[neskafeh]* any brand of instant coffee
ney reed flute
Nisan April
nohut *[nohoot]* chickpeas
nohutlu paça *[nohootloo pacha]* lamb's trotters with chickpeas
nohutlu yahni *[nohootloo yahnee]* lamb and chickpeas
normal 2/3 star, regular
normal konuşma normal call
nöbetçi eczane duty chemist
numara number

---

order of special characters: c ç g ğ ı i o ö s ş u ü

O

Ocak January
oda room
oda numarası room number
oda servisi room service
okul school
oldu *[oldoo]* OK, alright
olmaz *[olmaz]* it's not possible
olur *[oloor]* alright
omlet *[omlet]* omelet(te)
ordövr *[ordurvr]* hors d'oeuvres
orijinal original soundtrack
orman forest
orta boy *[orta]* medium sized (glass)
orta pişmiş *[orta peeshmeesh]* medium
orta şekerli kahve *[orta shekerlee kahveh]* medium sweet Turkish coffee
Osmanlı Ottoman
Osmanlıca Ottoman (*language*)
Osmanlı İmparatorluğu Ottoman Empire
otel hotel
otobüs bus
otobüs durağı bus stop
otobüs garajı bus/coach station
otogar bus station
otomobil car
otomobil kiralama servisi car rental service
otopark car park
oya hand-embroidered lace
oyun play
oyuncaklar toys
oyuncu actor; actress

Ö

ödeme payment
ödemeli konuşma reverse charge call, collect call
öğle yemeği lunch
öğrenci student
öğrenci geçiş yeri special young people's crossing
öğrenci yurdu student hostel (*some open to tourists during summer*)
Ölü Deniz Dead sea
ön cam windscreen, windshield
önde at the front
önden binilir entry at the front
ördek *[urrdek]* duck
ören yeri ruins
özel bakım ünitesi intensive care unit
özür dilerim *[ewzewr deelereem]* I'm sorry

P

paça *[pacha]* lamb's trotters
Padişah Sultan; ruler
paket servis *[paket serveess]* take away
palamut *[palamoot]* tunny
pamuk cotton
pancar *[panjar]* beetrot, red beet
pancar turşusu *[panjar toorshoossoo]* pickled beetroot/red beet
pansiyon bed only (*in a private house*)
papatya çayı *[papatya ch-'eye'-yuh]* camomile tea
papaz yahnisi *[papaz yahneessee]* stew with vegetables
parfümeri perfume shop
park edilmez no parking

park yapılmaz no parking
pasaj passage
pasaport kontrolü passport control
paskalya çöreği *[paskalya churreh-ee]* Easter bread — slightly sweetened bread in a plaited shape
pasta *[pasta]* cake
pasta(ha)ne cake shop; café
pastırma *[pastuhrma]* beef cured with cummin and garlic
pastırmalı yumurta *[pastuhrmaluh yoormoorta]* fried eggs with 'pastırma'
pastil pastilles, lozenges
patates *[patatess]* potatoes
patates kızartması *[patatess kuhzartmassuh]* chips, French fries
patates köftesi *[patatess kurftessee]* potato and cheese balls
patatesli *[patatesslee]* with potatoes
patates püresi *[patatess pewressee]* creamed potatoes
patates salatası *[patatess salatassuh]* potato salad
patiska cambric
patlıcan *[patluhjan]* aubergines, eggplants
patlıcan dolma turşusu *[patluhjan dolma toorshoossoo]* pickled stuffed aubergines/eggplants
patlıcan kebabı *[patluhjan kebabuh]* aubergine/eggplant wrapped around pieces of meat and roasted
patlıcan kızartması *[patluhjan kuhzartmassuh]* fried aubergines/eggplants
patlıcanlı pilav *[patluhjanluh peelav]* rice with aubergines/eggplants
patlıcan salatası *[patluhjan salatassuh]* aubergine/eggplant purée
pavurya *[pavoorya]* crab
payvon (cheap) night club; joint
Pazar Sunday
pazar market
Pazar günleri dışında except Sundays
pazarlık edilmez no bargaining
Pazartesi Monday
pazen brushed cotton
pembe şarap *[pembeh sharap]* rosé wine
pencere window
perde curtain; act
peribacası Fairy Chimney (*unusual geological formations in Cappadocia, Central Turkey*)
perma perm
peron platform, track
Perşembe Thursday
pestil *[pesteel]* sheets of dried fruit pulp
peşin in advance (*money*)
peşmelba *[peshmelba]* peach melba
peynir *[payneer]* cheese
peynirli *[payneerlee]* with cheese
peynirli sandviç *[payneerlee sandveech]* cheese roll
peynirli tepsi böreği *[payneerlee tepsee burreh-ee]* cheese pie
peynir tatlısı *[payneer tatluhssuh]* small cheese cakes in syrup
pezevenk *[pezevenk]* pimp (*term of abuse*)
pırasa *[puhrassa]* leek
pide *[peedeh]* pitta bread
pideli *[peedelee]* with pitta bread
pilaki *[peelakee]* cold white beans vinaigrette
pilav *[peelav]* rice cooked in butter
pilavlı tavuk *[peelavluh tavook]* chicken and rice
piliç *[peeleech]* chicken
piliç çevirme *[peeleech cheveermeh]* spit-roasted chicken
piliç ızgarası *[peeleech uhzgarassuh]* grilled chicken
piramit *[peerameet]* triangular-shaped cake
pirinç *[peereench]* rice (*uncooked*)
pirinç çorbası *[peereench chorbassuh]* rice soup
pirzola *[peerzola]* lamb chops
pisi *[peessee]* plaice
pişkin *[peeshkeen]* well-cooked
piyaz *[pee-yaz]* haricot bean salad
piyes play
PK (Posta Kutusu) PO box
plaj beach
poğaça *[po-acha]* pastries with meat or cheese filling
poliklinik out-patients' clinic
polis police
portakal *[portakal]* oranges
portakal reçeli *[portakal rechelee]* marmalade
portakal suyu *[portakal soo-yoo]* orange juice
posta kutusu PO box

postrestant post restante, general delivery
PTT (Posta, Telgraf, Telefon İşletmesi) post, telegraph and telephone office
puf böreği *[poof burreh-ee]* meat or cheese pasties
pul stamps
püre *[pewreh]* purée

R

rafadan *[rafadan]* soft-boiled egg
rakı *[rakuh]* Turkish national drink — distilled from grape juice and aniseed-flavo(u)red
Ramazan Moslem month of fasting
rebap gourd viol
reçel *[rechel]* jam
reçete prescription
reçete ile satılır prescription only
rehber guide
renkli colo(u)r
renkliler colo(u)rs
resepsiyon reception
resepsiyon memuru receptionist
restoran restaurant
revani *[revanee]* sweet semolina pastry
reyon department
rezervasyon reservation
rica ederim *[reeja edereem]* don't mention it
Rodos Rhodes
Romanya Rumania
roka *[roka]* kind of watercress
rokoko *[rokoko]* ice-cream tart
rom rum
rosto *[rosto]* roasted
röntgen x-ray
ruhsat tarihi date of licence/license to produce
Rum Greek (*ethnic: relates to Turkish subjects of Greek extraction*)
Rumca Greek language (*ethnic*)
Rumeli European Turkey (*as opposed to Asian*)
Rus Russian
rus salatası *[rooss salahtassuh]* Russian salad — mayonnaise, peas, carrots etc

S

saat time; clock, watch
sabun soap
saç kesme haircut (*for ladies*)
saç tıraşı haircut
sade *[sadeh]* plain
sade kahve *[sadeh kahveh]* Turkish coffee without sugar
sade pilav *[sadeh peelav]* plain rice pilav
sağa dönülmez no right turn
sağa viraj bend to right
sağdan gidiniz keep to the right
sahanda yumurta *[sahanda yoomorta]* fried eggs
sahil coast
sahil yolu coast road
sahlep *[sahlep]* drink made from sahlep root in hot milk and cinnamon
sahne stage
sakal tıraşı shave
sakızlı dondurma *[sakuhzluh dondoorma]* mastic-flavo(u)red ice cream
salam *[salam]* salami
salamlı *[salamluh]* with salami
salata *[salata]* salad
salatalık *[salataluhk]* cucumber
salça *[salcha]* with tomato sauce or paste
salçalı *[salchaluh]* with tomato sauce
salçalı köfte *[salchaluh kurfteh]* meatballs in tomato sauce
Salı Tuesday
salon lounge
salyangoz *[salyangoz]* snails

sanat galerisi art gallery
sandviç ekmeği *[sandveech ekmeh-ee]* rolls
santral memuru operator
saray palace
saray lokması *[sar-'eye' lokmassuh]* fried batter dipped in syrup
sardalya *[sardalya]* sardines
sarığı burma *[saruh-uh boorma]* 'Twisted Turban' — turban-shaped baklava
sarmısak *[sarmuhssak]* garlic
saz stringed instrument resembling the lute
sazan *[sazan]* carp
seans performance
sebze *[sebzeh]* vegetables
sebze çorbası *[sebzeh chorbassuh]* vegetable soup
sefer flight
sefer numarası flight number
sek şarap *[sharap]* dry wine
Selçuklular Selchuks (*a Turkish dynasty which ruled in Iran and Anatolia before the Ottomans*)
Sema whirling dance performed by Mevlevi dervishes
semizotu *[semeezotoo]* purslane — a herb mixed in salads or stewed
semt neighbo(u)rhood
serbest vacant, free
serseri *[serseree]* fool
sert dönüş/viraj sharp bend
servis dahildir service charge included
servis otobüsü shuttle bus
servis ücreti service charge
seyahat journey
seyahat çekleri traveller's cheques, traveler's checks
sıcak *[suhjak]* hot, warm
sığır eti *[suh-uhr etee]* beef
sıkmayınız do not wring
sınıf class
sigara böreği *[seegara burreh-ee]* cigarette-shaped fried pastry filled with cheese, parsley etc
sigara içenler smokers
sigara içilmez no smoking
sigara içmeyenler non-smokers
sigara içmeyiniz do not smoke
sigorta insurance; fuse
simit *[seemeet]* ring-shaped bread covered with sesame seeds
sinema cinema, movie theater
sirke *[seerkeh]* vinegar
sivil civilian
soğan *[so-an]* onions
soğan dolması *[so-an dolmassuh]* stuffed onions
soğuk *[so-ook]* cold
soğuk meşrubat *[so-ook meshroobat]* cold soft drinks
sokak road
sola dönülmez no left turn
sola viraj bend to left
som balığı *[baluh-uh]* salmon
son end
son durak last stop
son hareket last train
son kullanma tarihi use before
sos sauce
sosis *[sosseess]* sausage
sosisli sandviç *[sosseesslee sandveech]* hotdog
soslu *[sosloo]* with sauce
Sovyetler Birliği Soviet Union
soyadı surname
spor malzemeleri sports goods
stabilize yol macadam road
stadyum stadium
su *[soo]* water
su böreği *[soo burreh-ee]* layered pastry
sucuk *[soojook]* Turkish sausage with spices and garlic
sucuklu sandviç *[soojookloo sandveech]* roll with spicy Turkish sausage
sucuklu tost *[soojookloo]* toasted sandwich with spicy Turkish sausage
sumak *[soomak]* sumac — a herb eaten with kebabs
su muhallebisi *[soo moohal-lebeessee]* rice flour pudding with rosewater
supanglez *[soopanglez]* chocolate pudding
Suriye Syria
Suriyeli Syrian
suyla with water
... suyu ... juice
sülün *[sewlewn]* pheasant
süper 4 star, premium
Süryani Syriac (*a nationality in Southern Turkey, Syria and Iran which speaks the Syriac language*)
süt *[sewt]* milk
sütlaç *[sewtlach]* rice pudding

sütlü kahve *[sewtlew kahveh]* coffee with milk
sütun column
süzme yoğurt *[sewzmeh yo-oort]* strained yoghurt

Ş

şadırvan fountain (*in mosque*)
şalgam *[shalgam]* turnip
şam fıstığı *[sham fuhstuh-uh]* pistachio nuts
şam fıstıklı baklava *[sham fuhstuhkluh baklava]* pastry with pistachio nuts and syrup
şampuan shampoo
şam tatlısı *[sham tatluhssuh]* dessert with syrup
şarap *[sharap]* wine
şarküteri delicatessen
şeftali *[sheftalee]* peaches
şeftali suyu *[sheftalee soo-yoo]* peach juice
şehir city
şehiriçi local
şehirlerarası konuşma long-distance call
şehirlerarası otobüs işletmesi long distance coach/bus service
şehir merkezi city centre/center
şehir turu city tour
şehriye *[shehree-yeh]* vermicelli
şehriye çorbası *[shehree-yeh chorbassuh]* vermicelli soup with lemon
şehriyeli *[shehree-yelee]* with vermicelli
şehriyeli pilav *[shehree-yelee peelav]* pilav with vermicelli
şeker *[sheker]* sugar; candy
Şeker Bayramı festival at the end of Ramazan (*month of fasting*)
şekerleme *[shekerlemeh]* candy
şekerli *[shekerlee]* with sugar
şekerpare *[shekerpareh]* small cakes with syrup
şerbet *[sherbet]* sweetened and iced fruit juices
şesuar hairdryer (*for ladies*)
şıra *[shuhra]* grape juice
şilebezi cheesecloth
şiş *[sheesh]* cooked on a skewer
şişe *[sheesheh]* bottle
şişe suyu *[sheesheh soo-yoo]* bottled drinking water
şiş kebabı *[sheesh kebabuh]* small pieces of lamb grilled on skewers
şiş köfte *[sheesh kurfteh]* grilled meatballs on skewers
şofben water heater
şoför driver
şokolalı *[shokolaluh]* with chocolate
Şubat February
şube branch
şurup *[shooroop]* syrup

T

taahhütlü recorded delivery
tabii *[tabee-ee]* of course
taksi taxi
taksi durağı taxi rank/stand
taksimetre taximeter
talaş kebabı *[talash kebabuh]* lamb baked in pastry
tali yol kavşağı crossroads
tamam *[tamam]* OK
tambur long-necked stringed instrument
tam pansiyon full board, American plan
tam yağlı (süt) *[ya-luh (sewt)]* full cream (milk)
tandır kebabı *[tanduhr kebabuh]* meat roasted in an oven on the ground
tapınak temple
tarama *[tarama]* roe pâté
tarator *[tarator]* nut and garlic sauce
taratorlu karnıbahar *[taratorloo karnuhbahar]* cauliflower with nut

and garlic sauce
tarçın *[tarchuhn]* cinnamon
tarhana çorbası *[tarhana chorbassuh]* traditional soup with dried yoghurt, tomato and pimento
tarife charges; timetable, schedule
tarifeli sefer scheduled flight
tarih date
tarihi yerler historical sites
tas kebabı *[kebabuh]* diced lamb with rice
taşıt giremez no entry for vehicles
taşıt trafiğine kapalı yol closed to all vehicles
tatar böreği *[tatar burreh-ee]* ravioli
tatil köyü holiday village
tatlı *[tatluh]* sweet, dessert
tatlı şarap *[tatluh sharap]* dessert wine
tava (da) *[tava (da)]* fried
tavla backgammon
tavşan *[tavshan]* rabbit
tavuk *[tavook]* chicken
tavuk ciğeri ezmesi *[tavook jee-eree ezmessee]* chicken liver purée
tavuk çorbası *[tavook chorbassuh]* chicken soup
tavuk göğsü *[tavook ghur-sew]* chicken breast pudding — a creamy dessert made with rice flower and finely shredded chicken
tavuk ızgara *[tavook uhzgara]* barbecued chicken
tavuklu pilav *[tavookloo peelav]* chicken and rice
taze *[tazeh]* fresh
taze beyaz peynir *[tazeh bayaz payneer]* fresh white cheese
taze fasulye *[tazeh fassoolyeh]* runner beans in tomato sauce and olive oil
taze soğan *[tazeh so-an]* spring onions
TC (Türkiye Cumhuriyeti) Republic of Turkey
TCDD (Türkiye Cumhuriyeti Devlet Demiryolları) Turkish National Railways/Railroads
tehlike danger
tehlikeli eğim steep gradient
tekir *[tekeer]* striped mullet
tekke dervish monastery
tek kişilik oda single room
tek yönlü yol one-way street
teleferik cablecar
telefon kodu dialling code, area code
telefon konuşması telephone call
telefon numarası telephone number
telefon rehberi telephone directory
teleks telex
telgraf telegram
tel kadayıfı *[kad-'eye'-yuhfuh]* shredded wheat stuffed with nuts in syrup
Temmuz July
tepe hill
terbiye *[terbee-yeh]* egg and lemon sauce
terbiyeli *[terbee-yelee]* with egg and lemon sauce
terbiyeli haşlama *[terbee-yelee hashlama]* boiled lamb with egg and lemon sauce
terbiyeli köfte *[terbee-yelee kurfteh]* meatballs with egg and lemon sauce
tereyağı *[tereya-uh]* butter
tereyağlı *[tereya-luh]* with butter
terlik slippers
tersane shipyard
terzi tailor
teşekkür ederim *[teshek-kewr edereem]* thank you
THY (Türk Hava Yolları) Turkish Airlines
tiyatro theatre, theater
TL (Türk Lirası) Turkish Lira
top., toplam total
torik *[toreek]* large tunny
Toros Taurus
tost toasted sandwich
trança *[trancha]* sea bream
tren train
tren istasyonu train station
tren yolu geçidi level crossing, railroad crossing
triko knitwear
TRT (Türkiye Radyo Televizyon Kurumu) Turkish Radio and Television Company
Truva Troy
tuhafiyeci haberdashery, notions; fabrics
tulumba tatlısı *[tooloomba tatluhssuh]* semolina doughnut in syrup
tulum peyniri *[tooloom payneeree]* goat's milk cheese made in a skin
tur tour
turfanda *[toorfanda]* early fruit or vegetables
turistik otel tourist hotel
turizm bürosu tourist office

turna *[toorna]* pike
turnike turnstile
turp *[toorp]* radish
turşu *[toorshoo]* pickled vegetables
turşu suyu *[toorshoo soo-yoo]* juice of pickled vegetables
turta *[toorta]* pie, pastry
turunç *[tooroonch]* Seville oranges
tuvalet toilet, rest room
tuz *[tooz]* salt
tuzlu *[toozloo]* salty
tuzlu badem *[toozloo badem]* salted almonds
tükenmez *[tewkenmez]* eggs fried with tomatoes and sweet peppers
tünel tiny Istanbul underground train, subway
türbe tomb
Türk Turkish
Türkçe in Turkish
Türkiye Turkey
Türkiye Turing ve Otomobil Kurumu Turkish Touring and Automobile Association
Türkiye'ye giriş tarihi date of entry to Turkey
Türk sanat müziği Turkish classical music
türlü *[tewrlew]* meat and vegetable stew

U

uçak plane
uçakla airmail
uluslararası international
umumi hela public convenience
umumi telefon public telephone
un *[oon]* flour
un helvası *[oon helvassuh]* flour helva
un kurabiyesi *[oon koorabeeyessee]* cake with almonds or nuts
unvanı title
uskumru *[ooskoomroo]* mackerel
uskumru dolması *[ooskoomroo dolmassuh]* stuffed mackerel
uyruğu nationality
uzak dur keep out
uzun ömürlü süt *[oozoon urmewrlew sewt]* long life milk

Ü

ücret cost; fare
üçüncü kat (*UK*) third floor, (*US*) fourth floor
ülke country
üzüm *[ewzewm]* grapes
üzümlü kek *[ewzewmlew]* fruit cake

V

vadi valley
vagon carriage
vagon restoran dining car
vali governor of province
Van Gölü Lake Van
vanilya *[vaneelya]* vanilla
vapur passenger ferry
vapur gezisi cruise
vapur iskelesi landing stage for ferries
var yes; there is
varış arrival(s)
varış istasyonu destination
varış saati time of arrival
varyete floor show
vestiyer cloakroom, checkroom
vezne cash desk
veznedar cashier

viraj bend
viski *[veeskee]* whisky
vişne *[veeshneh]* black cherries
vites gears
votka *[votka]* vodka

Y

yağ *[ya]* oil, fat
yağlı güreş Turkish wrestling
yahni *[yahnee]* meat stew with onions
Yahudi Jew
yakında soon
yalı waterside mansion
yangın çıkışı fire exit
yangın muhbiri fire alarm
yanlış numara wrong number
yaprak dolması *[yaprak dolmassuh]* stuffed vine leaves
yarım pansiyon half board, European plan
yarım şişe *[yaruhm sheesheh]* half bottle
yasak forbidden
yastık cushion, pillow
yat yacht
yatak bed
yataklı vagon sleeping car
yavaş git slow
yaya geçidi pedestrian crossing
yayla plateau
yayla çorbası *[y-'eye'-la chorbassuh]* yoghurt soup
yaz türlüsü *[tewrlewssew]* stewed summer vegetables
yemeklerden önce before meals
yemeklerden sonra after meals
yemek listesi *[yemek listessee]* menu
yemekli vagon restaurant car
yemek salonu dining room
yemeni headscarf
yengeç *[yenghech]* crab
Yeniçeri Janissaries (*the Sultan's élite troops*)
yeraltı kilisesi catacomb
yeraltı şehri underground city
yerfıstığı *[yerfuhstuh-uh]* peanuts
yerlere çöp atmayınız don't throw rubbish on the ground
yeşil kart green card
yeşil mercimek çorbası *[yesheel merjeemek chorbassuh]* green lentil soup
yeşil salata *[yesheel salata]* green salad
yeşil zeytin *[yesheel zayteen]* green olives
yıkama ve mizanpli wash and set
yıldırım very urgent
yıldız star
yoğurt çorbası *[yo-oort chorbassuh]* yoghurt soup
yoğurtlu *[yo-oortloo]* with yoghurt
yoğurtlu biber *[yo-oortloo beeber]* green peppers in yoghurt
yoğurtlu kabak *[yo-oortloo kabak]* small marrows in yoghurt
yoğurtlu kebap *[yo-oortloo kebap]* kebab with pitta bread and yoghurt
yoğurtlu paça *[yo-oortloo pacha]* lamb's trotters with yoghurt and garlic
yok no; there isn't
yokuş hill
yol road; way
yolcular passengers
yolcu otobüsü coach, bus
yolda çalışma roadwork(s)
yol kapalı road closed
yol ver give way, yield
yukarı up
yumurta *[yoomoorta]* egg
yumurtalı *[yoomoortaluh]* with egg
yumurtalı çorba *[yoomoortaluh chorba]* soup with beaten eggs
Yunanistan Greece
Yunanlı Greek
yurt dışı abroad
yurt içi inland
yün wool
yünlü wool(l)en
yüzde yüz 100%
yüz numara toilet, rest room

Z

zemin kat (*UK*) ground floor, (*US*) first floor
zenci negro
zerde *[zerdeh]* saffron rice dessert
zeytin *[zayteen]* olives
zeytinyağı *[zayteenya-uh]* olive oil
zeytinyağlı *[zayteenya-**luh**]* in olive oil (*eaten cold*)
zeytinyağlı biber dolması *[zayteen-ya-**luh** beeber dolmass**uh**]* stuffed sweet peppers in olive oil
zeytinyağlı patlıcan pilavı *[zayteenya-**luh** patluhjan peelav**uh**]* rice with aubergines/eggplants in olive oil
zeytinyağlı taze bakla *[zayteenya-**luh** taz**eh** bakl**a**]* fresh broad beans in olive oil
zeytinyağlı yaprak dolması *[zayteenya-**luh** yapr**a**k dolmass**uh**]* vine leaves stuffed with rice, pine nuts and raisins
zeytinyağlı yeşil fasulye *[zayteenya-**luh** yesh**ee**l fass**oo**lyeh]* runner beans cooked in tomatoes and olive oil
zurna reed instrument resembling the oboe
züccaciye glassware

Reference Grammar

AGGLUTINATION

Turkish is what is called an 'agglutinative' language which means that endings or suffixes are added to words where several words would be used in English.

For example:

ev-im-den from my house (*literally* house-my-from)

VOWEL HARMONY

There are eight vowels in Turkish, four 'front' vowels (**e i ö ü**) and four 'back' vowels (**a ı o u**). As a general rule vowel harmony simply means that if the LAST vowel in a word is a front vowel, all endings to this word will also contain front vowels, and if the LAST vowel is a back vowel, all endings will contain back vowels. That is to say, front vowels cannot be followed by back vowels and vice versa.

	last vowel in a word	can only be followed by
back vowels	**a/ı** **o/u**	**a** or **ı** **a** or **u**
front vowels	**e/i** **ö/ü**	**e** or **i** **e** or **ü**

For example:

plaj	the beach	**Türkiye**	Turkey
plaja	to the beach	**Türkiye'ye**	to Turkey
havalimanı	the airport		
havalimanına	to the airport		

NOUNS

GENDER

There is no gender in Turkish.

PLURALS

There are two plural endings which can be added onto the end of a noun, depending on whether the last vowel in the noun is a front or a back vowel.

after front vowels **e i ö ü**	after back vowels **a ı o u**
-ler	**-lar**

For example:

adam-lar	men	(**a** is the last vowel in **adam** man)
çocuk-lar	children	(**u** is the last vowel in **çocuk** child)
gece-ler	nights	(**e** is the last vowel in **gece** night)
gün-ler	days	(**ü** is the last vowel in **gün** day)

In Turkish, a singular noun is sometimes used to express a plural (eg **elma** – apples) and a plural ending may be used where a singular would be used in English (eg **iyi günler!** – good day! (*literally* good days).

ARTICLES

THE INDEFINITE ARTICLE (A, AN)

The word for 'one' **bir** is used as the indefinite article.

For example:

bir dakika
just a minute
üzerinde bir leke var
there's a mark on it
bir dağ köyü
a mountain village

When a noun is used with an adjective the indefinite article usually comes between the adjective and the noun. For example:

başka bir otel
another hotel
çok nazik bir adam
he's such a gentleman

THE DEFINITE ARTICLE (THE)

There is no separate word for 'the' in Turkish, so for example **otel** can mean either 'hotel' or 'the hotel' depending on context.

CASES

There are six cases in Turkish – nominative, accusative, genitive, dative, locative and ablative, and their meanings are given in the tables below. The endings are regular, apart from changes to some consonants and the requirements of vowel harmony (see page 105).

	last vowel (if word ends in a consonant)			
	e or **i**	**a** or **ı**	**o** or **u**	**ö** or **ü**
nom.	**yer** (place)	**yıl** (year)	**yol** (road)	**köy** (village)
acc.	**yer-i**	**yıl-ı**	**yol-u**	**köy-ü**
gen. (of)	**yer-in**	**yıl-ın**	**yol-un**	**köy-ün**
dat. (to)	**yer-e**	**yıl-a**	**yol-a**	**köy-e**
loc. (at, in)	**yer-de**	**yıl-da**	**yol-da**	**köy-de**
abl. (from)	**yer-den**	**yıl-dan**	**yol-dan**	**köy-den**

	last vowel (if word ends in a vowel)			
	e or **i**	**a** or **ı**	**o** or **u**	**ö** or **ü**
nom.	**gemi** (ship)	**oda** (room)	**doğu** (east)	**ölçü** (measurement)
acc.	**gemi-yi**	**oda-yı**	**doğu-yu**	**ölçü-yü**
gen. (of)	**gemi-nin**	**oda-nın**	**doğu-nun**	**ölçü-nün**
dat. (to)	**gemi-ye**	**oda-ya**	**doğu-ya**	**ölçü-ye**
loc. (at, in)	**gemi-de**	**oda-da**	**doğu-da**	**ölçü-de**
abl. (from)	**gemi-den**	**oda-dan**	**doğu-dan**	**ölçü-den**

For example:

nom.	**oda çok iyi** the room is very nice	dat.	**odaya getirdi** he brought it to the room
acc.	**odayı görebilir miyim?** can I see the room?	loc.	**odada** in the room
gen.	**odanın ortasında** in the middle of the room	abl.	**odadan çıktım** I came out of the room

Consonant Changes					
	k ⟶ ğ	**p ⟶ b**	**ç ⟶ c**	**k ⟶ g**	**t ⟶ d**
nom.	**yemek** (meal)	**kitap** (book)	**ağaç** (tree)	**renk** (colour)	**yurt** (home country)
acc.	**yemeğ-i**	**kitab-ı**	**ağac-ı**	**reng-i**	**yurd-u**
gen.	**yemeğ-in**	**kitab-ın**	**ağac-ın**	**reng-in**	**yurd-un**
dat.	**yemeğ-e**	**kitab-a**	**ağac-a**	**reng-e**	**yurd-a**
loc.	**yemek-te**	**kitap-ta**	**ağaç-ta**	**renk-te**	**yurt-ta**
abl.	**yemek-ten**	**kitap-tan**	**ağaç-tan**	**renk-ten**	**yurt-tan**

For words ending with the consonants **ç, f, h, k, p, s, ş, t**, the locative and ablative case endings will take **t** instead of **d**.
For example:

sokakta on the street	**Ağustos'ta** in August

Plural endings are added to the word before case endings.
For example:

yollarda
on the roads

ADJECTIVES

Adjectives do not take any endings.

bu kahve soğuk
this coffee is cold
hava soğuk
the weather is cold
ellerim soğuk
my hands are cold

If an adjective is used before a noun with **bir**, meaning 'one' or 'a/an', **bir** may come between the adjective and the noun:

kırmızı kravat	a red tie
bir kırmızı kravat	a red tie
kırmızı bir kravat	a red tie

POSSESSIVE ADJECTIVES AND ENDINGS (MY, YOUR etc)

Rather than using possessive adjectives, Turkish uses special endings added onto nouns to express possession. There are possessive adjectives in Turkish, but these are used mainly for special emphasis. The possessive endings (which must also follow the rules of vowel harmony – see page 105) are given in the following tables. The words in brackets are the possessive adjectives.

		last vowel (if word ends in a consonant)			
		e or **i**	**a** or **ı**	**o** or **u**	**ö** or **ü**
		'house'	'name'	'arm'	'village'
my	**(benim)**	**ev-im**	**ad-ım**	**kol-um**	**köy-üm**
your (sing. familiar)	**(senin)**	**ev-in**	**ad-ın**	**kol-un**	**köy-ün**
his/her/its	**(onun)**	**ev-i**	**ad-ı**	**kol-u**	**köy-ü**
our	**(bizim)**	**ev-imiz**	**ad-ımız**	**kol-umuz**	**köy-ümüz**
your (pl. and polite)	**(sizin)**	**ev-iniz**	**ad-ınız**	**kol-unuz**	**köy-ünüz**
their	**(onların)**	**ev-leri**	**ad-ları**	**kol-ları**	**köy-leri**

		last vowel (if word ends in a vowel)			
		e or **i**	**a** or **ı**	**o** or **u**	**ö** or **ü**
		'mother'	'room'	'neighbour'	'measurement'
my	**(benim)**	**anne-m**	**oda-m**	**komşu-m**	**ölçü-m**
your (sing. familiar)	**(senin)**	**anne-n**	**oda-n**	**komşu-n**	**ölçü-n**
his/her/its	**(onun)**	**anne-si**	**oda-sı**	**komşu-su**	**ölçü-sü**
our	**(bizim)**	**anne-miz**	**oda-mız**	**komşu-muz**	**ölçü-müz**
your (pl. and polite)	**(sizin)**	**anne-niz**	**oda-nız**	**komşu-nuz**	**ölçü-nüz**
their	**(onların)**	**anne-leri**	**oda-ları**	**komşu-ları**	**ölçü-leri**

		Consonant Changes		
		k ⟶ ğ	**p ⟶ b**	**ç ⟶ c**
		'meal'	'book'	'tree'
		yemek	**kitap**	**ağaç**
my	**(benim)**	**yemeğ-im**	**kitab-ım**	**ağac-ım**
your (sing. familiar)	**(senin)**	**yemeğ-in**	**kitab-ın**	**ağac-ın**
his/her/its	**(onun)**	**yemeğ-i**	**kitab-ı**	**ağac-ı**
our	**(bizim)**	**yemeğ-imiz**	**kitab-ımız**	**ağac-ımız**
your (pl. and polite)	**(sizin)**	**yemeğ-iniz**	**kitab-ınız**	**ağac-ınız**
their	**(onların)**	**yemek-leri**	**kitap-ları**	**ağaç-ları**
		k ⟶ g	**t ⟶ d**	
		'colour'	'home country'	
		renk	**yurt**	
my	**(benim)**	**reng-im**	**yurd-um**	
your (sing. familiar)	**(senin)**	**reng-in**	**yurd-un**	
his/her/its	**(onun)**	**reng-i**	**yurd-u**	
our	**(bizim)**	**reng-imiz**	**yurd-umuz**	
your	**(sizin)**	**reng-iniz**	**yurd-unuz**	
their	**(onların)**	**renk-leri**	**yurt-ları**	

For example:

otelim
my hotel
adım
my name
adınız
your name
anne-m ve baba-m
my mother and my father
benim evimde yok
there isn't one in MY house

Plural endings are added to the noun BEFORE the possessive endings.
For example:

çanta-lar-ınız nerede?
where are your bags?
bizim bavul-lar-ımız
our suitcases

All other endings are added AFTER the possessive endings.
For example:

ceb-im-de
in my pocket
lüften yer-im-i tutar mısınız?
would you please keep my place for me?
araba-nız-ı oradan alır mısınız?
would you move your car?

COMPARATIVES (BIGGER, BETTER etc)
Comparatives are formed by placing **daha** 'more' before the adjective.

daha büyük	bigger
daha çabuk	faster

To say that something is 'more ... than ...' use the ablative case (**-den/-dan**) added to the noun (**daha** is optional).

benden (daha) büyük	bigger than me

SUPERLATIVES (BIGGEST, BEST etc)
The superlative is formed with **en**:
For example:

en çok bunu beğeniyorum
I like this one most
en güzel yer
the most beautiful place

PRONOUNS

PERSONAL PRONOUNS

nom.		acc.	
ben	I	**beni**	me
sen	you (sing. familiar)	**seni**	you
o	he/she/it	**onu**	him/her/it
biz	we	**bizi**	us
siz	you (pl. and polite)	**sizi**	you
onlar	they	**onları**	them

dat.		loc.		abl.	
bana	to me	**bende**	on/in me	**benden**	from me
sana	to you	**sende**	on/in you	**senden**	from you
ona	to him/her/it	**onda**	on/in him/her/it	**ondan**	from him/her/it
bize	to us	**bizde**	on/in us	**bizden**	from us
size	to you	**sizde**	on/in you	**sizden**	from you
onlara	to them	**onlarda**	on/in them	**onlardan**	from them

Personal pronouns are normally omitted unless special emphasis is required:

çok sıcak!
it's very hot!
yarın gidiyoruz
we're leaving tomorrow
ama o gitmiyor
but HE'S not leaving

YOU
There are two ways of expressing 'you' in Turkish. They are:

sen used to address a close friend, relative or child and also used between young people.
siz used to address more than one person or someone the speaker doesn't know very well or doesn't know at all.

EMPHATIC PRONOUNS (MYSELF, YOURSELF etc)

kendim	myself	**kendimiz**	ourselves
kendin	yourself (sing. familiar)	**kendiniz**	yourselves (pl. and polite)
kendi	himself, herself, itself	**kendileri**	themselves

For example: **kendiniz mi yapıyorsunuz?** do you make them yourself?

POSSESSIVE PRONOUNS (MINE, YOURS etc)

mine	**benim**	ours	**bizim**
yours (sing. familiar)	**senin**	yours (pl. and polite)	**sizin**
his/hers/its	**onun**	theirs	**onların**

For example: **o bardak sizin mi? – hayır, onun** is that your glass? – no, it's his/hers

VERBS

Verbs always come at the end of a sentence. Except for the consonant changes **t ⟶ d (et-mek – ediyor, git-mek – gidiyor** etc) all verbs in Turkish are regular.

The personal pronouns (I, you etc), which are given in the following tables in brackets, are only used for emphasis.

PRESENT TENSE (I am ...ing etc)

		last vowel in stem is			
		e or **i**	**a** or **ı**	**o** or **u**	**ö** or **ü**
		bil-mek to know	**al-mak** to take	**konuş-mak** to speak	**gör-mek** to see
(ben)	I	**bil-iyorum**	**al-ıyorum**	**konuş-uyorum**	**gör-üyorum**
(sen)	you	**bil-iyorsun**	**al-ıyorsun**	**konuş-uyorsun**	**gör-üyorsun**
(o)	he/she/it	**bil-iyor**	**al-ıyor**	**konuş-uyor**	**gör-üyor**
(biz)	we	**bil-iyoruz**	**al-ıyoruz**	**konuş-uyoruz**	**gör-üyoruz**
(siz)	you	**bil-iyorsunuz**	**al-ıyorsunuz**	**konuş-uyorsunuz**	**gör-üyorsunuz**
(onlar)	they	**bil-iyorlar**	**al-ıyorlar**	**konuş-uyorlar**	**gör-üyorlar**

		verb stem ends in a vowel			
		e or **i**	**a** or **ı**	**o** or **u**	**ö** or **ü**
		bekle-mek to wait	**başla-mak** to begin	**uyu-mak** to sleep	**yürü-mek** to walk
(ben)	I	**bekl-iyorum**	**başl-ıyorum**	**uyu-yorum**	**yürü-yorum**
(sen)	you	**bekl-iyorsun**	**başl-ıyorsun**	**uyu-yorsun**	**yürü-yorsun**
(o)	he/she/it	**bekl-iyor**	**başl-ıyor**	**uyu-yor**	**yürü-yor**
(biz)	we	**bekl-iyoruz**	**başl-ıyoruz**	**uyu-yoruz**	**yürü-yoruz**
(siz)	you	**bekl-iyorsunuz**	**başl-ıyorsunuz**	**uyu-yorsunuz**	**yürü-yorsunuz**
(onlar)	they	**bekl-iyorlar**	**başl-ıyorlar**	**uyu-yorlar**	**yürü-yorlar**

For example:

Türkçe biliyor
he knows Turkish

AORIST TENSE (take etc)
There are six endings. First person singular endings are:

after verb stems	in **a/ı/o/u**	**-arım/-ırım/-urum**
	in **e/i**	**-erim/-irim**
	in **ö/ü**	**-ürüm**

To find the verb stem remove **-mak** or **-mek** from the verbs as given in column 1 on page 116.

If the verb stem ends in a **t** this changes to **d** (**gitmek – giderim**). If the verb stem ends in a vowel no additional vowel is put before the **r** (see **ye-mek**)

		bil-mek to know	**al-mak** to take	**sor-mak** to ask	**gör-mek** to see
(ben)	I	**bil-irim**	**al-ırım**	**sor-arım**	**gör-ürüm**
(sen)	you	**bil-irsin**	**al-ırsın**	**sor-arsın**	**gör-ürsün**
(o)	he/she/it	**bil-ir**	**al-ır**	**sor-ar**	**gör-ür**
(biz)	we	**bil-iriz**	**al-ırız**	**sor-arız**	**gör-ürüz**
(siz)	you	**bil-irsiniz**	**al-ırsınız**	**sor-arsınız**	**gör-ürsünüz**
(onlar)	they	**bil-irler**	**al-ırlar**	**sor-arlar**	**gör-ürler**
		geç-mek to pass	**sat-mak** to sell	**uyu-mak** to sleep	**ye-mek** to eat
(ben)	I	**geç-erim**	**sat-arım**	**uyu-rum**	**ye-rim**
(sen)	you	**geç-ersin**	**sat-arsın**	**uyu-rsun**	**ye-rsin**
(o)	he/she/it	**geç-er**	**sat-ar**	**uyu-r**	**ye-r**
(biz)	we	**geç-eriz**	**sat-arız**	**uyu-ruz**	**ye-riz**
(siz)	you	**geç-ersiniz**	**sat-arsınız**	**uyu-rsunuz**	**ye-rsiniz**
(onlar)	they	**geç-erler**	**sat-arlar**	**uyu-rlar**	**ye-rler**

The aorist tense is commonly used for general statements, requests and promises. For example:

çay severim
I like tea
kahve içer misiniz?
would you like some coffee?
yarın gelirim
I'll come tomorrow

PAST TENSE

last vowel in verb stem			
a, ı	**e, i** **ver-mek** to give	**ö, ü** **gör-mek** to see	**o, u** **uyu-mak** to sleep
al-dım **al-dın** **al-dı** **al-dık** **al-dınız** **al-dılar**	**ver-dim** **ver-din** **ver-di** **ver-dik** **ver-diniz** **ver-diler**	**gör-düm** **gör-dün** **gör-dü** **gör-dük** **gör-dünüz** **gör-düler**	**uyu-dum** **uyu-dun** **uyu-du** **uyu-duk** **uyu-dunuz** **uyu-dular**

If the last consonant in a verb stem is **ç, f, h, k, p, s, ş, t** then the **d** in the past tense will change to a **t**.
For example:

git-tim	I went *or* I have gone
konuş-tum	I spoke *or* I have spoken
iç-tim	I drank *or* I have drunk

IMPERFECT TENSE
This tense is formed by adding the following endings, which are the same for all verbs, to the verb stem:

(ben)	**gel-iyor-dum**	I was coming
(sen)	**gel-iyor-dun**	you were coming
(o)	**gel-iyor-du**	he/she/it was coming
(biz)	**gel-iyor-duk**	we were coming
(siz)	**gel-iyor-dunuz**	you were coming
(onlar)	**gel-iyor-lardı**	they were coming

FUTURE TENSE

	last vowel in verb stem (if it ends in a consonant)		(if it ends in a vowel)	
	e, i, ö, ü	**a, ı, o, u**	**e, i, ö, ü**	**a, ı, o, u**
(ben)	**-eceğim**	**-acağım**	**-yeceğim**	**-yacağım**
(sen)	**-eceksin**	**-acaksın**	**-yeceksin**	**-yacaksın**
(o)	**-ecek**	**-acak**	**-yecek**	**-yacak**
(biz)	**-eceğiz**	**-acağız**	**-yeceğiz**	**-yacağız**
(siz)	**-eceksiniz**	**-acaksınız**	**-yeceksiniz**	**-yacaksınız**
(onlar)	**-ecekler**	**-acaklar**	**-yecekler**	**-yacaklar**

If the final vowel of the stem is **e** or **a**, it is narrowed into **i** or **ı**.

For example:

ye-mek	to eat	**yi-yecek**	he will eat
anla-mak	to understand	**anlı-yacak**	he will understand

TO BE

The Turkish equivalent for the verb 'to be' is formed by using a set of endings which are attached to the adjective or noun and which follow the rules of vowel harmony (see page 105).

		last vowel (if word ends in a consonant)			
		e or i	**a or ı**	**o or u**	**ö or ü**
		English	German	tired	Turkish
(ben)	I	**Ingiliz-im**	**Alman-ım**	**yorgun-um**	**Türk-üm**
(sen)	you are	**Ingiliz-sin**	**Alman-sın**	**yorgun-sun**	**Türk-sün**
(o)	he/she/it is	**Ingiliz**	**Alman**	**yorgun**	**Türk**
(biz)	we are	**Ingiliz-iz**	**Alman-ız**	**yorgun-uz**	**Türk-üz**
(siz)	you are	**Ingiliz-siniz**	**Alman-sınız**	**yorgun-sunuz**	**Türk-sünüz**
(onlar)	they are	**Ingiliz-ler**	**Alman-lar**	**yorgun-lar**	**Türk-ler**

	last vowel (if word ends in a vowel)			
	well **e, i**	ill **a, ı**	happy **o, u**	villager **ö, ü**
(ben)	**iyi-yim**	**hasta-yım**	**mutlu-yum**	**köylü-yüm**
(sen)	**iyi-sin**	**hasta-sın**	**mutlu-sun**	**köylü-sün**
(o)	**iyi**	**hasta**	**mutlu**	**köylü**
(biz)	**iyi-yiz**	**hasta-yız**	**mutlu-yuz**	**köylü-yüz**
(siz)	**iyi-siniz**	**hasta-sınız**	**mutlu-sunuz**	**köylü-sünüz**
(onlar)	**iyi-ler**	**hasta-lar**	**mutlu-lar**	**köylü-ler**

The following consonant changes take place when words end in **k, p, ç** or **t** (**k ⟶ ğ, p ⟶ b, ç ⟶ c, t ⟶ d**).

For example:

> **Ingilizim**
> I am English

PAST TENSE OF 'TO BE'

		last vowel (if word ends in a consonant)			
		e or **i**	**a** or **ı**	**o** or **u**	**ö** or **ü**
(ben)	I was	**-dim**	**-dım**	**-dum**	**-düm**
(sen)	you are	**-din**	**-dın**	**-dun**	**-dün**
(o)	he/she/it/was	**-di**	**-dı**	**-du**	**-dü**
(biz)	we are	**-dik**	**-dık**	**-duk**	**-dük**
(siz)	you are	**-diniz**	**-dınız**	**-dunuz**	**-dünüz**
(onlar)	they are	**-diler**	**-dilar**	**-dular**	**-düler**
		last vowel (if word ends in a vowel)			
		e or **i**	**a** or **ı**	**o** or **u**	**ö** or **ü**
(ben)		**-ydim**	**-ydım**	**-ydum**	**-ydüm**
(sen)		**-ydin**	**-ydın**	**-ydun**	**-ydün**
(o)		**-ydi**	**-ydı**	**-ydu**	**-ydü**
(biz)		**-ydik**	**-ydık**	**-yduk**	**-ydük**
(siz)		**-ydiniz**	**-ydınız**	**-ydunuz**	**-ydünüz**
(onlar)		**-ydiler**	**-ydılar**	**-ydular**	**-ydüler**

If the last letter of an adjective is **ç, f, h, k, p, s, ş** or **t**, then the **d** of the past tense will change to **t**.

For example:

yorgundum
I was tired

TO HAVE
This is formed by adding the possessive endings (see pages 107–108) to the thing possessed and adding **var** to the sentence to mean 'have' or **yok** to mean 'have not'.

For example:

(benim) arabam var	I have a car
(onun) arabası yok	he doesn't have a car

PAST TENSE OF 'TO HAVE'
This is formed as for the present except that the past tense ending **-dı** is added to **var** and **-tu** to **yok**.

For example:
(benim) arabam var-dı
I had a car
(onun) arabası yok-tu
he didn't have a car

VERBS
Here are some of the most commonly used verbs in the first person (I).

Infinitive		Present	Aorist	Past	Future
açmak	*to open*	açıyorum	açarım	açtım	açacağım
almak	*to take*	alıyorum	alırım	aldım	alacağım
bakmak	*to look*	bakıyorum	bakarım	baktım	bakacağım
başlamak	*to begin*	başlıyorum	başlarım	başladım	başlayacağım
beklemek	*to wait*	bekliyorum	beklerim	bekledim	bekleyeceğim
bırakmak	*to leave*	bırakıyorum	bırakırım	bıraktım	bırakacağım
bilmek	*to know*	biliyorum	bilirim	bildim	bileceğim
bulmak	*to find*	buluyorum	bulurum	buldum	bulacağım
çalışmak	*to work*	çalışıyorum	çalışırım	çalıştım	çalışacağım
çıkmak	*to go out*	çıkıyorum	çıkarım	çıktım	çıkacağım
demek	*to say*	diyorum	derim	dedim	diyeceğim
duymak	*to hear, feel*	duyuyorum	duyarım	duydum	duyacağım
etmek	*to do (in compounds)*	ediyorum	ederim	ettim	edeceğim
geçmek	*to pass*	geçiyorum	geçerim	geçtim	geçeceğim
gelmek	*to come*	geliyorum	gelirim	geldim	geleceğim
getirmek	*to bring*	getiriyorum	getiririm	getirdim	getireceğim
gezmek	*to go about*	geziyorum	gezerim	gezdim	gezeceğim
girmek	*to enter*	giriyorum	girerim	girdim	gireceğim
gitmek	*to go*	gidiyorum	giderim	gittim	gideceğim
giymek	*to wear*	giyiyorum	giyerim	giydim	giyeceğim
göndermek	*to send*	gönderiyorum	gönderirim	gönderdim	göndereceğim
görmek	*to see*	görüyorum	görürüm	gördüm	göreceğim
içmek	*to drink*	içiyorum	içerim	içtim	içeceğim
istemek	*to want*	istiyorum	isterim	istedim	isteyeceğim
işitmek	*to hear*	işitiyorum	işitirim	işittim	işiteceğim
kalmak	*to stay*	kalıyorum	kalırım	kaldım	kalacağım
kapamak	*to close*	kapayorum	kaparım	kapadım	kapayacağım
kaybetmek	*to lose*	kaybediyorum	kaybederim	kaybettim	kaybedeceğim
kırmak	*to break*	kırıyorum	kırarım	kırdım	kıracağım
koymak	*to put*	koyuyorum	koyarım	koydum	koyacağım
konuşmak	*to speak*	konuşuyorum	konuşurum	konuştum	konuşacağım
okumak	*to read*	okuyorum	okurum	okudum	okuyacağım
olmak	*to become*	oluyorum	olurum	oldum	olacağım
oturmak	*to live, sit*	oturuyorum	otururum	oturdum	oturacağım
öğrenmek	*to learn*	öğreniyorum	öğrenirim	öğrendim	öğreneceğim
ölmek	*to die*	ölüyorum	ölürüm	öldüm	öleceğim
satmak	*to sell*	satıyorum	satarım	sattım	satacağım
sevmek	*to love*	seviyorum	severim	sevdim	seveceğim
sormak	*to ask*	soruyorum	sorarım	sordum	soracağım
söylemek	*to say, tell*	söylüyorum	söylerim	söyledim	söyleyeceğim
taşımak	*to carry*	taşıyorum	taşırım	taşıdım	taşıyacağım
tutmak	*to hold*	tutuyorum	tutarım	tuttum	tutacağım
unutmak	*to forget*	unutuyorum	unuturum	unuttum	unutacağım
uyumak	*to sleep*	uyuyorum	uyurum	uyudum	uyuyacağım
varmak	*to arrive*	varıyorum	varırım	vardım	varacağım
vermek	*to give*	veriyorum	veririm	verdim	vereceğim
yapmak	*to make, do*	yapıyorum	yaparım	yaptım	yapacağım
yatmak	*to lie down*	yatıyorum	yatarım	yattım	yatacağım
yazmak	*to write*	yazıyorum	yazarım	yazdım	yazacağım
yemek	*to eat*	yiyorum	yerim	yedim	yiyeceğim

NEGATIVES

Negative of verbs are formed by adding **-me/-ma** after the verb stem and before other endings (before **y** of the present tense this is narrowed to **-mi/-mı/-mü/-mu**).

For example:

last vowel in verb stem				
	e, i	**a, ı**	**o, u**	**ö, ü**
Present Tense:	**bil-mi-yorum**	**al-mı-yorum**	**konuş-mu-yorum**	**gör-mü-yorum**
Past Tense:	**bil-me-dim**	**al-ma-dım**	**konuş-ma-dım**	**gör-me-dim**
Imperfect Tense:	**bil-mi-yordum**	**al-mı-yordum**	**konuş-mu-yordum**	**gör-mü-yordum**
Future Tense:	**bil-mi-yeceğim**	**al-mı-yacağım**	**konuş-ma-yacağım**	**gör-mi-yeceğim**

The negative of the Aorist Tense is irregular:

verb stems ending in		
	e i ö ü	**a ı o u**
(ben)	**-me-m**	**-mam**
(sen)	**-mez-sin**	**-maz-sın**
(o)	**-mez**	**-maz**
(biz)	**-me-yiz**	**-mayız**
(siz)	**-mez-siniz**	**-maz-sınız**
(onlar)	**-mez-ler**	**-maz-lar**

For example:

biliyorum
I know

bilmiyorum
I don't know

sizi anlıyorum
I understand you

sizi anlamıyorum
I don't understand you

gelmem
I don't/won't come

gitmez
he/she doesn't/won't go

NEGATIVE OF 'TO BE'

The negative of the verb 'to be' is formed by using the following words which are placed after the respective adjective etc.

I am not	**değil-im**
you are not	**değil-sin**
he/she/it is not	**değil**
we are not	**değil-iz**
you are not	**değil-siniz**
they are not	**değil-ler**

For example:

Alman değilim
I am not German

fena değil
it's not bad

QUESTIONS

These are formed by using one of the particles **mi/mı/mü/mu**, which follow the vowel harmony of the preceding vowel (see page 105). To form a question separate off the verb ending as given in the preceding tables and add one of these particles to the front of it, for example:

Present Tense	**geliyor musunuz?**	are you coming?
Aorist Tense	**gelir misiniz?**	would you come?
Past Tense	**geldiniz mi?**	did you come?
Imperfect Tense	**geliyor muydunuz?**	were you coming?
Future Tense	**gelecek misiniz?**	will you come?

geliyorsunuz you are coming	**geliyor** he/she is coming
geliyor musunuz? are you coming?	**geliyor mu?** is he/she coming?

IMPERATIVE (GIVING COMMANDS)

The polite form of the imperative is formed by adding the following endings to the verb stem:

last vowel of verb stem (if ending in a consonant)			
e or **i**	**a** or **ı**	**o** or **u**	**ö** or **ü**
-in	**-ın**	**-un**	**-ün**
(if verb stem ends in a vowel)			
-yin	**-yın**	**-yun**	**-yün**

For example:

girin! come in!	**oturun** sit down	**bekleyin!** wait!

To form the negative imperative take the verb stem (column 1 in the verb tables on page 116 minus **-mak** or **-mek**) and add **-me** or **-ma** according to the rules of vowel harmony (see page 105). Then add on the endings as in the above table:

girmeyin! don't come in!	**beklemeyin** don't wait

ALSO, TOO

There are two words for 'also' and 'too': **de** and **da**. The one to be used depends on the last vowel of the preceding word (see vowel harmony page 105).

last vowel of preceding word	
a ı o u	**e i ö ü**
da	**de**

For example:

ben de	I too	**o da**	she/he too	**siz de**	you too

CAN

This is formed by using the verb **bilmek** 'to know' which is added to the verb stem with either an **e** or a **a** first (depending on the previous vowel) and also a **y** if the verb stem ends in a vowel. **Bilmek** is then conjugated like a normal verb.

last vowel in verb stem	
a ı o u	**e i ö ü**
-abil-	**-ebil-**

For example:

al-a-bilmek to be able to take
gel-e-bilmek to be able to come

gelebilir miyim?
can I come?

bana yardım edebilir misiniz?
can you help me?

TELLING THE TIME

what time is it?	**saat kaç?** *[sa-at kach]*
it is ...	**saat ...**
one o'clock	**saat bir** *[beer]*
seven o'clock	**saat yedi** *[yedee]*
one a.m.	**sabah saat bir** *[sabah]*
seven a.m.	**sabah saat yedi**
one p.m.	**öğleden sonra saat bir** *[urleden sonra]*
seven p.m.	**akşam saat yedi** *[aksham]*
midday	**öğleyin** *[urlayeen]*
midnight	**gece yarısı** *[yaruhssuh]*
five past eight	**sekizi beş geçiyor** *[sekeezee besh ghechee-yor]*
five to eight	**sekize beş var** *[sekeezeh]*
half past ten	**on buçuk** *[boochook]*
twenty-five to ten	**ona yirmi beş var** *[ona yeermee]*
twenty-five past ten	**onu yirmi beş geçiyor** *[onoo]*
quarter past eleven	**onbiri çeyrek geçiyor** *[onbeeree chayrek]*
quarter to eleven	**onbire çeyrek var** *[onbeereh]*

CONVERSION TABLES

1. LENGTH

centimetres, centimeters
1 cm = 0.39 inches

metres, meters
1 m = 100 cm = 1000 mm
1 m = 39.37 inches = 1.09 yards

kilometres, kilometers
1 km = 1000 m
1 km = 0.62 miles = 5/8 mile

km	1	2	3	4	5	10	20	30	40	50	100
miles	0.6	1.2	1.9	2.5	3.1	6.2	12.4	18.6	24.9	31.1	62.1

inches
1 inch = 2.54 cm

feet
1 foot = 30.48 cm

yards
1 yard = 0.91 m

miles
1 mile = 1.61 km = 8/5 km

miles	1	2	3	4	5	10	20	30	40	50	100
km	1.6	3.2	4.8	6.4	8.0	16.1	32.2	48.3	64.4	80.5	161

2. WEIGHT

gram(me)s
1 g = 0.035 oz

g	100	250	500
oz	3.5	8.75	17.5 = 1.1 lb

kilos
1 kg = 1000 g
1 kg = 2.20 lb = 11/5 lb

kg	0.5	1	1.5	2	3	4	5	6	7	8	9	10
lb	1.1	2.2	3.3	4.4	6.6	8.8	11.0	13.2	15.4	17.6	19.8	22

kg	20	30	40	50	60	70	80	90	100
lb	44	66	88	110	132	154	176	198	220

tons
1 UK ton = 1018 kg
1 US ton = 909 kg

tonnes
1 tonne = 1000 kg
1 tonne = 0.98 UK tons = 1.10 US tons

ounces
1 oz = 28.35 g

pounds
1 pound = 0.45 kg = 5/11 kg

lb	1	1.5	2	3	4	5	6	7	8	9	10	20
kg	0.5	0.7	0.9	1.4	1.8	2.3	2.7	3.2	3.6	4.1	4.5	9.1

stones
1 stone = 6.35 kg

stones	1	2	3	7	8	9	10	11	12	13	14	15
kg	6.3	12.7	19	44	51	57	63	70	76	83	89	95

hundredweights
1 UK hundredweight = 50.8 kg
1 US hundredweight = 45.36 kg

3. CAPACITY

litres, liters
1 l = 1.76 UK pints = 2.13 US pints
½ l = 500 cl
¼ l = 250 cl

pints
1 UK pint = 0.57 l
1 US pint = 0.47 l

quarts
1 UK quart = 1.14 l
1 US quart = 0.95 l

gallons
1 UK gallon = 4.55 l
1 US gallon = 3.79 l

4. TEMPERATURE

centigrade/Celsius
C = (F − 32) × 5/9

C	−5	0	5	10	15	18	20	25	30	37	38
F	23	32	41	50	59	64	68	77	86	98.4	100.4

Fahrenheit
F = (C × 9/5) + 32

F	23	32	40	50	60	65	70	80	85	98.4	101
C	−5	0	4	10	16	20	21	27	30	37	38.3

NUMBERS

0	sıfır *[suhf**uh**r]*
1	bir *[beer]*
2	iki *[eek**ee**]*
3	üç *[ewch]*
4	dört *[durt]*
5	beş *[besh]*
6	altı *[alt**uh**]*
7	yedi *[yed**ee**]*
8	sekiz *[sek**ee**z]*
9	dokuz *[dok**oo**z]*
10	on *[on]*
11	on bir *[on beer]*
12	on iki *[on eek**ee**]*
13	on üç *[on ewch]*
14	on dört *[on durt]*
15	on beş *[on besh]*
16	on altı *[on alt**uh**]*
17	on yedi *[on yed**ee**]*
18	on sekiz *[on sek**ee**z]*
19	on dokuz *[on dok**oo**z]*
20	yirmi *[yeerm**ee**]*
21	yirmi bir *[yeerm**ee** beer]*
22	yirmi iki *[yeerm**ee** eek**ee**]*
30	otuz *[ot**oo**z]*
31	otuz bir *[ot**oo**z beer]*
32	otuz iki *[ot**oo**z eek**ee**]*
40	kırk *[kuhrk]*
50	elli *[el-l**ee**]*
60	altmış *[altm**uh**sh]*
70	yetmiş *[yetm**ee**sh]*
80	seksen *[sekss**e**n]*
90	doksan *[dokss**a**n]*
100	yüz *[yewz]*
110	yüz on *[yewz on]*
200	iki yüz *[eek**ee** yewz]*
1,000	bin *[been]*
3,000	üç bin *[ewch been]*
1989	bin dokuz yüz seksen dokuz *[been dok**oo**z yewz sekssen dok**oo**z]*

1st	birinci *[beer**ee**njee]*
2nd	ikinci *[eek**ee**njee*
3rd	üçüncü *[ewch**ew**njew]*
4th	dördüncü *[durd**ew**njew]*
5th	beşinci *[besh**ee**njee]*
6th	altıncı *[alt**uh**njuh]*
7th	yedinci *[yed**ee**njee]*
8th	sekizinci *[sekeez**ee**njee]*
9th	dokuzuncu *[dokooz**oo**njoo]*
10th	onuncu *[on**oo**njoo]*

1,000,000 bir milyon *[beer meel-y**o**n]*